HISTORY OF IDEAS
IN
ANCIENT GREECE

HISTORY OF IDEAS
IN
ANCIENT GREECE

Advisory Editor

Gregory Vlastos

The

PLATONIC EPISTLES

Translated with Introduction
and Notes

by

J. HARWARD

ARNO PRESS

A New York Times Company

New York / 1976

Editorial Supervision: EVE NELSON

————◆————

Reprint Edition 1976 by Arno Press Inc.
First published 1932

Reprinted by permission of
  Cambridge University Press

Reprinted from a copy in
  The Princeton University Library

HISTORY OF IDEAS IN ANCIENT GREECE
ISBN for complete set: 0-405-07285-6
See last pages of this volume for titles.

Manufactured in the United States of America

————◆————

Library of Congress Cataloging in Publication Data

Plato. Spurious and doubtful works.
    The Platonic epistles.

    (History of ideas in ancient Greece)
    Reprint of the 1932 ed. published by the Univer-
sity Press, Cambridge, Eng.
    Bibliography: p.
    I. Harward, John, 1858-   II. Title. III. Se-
ries.
B391.E8H3   1975   184   75-13287
ISBN 0-405-07330-5

THE PLATONIC EPISTLES

LONDON
Cambridge University Press
FETTER LANE

NEW YORK . TORONTO
BOMBAY . CALCUTTA . MADRAS
Macmillan

TOKYO
Maruzen Company Ltd

The
PLATONIC EPISTLES

Translated with Introduction
and Notes

by

J. HARWARD, M.A. (Oxon)

Late Director of Education
Ceylon

σχεδὸν γὰρ εἰκόνα ἕκαστος τῆς ἑαυτοῦ
ψυχῆς γράφει τὴν ἐπιστολήν.

Demetrius, περὶ ἑρμηνείας, § 227

CAMBRIDGE
AT THE UNIVERSITY PRESS
1932

CONTENTS

PREFACE

This Translation was made in 1919 at the request of a friend whose Greek was getting rusty, and who wished to read the Platonic Epistles. I tried to make it readable; but the main object was to reproduce as faithfully as possible what seemed to be the thought of the original, without removing all traces of peculiarities of style. Extensive selections from the translation were embodied in a paper entitled "The Story of the Platonic Epistles", which was read to the Melbourne Classical Society in 1920.

The Epistles present many problems to the translator, and any fidelity which this version has attained will be largely due to the help of Professor A. E. Taylor, who in 1922 very kindly read through the whole of it, suggested many corrections, and threw light on many dark places. I have also compared it throughout with that of R. G. Bury, and, in many parts, with that of L. A. Post; and am indebted to both of these for corrections.

The Translation follows the text of Volume v of the Clarendon Press Edition, edited by J. Burnet in 1913, and all references to the Greek follow the divisions there shown. In one passage (359 a 3) my rendering implies a slight alteration in the Greek, and in five others (313 a 2, 335 a 7, 338 a 5, 345 a 6, 351 a 4) changes of punctuation. All of these are dealt with in the Notes.

The work was begun with a strong conviction of the genuineness of the 7th Epistle, but with an open mind as regards the other twelve. I must confess to some changes of opinion during the interval. The conservative view of all the letters except the 1st, to which I have finally inclined, has, I think (so far as a man can trace the origin of his own beliefs), been the result of impressions formed by repeated study of the original. Doubts which have suggested themselves, or have been suggested by others, have usually been removed by a more careful reading of the Greek. The view thus formed has been confirmed by such study as I have been able to give to the subject-matter of the Epistles and to their historical setting.

When my first approaches to the Epistles were made, the only English edition or translation was, I believe, that published in the Bohn Series, and none had appeared on the Continent for a considerable time. Since then six translations have appeared, three German, two English, and one French. It may be thought that there is no call for a seventh. But whatever other merits these editions have, none of them has the fullness which so important a subject calls for. In all of them the historical setting of the Epistles is treated with extreme brevity, and only one of them, that of M. Souilhé, handles the question of genuineness with much thoroughness of detail.

Since placing this work in the hands of the publishers I have received another edition, that of F. Novotný, published at Brno in 1930, which comprises the Greek text of the Epistles with a commentary which in fullness of detail far exceeds any of the other editions. The writer does not give any detailed account of the historical setting, nor does he enter fully into the question of genuineness, except in the case of the 1st and 12th Epistles. But his commentary is full of valuable matter, and evidently embodies the results of a prolonged and original study of the work. It is a pleasure to find that Novotný has arrived at the same conclusion on the question of genuineness as that which is adopted in this edition. Time has not allowed of my doing more than to make in my proofs a few corrections suggested by his notes, and to append a short Addendum dealing with a few points which seemed to call for separate mention.

I have to thank Professor A. E. Taylor, not only for the revision of my Translation, which I have mentioned above, but for the constant encouragement and information on questions connected with Platonism, which I have now for some years received from him. It is not necessary to dwell on the value of such help to a student working in a country town in Australia. I am also indebted for help to two friends at the University of Queensland, Professor J. L. Michie and Mr S. Castlehow; and to the authorities of the Library of the University of Queensland and of the Fisher Library of the University of Sydney for their constant kindness in forwarding to me books, without which the work could not have been attempted. Last, but not least, I have to thank the Syndics of the Cambridge University Press for their kindness in undertaking the publication of this work. To the careful revision which it received throughout from their corrector, before proofs were forwarded to me in Australia, I am also indebted for the removal of not a few blemishes and errors.

J. HARWARD

Warwick
Queensland
29th September 1931

BOOKS & MONOGRAPHS CONSULTED

ADAM, R. *Die Echtheit der platonischen Briefe.* Berlin, 1906.
ANDREAE, W. Die philosophische Probleme in den platonischen Briefen. *Philologus*, 1922, vol. LXXVIII.
—— *Platons Staatschriften.* Erster Teil: Briefe. Jena, 1923.
APELT, O. *Platons Briefe, übersetzt und erläutert.* Leipzig, 1918.
BENTLEY, R. *Dissertations upon the Epistles of Phalaris, Themistocles,* etc. Dyce's edition. 1836.
—— *Remarks on a late Discourse of Free Thinking.* Dyce's edition of Bentley's Works, vol. III, pp. 410 ff.
BIEDENWEG, W. *Plutarchs Quellen in den Lebensbeschreibungen des Dion und Timoleon.* Leipzig, 1884.
BILLIG, L. Clausulae and Platonic Chronology. *Journal of Philology,* vol. XXXV, no. 70.
BRINKMANN, A. Ein Brief Platons. *Rhein. Mus.* N.F. vol. LXVI. (A reply to Boeckh's attack on Plat. *Ep.* VI.)
BURNET, J. *Greek Philosophy from Thales to Plato.* London, 1914.
—— *Platonism.* Berkeley, California, 1928.
BURY, R. G. Plato. Vol. VII. Loeb Classical Library, 1929.
Cambridge Ancient History, vol. VI. Cambridge, 1928.
DITTENBERGER, W. *Sylloge Inscriptionum Graecarum.*
EGERMANN, F. *Die Platonischen Briefe VII und VIII.* Dissert. Vienna, 1928.
FIELD, G. C. *Plato and his Contemporaries.* London, 1930.
FREEMAN, E. A. *History of Sicily,* vol. IV.
GROTE, G. *History of Greece.*
—— *Plato and the Companions of Socrates.*
HACKFORTH, R. *Authorship of the Platonic Epistles.* Manchester, 1913.
HERCHER, R. *Epistolographi Graeci.* Paris, 1871.
HOLM, A.* *Geschichte Siciliens.* Vol. II. Leipzig, 1874.
HOWALD, E. *Die Briefe Platons.* Zürich, 1923.
IMMISCH, O. Der erste Platonische Brief. *Philologus,* vol. LXXII.
JOWETT, B. Translation of Plato's Dialogues, Prefaces to the second and third editions.
KARSTEN, H. T. *De Epistolis quae feruntur Platonicis.* Utrecht, 1864.
MEYER, E. *Geschichte des Altertums.* Vol. V.
NOVOTNÝ, F. *Platonis Epistulae commentariis illustratae.* Brno, 1930.
ODAU, M. *Quaestionum de Septima et Octava Platonis Epistola.* Dissert. Königsberg, 1906.
POST, L. A. *Thirteen Epistles of Plato.* Oxford, 1925.
—— A supposed discrepancy in the Platonic Epistles. *American Journ. of Phil.* Vol. XLV.

* For Sicilian affairs Holm is still the safest guide.

RAEDER, H. Über die Echtheit der Platonischen Briefe. *Rhein. Mus.* vol. LXI, 1906.

RICHARDS, H. *Platonica.* London, 1911.

RITTER, C. *Untersuchungen über Platon.* Stuttgart, 1888.

—— *Kommentar zu Platons Gesetzen.* Anhang, p. 367. Leipzig, 1896.

—— *Neue Untersuchungen über Platon.* Munich, 1910.

SILL, H. A. *Untersuchungen über die platonischen Briefe.* I Teil. Dissert. Halle, 1901.

SOUILHÉ, J. *Platon, Œuvres Complètes.* Tome XIII, 1re Partie, Lettres. Paris, 1926.

SUSEMIHL, F. *Gesch. der griech. Lit. in der alexandr. Zeit.* Leipzig, 1892.

TAYLOR, A. E. The ἐπιστήμη in the 7th Platonic Epistle. *Mind*, N.S. No. 83, 1912.

—— *Varia Socratica.* Oxford, 1911.

—— *Plato: The Man and his Work.* London, 1926.

UNGER, G. F. Paper on Eudoxos. *Philologus*, N.F. vol. IV, 1891.

WILAMOWITZ-MOELLENDORFF, U. VON. *Platon.* Vols. I and II. 1920.

—— *Antigonos von Karystos.* Berlin, 1881.

INTRODUCTION

The thirteen Platonic Epistles are concerned almost exclusively
with Sicily and its affairs. Of the five longer and more important
letters, three, the 2nd, 3rd, and 13th, are addressed to the
younger Dionysios, and the other two, the 7th and 8th, to the
relatives and friends of Dion after his death. These with the 4th,
a shorter letter addressed to Dion himself, make up about nine-
tenths of the text of the collection. Of the other seven letters
only one, the 6th, has any importance for the life of Plato. The
Sicilian letters only become intelligible when studied in their
proper historical setting. An attempt to supply this is made in
the first three Sections of this Introduction. Their contents are:

I. A short survey of such of the earlier events as throw light
on the state of affairs which Plato found in Sicily at the time of
his visits to the elder Dionysios and his son, on the problems
with which he was confronted in his relations with the latter, and
on the local scenery of the drama.

II. An account of Plato's three visits to Sicily, which will
serve to supplement the narrative given in the 3rd and 7th
Epistles by particulars drawn from other authorities and by
suggesting possible reasons for his conduct.

III. An account of Dion's expedition and of the events which
followed his overthrow of the monarchy and led up to his own
murder.

The third of these Sections errs perhaps on the side of fullness; but it is not unnecessary. Plato's narrative gives us in
Dion's death the catastrophe of a tragedy, but leaves us without
information as to its causes. A Note on the lost Epistles of
Timonides is attached to this Section. If these were nothing
more than a novel in the form of letters, what we know of Dion
at first hand shrinks to very little.

Section IV of the Introduction deals in general terms with the
question of the genuineness of the collection regarded as a
whole. The discussion of the evidence for or against each of the

letters individually is reserved for the Notes. This Section is followed by a Note on the Sokratic Epistles, and another on the literary style of the Platonic Epistles.

§ I

SICILIAN AFFAIRS DOWN TO THE DEATH OF THE ELDER DIONYSIOS

The Greek colonies of Sicily and southern Italy were a New World, which, in matters of sentiment, culture and intercourse, bore to the older States of Hellas a relation not unlike that which existed a century ago between England and her earlier settlements on the other side of the Atlantic. In both cases movement was more rapid in the younger settlements than in the mother country, and new types were developed in politics, religion and philosophy. Syracuse, with which we are mainly concerned, was a colony of Dorians from Corinth. Some of the best families of Corinth took part in its foundation, and the tie which connected the colony with its mother city was never forgotten. It was to Corinth that Dion looked for help in drawing up his new constitution, and to Corinth that the Syracusans appealed when they wanted a deliverer from the second tyranny of the younger Dionysios. And, a century later, Syracusan families of the better sort, even after migrating to Alexandria, were still proud of their Corinthian pedigrees and Doric dialect.*

Sicily far surpassed the older Hellas in fertility and natural resources, and the Greeks knew how to make the most of such advantages. But increasing wealth brought with it habits of luxury with their inevitable train of vices and excesses. Sicilian banquets became a proverb among those who were used to the simple and hardy life which continued to be practised in most of the older States of Hellas. If wealth accumulated in the hands of individuals in Sicily, it did so still more in the hands of the despots of such cities as Syracuse and Akragas. These monarchs made a great show at gatherings such as the Olympic Games; and their victories are celebrated in some of the finest of the Odes

* Theokr. *Id.* xv, 90.

of Pindar. The Gods were not neglected, and the ruins of the temples of Akragas and Selinous are still among the most extensive remains of Greek architecture. But a vein of frivolity was characteristic of the people, and their principal contributions to literature were the comic drama and the mime or comic sketch.

At the same time, however, a spirit of enquiry was developed, and some of the greatest names in Greek philosophy and science belong to Italy and Sicily—Pythagoras, Parmenides, Zeno, Empedokles, Philolaos, Archimedes—whose contributions, not only to philosophy, but to mathematics, music and medicine, were of the highest importance. To the student of the Platonic Epistles Pythagoras is important, because they contain passages which show the influence of Pythagorean teaching on the mind of Plato, and because he founded a School of study, which, transferred later to Taras, did valuable work in the development of mathematics and in other directions. Plato's first introduction to Sicily arose from a visit to this School.

The brilliant period of the early despots coincided with that of the Persian Wars, and the Carthaginians, whose action was, no doubt, inspired by Persia, invaded Sicily with an overwhelming force in the same year in which Xerxes invaded Greece. But Gelon, the despot of Syracuse, was able to put an army of 50,000 men into the field, and at the battle of Himera (480 B.C.) defeated the invaders so decisively that for more than seventy years Carthage was content with maintaining her settlements at the western end of Sicily, and left the Greek colonies unmolested. But she remained a formidable neighbour, and they had had a narrow escape. They owed their survival mainly to the fact that the development of the population and resources of Syracuse under Gelon's rule enabled him to put a large and united force into the field. He had in fact converted a small town into one of the largest cities of the Greek world.

The earlier Syracuse was, like the modern city, a town of modest dimensions on the island of Ortygia (see Plan), which was separated from the mainland by a narrow channel, and commands two harbours, a large one on the west, and a smaller one on the east. The site was an ideal one for a small city of about 20,000 inhabitants, but allowed of no expansion. At an early date the island was connected with the mainland by a mole, which in time became an isthmus, converting it into a peninsula. Before Gelon's time a suburb, Achradina, had been formed on the higher ground of the seaward end of the blunt peninsula which adjoins Ortygia on the north. This new quarter, together with the low ground between it and Ortygia, Gelon protected by a wall running from the sea on the north to the shore of the Great Harbour near the point where the isthmus branches off. Thus the whole of the butt-end of the broad peninsula, which was also protected by a wall on its seaward sides, formed, with Ortygia, a single great city.

Gelon himself only survived his victory for about a year; but the splendour of his rule was maintained by his brother Hieron, who succeeded him. The coinage is still a convincing evidence of the immense prosperity of the leading Greek States of Sicily during the next seventy years. The large silver tetradrachms with the majestic four-horsed chariot on the reverse, which were struck by Gelon in commemoration of his victory, set a fashion which was followed in the beautiful coins struck by Syracuse and other Sicilian cities during this period. The visits of poets such as Pindar, Simonides, Bacchylides and Aeschylus, are another sign of the splendour of the age.

Fifteen years after the battle of Himera the Syracusans overthrew the despotism and established popular government. Their example was followed by the other Sicilians, and for the next sixty years the personal rule of tyrants disappears from Sicily. At Syracuse towards the close of this period the power was in the hands of the nobles, and Hermokrates, under whose able leadership the Syracusans defeated and destroyed the invading forces of Athens (415–413 B.C.), was at the head of the aristocratic party. But this national victory was followed by an outburst of democratic feeling. It was the moment of which Plato speaks (354 a), when the citizens of Syracuse "carried to excess their opposition to authority, and were victims of a passion for liberty which knew no bounds".

The democratic party obtained the control of affairs and

Hermokrates was banished. He tried to reinstate himself by force, was defeated, and lost his life; his supporters had to retire into exile. Among those who fought desperately for him, and, though wounded, escaped with his life, was Dionysios, a young man of humble origin, who with a few others of the wounded escaped banishment, because their friends gave out that they were dead. Dionysios had the ability and courage of Hermokrates, but none of his public spirit. His aims were purely personal, and he was untroubled by scruples of any kind.

It was one of those times of crisis and imminent danger which give an opportunity to the adventurer. The collapse of Athenian prestige, when their expeditionary force was annihilated in 413 B.C., was followed almost at once by renewed activity on the part of the barbarians both in the east and the west. In the following year the Persians were attacking the Athenians' dependencies in Asia Minor, and three years later (409 B.C.) a large Carthaginian army landed in western Sicily. The two movements were probably the results of concerted policy.

The Carthaginians brought with them all the appliances for taking walled cities, and Selinous and Himera, the two cities nearest their own settlements, were taken by storm and destroyed. At Himera all the male captives, 3000 in number, were sacrificed on the spot where the Carthaginian general had fallen in 480 B.C. Three years later (406 B.C.) another invasion took place on a larger scale, and Akragas, one of the wealthiest cities of the Greek world, fell after a seven months' siege. On this occasion a strong relieving force was sent from Syracuse, and with proper co-operation between this and the Akragantine troops the city might have been saved. But the generals of both forces were suspected of treachery and collusion with the enemy. The Akragantines put their five generals on trial, and stoned four of them to death. The only thing accomplished by the Syracusans was to cover the flight of the citizens, who evacuated the city by night, when their food was exhausted. Akragas was left to be plundered by the Carthaginians, who took up their winter quarters in the city.

The fall of Akragas, which must have been a great shock to

the Greek world, gave Dionysios his opportunity. He denounced the Syracusan generals as traitors, urging the people to lay hands on them and put them to death without waiting for a trial. He was backed by Philistos, a wealthy man who was afterwards the most consistent supporter, and the historian, of the Dionysian dynasty. The people were not disposed to follow the example of the Akragantines; but they deposed the generals and appointed ten successors, of whom Dionysios was one. He was not content with this, and when the force of Syracuse took the field in defence of Gela, which was the next place attacked by the invaders, he appeared before the Assembly with charges of treachery against his colleagues, and at the same time obtained a vote for the recall of exiled members of the party of Hermokrates.

He had now a strong body of supporters at his back, of whom the most prominent was Hipparinos, a noble with powerful connections. They had learnt a lesson from the failure of Hermokrates, and were convinced that absolute power resting on armed force was the only means of securing stable government for Syracuse. A dispassionate view of the facts, as they then stood, and of the heterogeneous nature of the population of Syracuse, suggests that there was much to be said for this view.

With the aid of his new supporters, Dionysios was able to induce the Assembly to depose his nine colleagues and appoint him sole General with Full Powers (αὐτοκράτωρ στρατηγός). His next step, the usual one in a despot's progress, was to trick the troops into allowing him a bodyguard of 600 mercenaries, which he at once strengthened to 1000. He was then able to seize the citadel and rule as autocrat without disguise. He still had to reckon with the Carthaginians. Only two unconquered cities, Gela and Kamarina, were left between their forces and Syracuse, and they were already besieging Gela. A large force of allies from southern Italy had arrived to help in stemming the tide of invasion, and Dionysios took the chief command. Again, as at Akragas, an attempt at decisive action on the part of the combined forces failed, and in this case the failure was due to the fact that Dionysios had not brought up his contingent at the

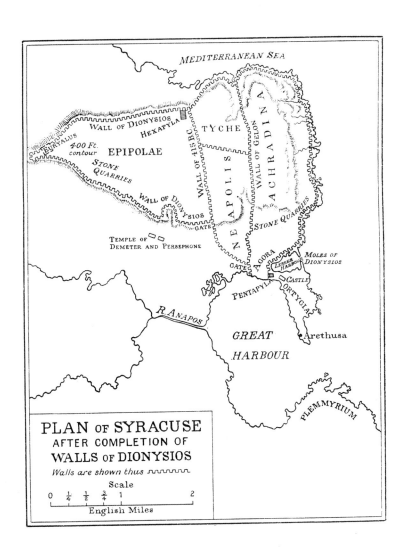

MEDITERRANEAN SEA

WALL OF DIONYSIOS

HEXAPYLA

TYCHE

EURYALUS

400 Ft. *contour*

EPIPOLAE

STONE QUARRIES

WALL OF 415 B.C.

WALL OF GELON

NEAPOLIS

ACHRADINA

WALL OF DIONYSIOS

GATE

STONE QUARRIES

TEMPLE OF DEMETER AND PERSEPHONE

AGORA

GATE

LESSER HARBOUR

MOLES OF DIONYSIOS

CASTLE

PENTAPYLA

ORTYGIA

R. ANAPOS

GREAT

HARBOUR

Arethusa

PLEMMYRIUM

PLAN of SYRACUSE
AFTER COMPLETION OF
WALLS of DIONYSIOS

Walls are shown thus ᠕᠕᠕᠕᠕

Scale

0   ¼   ½   ¾   1   2

English Miles

proper time. There is little doubt that it was he who was now in collusion with the Carthaginians. After the defeat the city was evacuated by night, and the Geloans were marched towards Syracuse. The Kamarineans were compelled to join the wretched column of fugitives, and both cities were left to be plundered by the Carthaginians.

The allies now went home in disgust, and some of the Syracusans made a fruitless attempt at mutiny. They succeeded in seizing and holding the city and citadel for a few hours. But Dionysios was soon master of the position again, and instituted a house-to-house search, during which many of his principal enemies were despatched. It was not long before he came to terms with the Carthaginians. The treaty between them left the enemy in possession of all that they had taken, including the whole south coast of Sicily, and provided for the independence of the Greek cities in the east of the island and of the native tribes of the interior, leaving only Syracuse to Dionysios. But he was recognised as the ruler of Syracuse, and we may assume that this was the price which he received for his treachery at Gela. It was all that he wanted for the moment; for it gave him time to secure and consolidate his rule.

The steps which he took for this purpose included wholesale changes in the city and citadel. The whole of Ortygia was appropriated for the residence of the royal family with its guards and attendants, and was protected on the landward side by a high wall across the isthmus with numerous and lofty towers. Admission could be obtained only through the Pentapyla, a long entrance-way with five successive gates. Within these fortifications and close by them was the private castle of Dionysios, a massive and impregnable stronghold from which the despot could control Ortygia and the harbours on either side of it. It had, no doubt, extensive grounds, and in the Epistles we have mention of gardens with shrubberies, and a garden-house, which was assigned to Plato for his quarters (Ep. II, 313 a, III, 319 c, VII, 347 a, 348 c, 349 c, d). New docks were constructed in the Lesser Harbour within the line of fortifications; and the mouth of the harbour was closed by a wall with gates, which admitted only one ship at a time. What is said in the 7th Epistle about Plato's difficulty in getting away from Syracuse (347 a) shows how completely all the shipping was under the monarch's control. These works secured Dionysios against enemies within. He had also to make the city impregnable against foreign foes; for his policy of submission to Carthage was only a temporary measure to be changed for one of aggression as soon as circumstances allowed. The existing fortifications left the upper city, built on the slopes of Epipolae, exposed to attack from the higher ground to the west of them, which rose in a long triangle, inadequately protected by the outlying fort Euryalos at its apex about two miles from the city walls. The only way of completing the defences satisfactorily was to build walls from Euryalos, running north-east and south-east, so as to enclose the whole of the triangle. This was what Dionysios did. He was a great builder, and his huge walls of magnificent masonry, of which large parts are still standing, with the massive works which he constructed at Euryalos, have ever since been the most effective memorial of his rule (see Plan).

Not less impressive for a contemporary were the military and naval forces which he got together, the "fetters of adamant" by which his power was secured. The catalogue is repeated in almost the same terms by three ancient authorities*—400 triremes and quinqueremes, 100,000 infantry, 10,000 cavalry, and 10,000 mercenaries.† Round numbers of this sort must not be taken too seriously. The whole navy was not kept permanently in commission, and there is probably much exaggeration in the numbers given for the citizen forces. But there is no doubt about the mercenaries; and the spectacle of a despot supported by a standing army of professional soldiers on so large a scale was something new in the Greek world.

The rule of Dionysios was on the whole a mild one; but he

---

* Plutarch, *Dion*, 14; Aelian, *V.H.* vi, 12; Nepos, *Dion*, 5.
† Plato's narrative (348 b, 350 a) makes it clear that the quarters of the main body of the mercenaries were, under ordinary circumstances, outside the akropolis. There must have been quarters for them inside also, to which they would be moved in case of a siege. They were evidently within the akropolis during the struggle with Dion.

intended to make it hereditary, and set to work in a methodical way to found a royal family. His first wife, the daughter of Hermokrates, lost her life during the mutiny mentioned above. When his power was more firmly established, he followed the practice of oriental monarchs, and took two consorts. One of these was Aristomachê, the daughter of Hipparinos, whose family he henceforth associated closely with his own. The other, chosen to strengthen his hands in southern Italy, was Doris, daughter of one of the leading citizens of Lokroi. He astonished the Greek world by marrying these two wives on the same day (398 B.C.).

By Doris he had two sons, Dionysios, who succeeded him, and Hermokritos, and one daughter, Dikaiosynê (Justice); Aristomachê remained childless for some years, and then presented him with two sons, Hipparinos and Nysaios, and two daughters, Sophrosynê (Temperance) and Aretê (Virtue). The daughters, as soon as they were of marriageable age, he assigned to members of his new royal family—Dikaiosynê to his brother, Leptines, Sophrosynê to his son, Dionysios, Aretê first to his brother, Thearidas, and, after his death, to her uncle, Dion, the brother of Aristomachê (see Genealogical Table).

In foreign policy the principal incidents of his long reign were his wars with Carthage. At one moment it seemed as if he was bringing the Carthaginian power in Sicily entirely to an end. But Carthage had great reserves of power, and was not likely to submit to complete loss of so important a trade centre. Perhaps, too, Dionysios thought that his position would be less secure if his subjects were relieved of all outside dangers. On a view of the whole struggle, he has some claims to the gratitude of Europe for having checked the encroachments of an oriental power. He left the Greeks in possession of much, though not quite all, which they had possessed before the invasions of Carthage in 409 and 406 B.C.

But, while he thus recovered lost ground, he left it doubtful whether the Sicilian Greeks would not have been better off as subjects of Carthage than under his rule. Plato says (332 c) that he gathered the whole of Sicily into a single city. This is a mild description of his policy. Before the end of his reign he had either sold into slavery or transferred to Syracuse the population of all the other cities of eastern Sicily. Naxos was destroyed and its inhabitants sold into slavery. The same fate befell the citizens of Katana. Those of Leontinoi were more mercifully treated and transferred to Syracuse. These two cities were utilised for settlements of Campanian mercenaries. Messana received new settlers from southern Italy, and her own citizens were left to wander homeless. The abandoned sites of Akragas, Gela and Kamarina were within his sphere of territory, but no attempt was made to resettle them. Bands of homeless refugees from these places and from Syracuse itself were wandering about the interior, finding shelter where they could, or living by plunder. These facts are sufficient commentary on the passages in the Epistles (315 d 2, 332 e 3, 336 a 6, 337 a, b), in which proposals for the resettlement of the cities of Sicily are spoken of as the first step to be looked for from a reformed government at Syracuse.

Dionysios formed, and in some measure carried out, imperial schemes which went far beyond his dominions in Sicily. The presence of independent cities on the other side of the Straits of Messana was an immediate danger to his power, and it was necessary for him to secure the whole of the south-western corner of Italy. Here, as in Sicily, his policy was to confine political independence to a single city. Lokroi, connected with him by marriage, was allowed to retain its freedom. All the other cities, even the once-powerful Kroton, were captured and either left desolate or reduced to the position of subjects.

The Greek colonies in the south-east of Italy had formed a confederacy under the presidency of Taras, which was guided largely by the counsel of the philosopher Archytas. He held the chief magistracy in his own city seven times, and enjoyed a permanent ascendancy like that of Perikles at Athens. Taras and the States in league with her were treated with respect by Dionysios, and continued to enjoy their freedom; his relation to them was probably that of a mild protectorate.

The navy of Dionysios enabled him to exercise control much

FAMILY OF DIONYSIOS

(From Holm, vol. II, p. 451.)

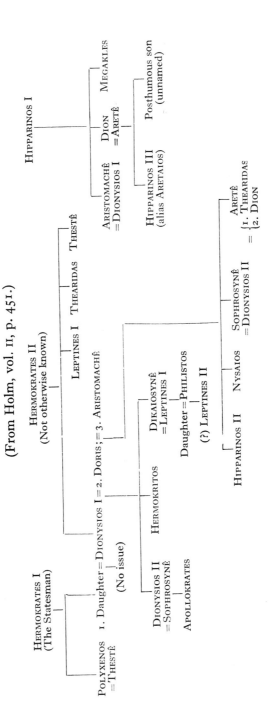

farther than Taras. The trade of the Adriatic was important for Syracuse, and one of the objects of his policy was to secure it by settlements at convenient points. He founded colonies at Issa, an island half way up the sea, and at Adria in the extreme north. Ankon also (the modern Ancona) was founded at the same time; and though Strabo attributes this settlement to refugees from the power of Dionysios, we may safely assume that it was made with his permission.

As the reign of Dionysios went on, the feeling of alarm which his power inspired among the older States of Hellas in a great measure subsided. At first platform orators and publicists had pointed to his tyranny in the west and to the Persian monarchy in the east, as the two sources of danger to a free Hellas of the old type. Lysias had spoken against him at the Olympic Games, and had urged the spectators to attack the gorgeous tents in which the emissaries and competitors sent by him were housed. The date is doubtful; but it was either 388 or 384 B.C. Again in 380 B.C. Isokrates in his *Panegyrikos* urged Athens and Sparta to combine in repelling the danger which threatened Hellas from the monarchies of the east and of the west, Persia and Syracuse. But such appeals did not belong to practical politics. Sparta had rendered material help to Dionysios in his early struggles with the citizens of Syracuse, and remained his close ally throughout his reign. Dionysios sent naval contingents and mercenaries to her aid on more than one occasion.

Athens, in spite of the fine language of her orators, is proved by inscriptions to have been ready to coquet with the tyrant. As early as 393 B.C., when her naval power was being revived, a complimentary decree was passed in honour of Dionysios, his brothers Leptines and Thearidas, and his brother-in-law Polyxenos.* This was an attempt to detach the monarch from Sparta, and it led to no result. But towards the close of his reign, when Sparta had been humbled by Thebes and was in alliance with Athens, the Athenian overtures were more successful. An inscription of 369 B.C.† shows that the citizenship of Athens was

* Dittenberger, *Syll.* vol. I, No. 66 (= *C.I.A.* II, 8).
† Dittenberger, *ib.* No. 89 (= *C.I.A.* II, 51).

conferred on Dionysios and his sons, Dionysios and Hermokritos, in recognition of his services at the ineffectual Peace
Congress held at Delphi in that year. The award of the first
prize to his tragedy, *The Ransom of Hector*, at the Lenaea of
January 367 B.C., was probably not unconnected with these
political combinations; for an inscription of February 367 B.C.*
records the conclusion of a defensive alliance between Athens
and Dionysios. The death of Dionysios followed shortly after
this. The narrative of Diodoros (xv, 73, 74), which attributes it
to excesses at the banquets given in celebration of his poetical
victory, is sufficiently disproved by the date of this inscription.†
The habitual temperance of Dionysios ought to have made
historians cautious about accepting this story, which is brought
in by Diodoros as a proof of the fulfilment of an oracle. It is not
mentioned by Plutarch, and there is no allusion to it in the
Platonic Epistles, the only contemporary document which we
have.

   The death of Dionysios came when his prestige stood at its
highest point. Monarchy was beginning to be regarded with less
disfavour by political writers of various shades of opinion.
Isokrates, who in 380 B.C. had denounced Dionysios as an enemy
to Hellenism, addressed a letter to him in 369 B.C., of which the
opening pages are still extant. The tyrant is appealed to as
the man who stands first and is most powerful among the
Greek race (Isokr. *Ep.* 1, 7), and it was clearly the writer's
intention to invite him to lead the Greek States in an attack on
Persia.

   Xenophon, a friend to monarchy, devoted to Sicily a dialogue,
the *Hiero*, written probably just after the death of Dionysios, and
before the power left by him had been weakened. In the earlier
part of it Hiero expounds to the poet, Simonides, the drawbacks
under which the life of a tyrant, even if successful, suffers; the
details throughout belong to the reign of Dionysios, and the
picture is so drawn as to be unmistakeable to a contemporary.
The concluding pages come as a surprise; for the poet replies by

describing the benefits which may be conferred on a State, not by a hereditary king, but by an enlightened and benevolent despot.

Plato's Dialogues show that his views, like those of Isokrates, changed in his later years. In middle life he drew in his *Republic* a dark picture of the despot, which must have been either written or retouched in the light of his own experiences at Syracuse in 388 B.C. Many touches belong unmistakeably to the elder Dionysios, and there is no hint that a tyranny might be developed into a better form of government. It is something irremediably evil, and even the poets, who, like Euripides, have praised it, must be banished from the State.

The *Politikos*, written fifteen or twenty years later, shows a different attitude. Here the ideal form of government, if it were attainable, is that of the absolute monarch, who is uncontrolled by laws, but knows the art of ruling, and settles all details in accordance with it. But as this is beyond human powers, the next best constitution is that of the king who governs in accordance with laws.

In the *Laws*, his last work, the constitution which he constructs is not monarchical, but an aristocracy of a rather narrow type. But he is not the less alive to the advantages of a limited or constitutional monarchy; and the best chance, which he can see in practice, for the actual establishment of such a State as he would desire, is that there should be a young tyrant willing to listen to the advice of a wise lawgiver (see 709 c ff.). Most striking is the language in which he describes the efficiency of work done under the orders of a competent despot; and it is clear that he was fully conscious of the practical advantages of this form of government. He thought that the advantages might still be secured if the despotism were converted into a limited monarchy. It may be safely inferred that he went to Sicily, on his first invitation from the younger Dionysios, with the intention of playing the part of the lawgiver described in this passage, and of converting the despotism into a monarchy limited by laws. But the change was one which he would not have made hastily, nor without some education of the young monarch. This preliminary education was the rock on which Plato's scheme was wrecked.

To understand Plato's language, it must be remembered that in three of his works, the *Politikos*, the *Laws*, and the 7th Epistle, there is mention of a "best thing" and a "second-best thing", and that the things which are best and second-best are not the same in each case. In the *Politikos* the "best thing" is the rule of the beneficent super-man, unhampered by laws, and the "second-best thing" the rule of the constitutional monarch under unalterable laws. In the *Laws* the "second-best thing" is the non-communistic aristocracy there mapped out, while the "best thing" is the communistic State which he had described in the *Republic*. In both these cases the thing which would be best is put aside as unattainable. But in the 7th Epistle the "best thing" was for a moment actually attainable. It was the rule which the younger Dionysios might have introduced, if he had followed Plato's counsels (see 335 d, 337 d). It was attainable so long as the power of the monarchy remained intact. With the aid of that power changes might have been made so radical that they would have formed a foundation for a new type of State, which would have succeeded in developing virtuous-minded citizens. After the overthrow of this power, Plato thought it still possible, if his advice were followed, to found a reformed State, which would have political stability; but it could no longer be expected to produce the same far-reaching moral reformation. This is the "second-best" thing of the 7th Epistle, and the 8th gives the form which he thought such a State might take.

§ II

PLATO'S VISITS TO SICILY

That Plato's first journey to Italy and Sicily took place in 388/7 B.C. may be inferred from what he says about his own age and that of Dion at the time (324 b, c). His account of it (326 b 5–327 b 4) follows the remarkable climax which closes the narrative of his early life. He had been anxious, he says, from the first, to take part in political life, and had waited and watched for opportunities of doing so; but the general and increasing disorganisation of public affairs at Athens and elsewhere had forced upon him the conviction that "there will be no cessation of evils for mankind till either those who have attained a right and true philosophy receive sovereign power in the States, or those in power in the States by some dispensation of Providence become true philosophers" (326 b).

It is clear that he regarded the journey as a turning-point both in his own career and in the history of Sicily. For himself it marked the final abandonment of all intention of taking part in the political life of Athens. This did not mean that he had given up the intention of working for others, but that in future his energies were to be devoted to teaching others to do that which he had been prevented from doing himself, and to giving to the future statesmen of Hellas that training in philosophy which he believed to be the only sure foundation for political activity.* For Sicily the journey was the first link in the chain of events which was destined to lead to the fall of the monarchy founded by Dionysios.

We can hardly be wrong in connecting his travels with the School which he established on his return. Plato's School was not an entirely new departure. Isokrates was in the field before him, and was training young men for public life by a course of instruction to which he also gave the name of philosophy. To Isokrates "philosophy" meant the skilful use of language, combined with such general culture as fits men for handling public affairs. Plato's "philosophy" required as its first step a training in pure science, that is, in mathematical science.

During the ten years which followed the death of Sokrates Plato must have been occupied, not merely with the composition of the Dialogues which were given to the public during that period, but with the study of those mathematical subjects which were to form so important a part of the work of the Academy, so far as this could be carried on at Athens. It was not the age of

* For the political influence thus exercised by Plato's teaching see Burnet, *Phil.* pp. 302 ff.

text-books, and if he was to learn the results of the researches of others, this could only be done by personal contact with those mathematicians who had worked out the higher parts of the subject. The best mathematical School of the day was that of the Pythagoreans of Taras, whose leader, Archytas, was a man of about the same age as Plato.*

Plato's account of his movements only tells us that he went to Italy and Sicily. But his visit to Syracuse evidently followed a stay at Taras long enough for him to establish friendly relations with Archytas, and learn what was to be learned from him. His visit must have made some stir in the Greek world of the west. His earlier Dialogues were probably in circulation at Taras and Syracuse; his name was, no doubt, well known as that of a new writer of remarkable genius. Some of his more recent works were perhaps communicated by his own reading to philosophical circles at both cities. The interest aroused by his visit must have resembled that created by the tours of Dickens and Thackeray in the United States.

Plato says nothing about his reasons for crossing from Italy to Sicily, beyond a remark that the act seemed to be due to the working of Providence. He may, as his biographers say, have wished to visit the scene of the eruptions of Etna. But there can be little doubt that his visit to Syracuse was preceded by correspondence between Archytas and Dionysios, and it is worth noting that it followed very shortly after the annihilation by Dionysios of Rhegion and other cities of south-western Italy. The "frightfulness" of his treatment of some of these conquered enemies must have been fresh in men's minds.

* There is no reason to doubt the tradition that it was the Pythagoreans who first solved the problem of constructing and inscribing in the sphere three of the five "regular solids", the tetrahedron, the cube, and the dodekahedron, and that the geometry of what were afterwards known as the "Platonic Solids" was completed in the Academy by Theaitetos. (For the evidence see A. E. Taylor's *Commentary on Plato's Timaeus*, pp. 358–9.) It is scarcely possible to over-rate the importance of these extensions of knowledge. (See my edition of Plato's *Epinomis*, Introduction, Section VI.) Those who followed the movement felt that new worlds were being opened to them. Geometry for the moment was in the same position in which Relativity has been in our day.

Cumae Neapolis
Capreae I.
Posidonia
Elea
Palinuri Pr.
Thurii
Brundisium
Metapontum Taras
Heraklea
Siris
Sybaris
Kroton
Skylletion
Pelorum Pr.
Hipponion
Kaulonia
Lokri
Messana
Panormus
Rhegion
Himera
Egesta
Motya
Lilybaeum
Mt. Aetna
Tauromenion
Naxos
Selinous
Halykos Fl.
Enna
Katana
Heraklea
Minoa
Akragas
Leontini
Gela
Anapos Fl.
Megara Hyblaea
Syracuse
Eknomos Pr.
Kamarina
Pachynum Pr.

SOUTHERN ITALY
AND
SICILY
IN THE TIME OF
PLATO AND DION
Scale
0 10 20 30 40 50 60 70 80
English Miles

Plato's account of his visit falls into two parts. The first gives a striking picture of those social and moral excesses which had made the name of Sicily a by-word. The second tells of his personal intercourse with Dion, and the permanent effect produced by it on the young man's life and character. In the first part he lays stress on the uselessness of political reforms, unless they are accompanied by a reform in morals. In the second it is again the moral side of the young man's character to which he draws special attention.

What is said about the relations between Plato and Dion as teacher and pupil presupposes, on Plato's part, a stay at Syracuse of some little duration. Dion was at this time a young man of about twenty. From other sources we learn that he had a commanding figure and striking features (Nep. *Dion*, 2). Plato testifies to his remarkable mental gifts, and his enthusiasm for all that was good and noble (327 a 6). Dion became for him the ideal pupil, the disciple and friend, for whom he never ceased to feel a love passing the love of women.*

Plato makes no mention of any personal intercourse between himself and Dionysios; but he was capable of great reticence on such matters. If his readings at Syracuse included selections from the *Gorgias*, his views might well be regarded by the monarch as dangerous. The details which later writers give of the conversations between the two men may be dismissed as legendary. But there can be no doubt that there were conversations. Dionysios was fond of conversing with the literary men who were attracted to his court. He was, however, always on the watch for anything which might be dangerous to his rule.

* The epitaph on Dion, written in Plato's name and preserved by Diog. Laert. III, 30, deserves quotation, though the last line has made critics doubtful about its authorship.

Δάκρυα μὲν 'Εκάβῃ καὶ 'Ιλιάδεσσι γυναιξὶ
 Μοῖραι ἐπέκλωσαν δή ποτε γεινομέναις.
σοὶ δέ, Δίων, ῥέξαντι καλῶν ἐπινίκιον ἔργων
 δαίμονες εὐρείας ἐλπίδας ἐξέχεαν.
κεῖσαι δ' εὐρυχόρῳ ἐν πατρίδι τίμιος ἀστοῖς,
 ὦ ἐμὸν ἐκμήνας θυμὸν ἔρωτι Δίων.

For a fine rendering in German see Wilamowitz, *Platon*, 1, 644.

Plato had the courage of his opinions, and it is quite likely that his outspokenness may have led to his deportation.

Most of the recent critics reject the story of the sale of Plato in the slave-market. Is not this carrying scepticism too far? In any case it is too interesting to be passed over. It is told in two forms, which must come from independent sources. Diodoros (XV, 7) makes the sale take place at Syracuse and connects it with a series of anecdotes about the dithyrambic poet, Philoxenos, one of the literary visitors of Dionysios, whose jests at the expense of the tyrant's poems led to his imprisonment in the stone quarries. "A similar thing," he says, "happened to the philosopher Plato. For, having sent for this man, he at first gave him a great reception, because he had a freedom of speech worthy of a philosopher. But subsequently he took offence at some of his language, and had him taken to the slave-market and sold for twenty minae. His friends, however, got together, and purchased him, and sent him away to Greece, adding this friendly advice, that a wise man either avoids as far as possible the society of tyrants, or makes himself as agreeable as possible to them."

Plutarch (Dion, 4, 5) gives details of the conversation which made Dionysios lose his temper.* According to him Plato's friends after the interview arranged for his departure by the ship in which the Spartan emissary, Pollis, was returning to Greece. But Dionysios gave his own instructions to Pollis that Plato should either be killed on the journey or be sold as a slave. Plato was put on shore at Aegina, which was at the moment at war with Athens, and was there sold as a slave. Plutarch does not add anything about his redemption and return to Athens.

The story is also told by Diogenes Laertius (III, 20), who agrees with Plutarch in representing Plato as sold by Pollis in Aegina, and with Diodoros in giving twenty minae as his price. His redemption is ascribed to Annikeris of Kyrene, and the purchase money, when refunded by Plato's friends, was devoted

* Plutarch's authority is probably Timaios for most of the details which I have taken from him in this section.

by Annikeris to buying for Plato the land on which the Academy was established.

Legendary embellishments should not always be allowed to discredit the incidents to which they are attached. It is quite likely that Philoxenos was imprisoned in the stone quarries, and that Dionysios contrived, as an unpleasant surprise for Plato, that he should be put up for sale in a slave-market. Such an act is in accordance with the vindictiveness of his character. Aegina was at war with Athens at the time (388/7 B.C.), and Dionysios was in alliance with the Spartans and in frequent communication with them. Pollis may very well have obliged him by arranging in this way for the sale of Plato. Such an incident would inevitably receive legendary accretions. The twenty minae and the subsequent use made of the money for the purchase of the site of the Academy may be mythical; but the central incident to which they are attached is probably founded in fact.* What is more important is that the Academy must have been opened by Plato very shortly after his return.

Plato passes over the period of nearly twenty years between his first visit to Syracuse and the death of Dionysios I (368/7 B.C.) with the remark that Dion's strict morals made him rather unpopular at court. The interval was an important one for both men. Dion became the chief minister of Dionysios, and was more closely allied to the royal family by his marriage with the monarch's daughter Areté, after the death of her first husband, Thearidas. Dionysios was a good judge of men, and Dion, though events showed that he was not a great political leader, had in a high degree the qualities which fit a man for the post of a second in command in dealing with great affairs. Like the Emperor Galba, he was "omnium consensu capax imperii, nisi imperasset".

Plato during the same years was engaged in what he, no doubt, regarded as the most important work of his life, the foundation

* One is reminded of the purchase of the "Potter's Field" with the thirty pieces of silver received by Judas, where also the story appears in different forms (Matt. xxvii, 7, Acts i, 18), and where, surely, one may recognise that legend has been at work, without abandoning the belief that a betrayal actually took place.

and development of his new School. Twenty years of such work
must have left their mark on him. If we are to understand the
Plato of the Letters and the later Sicilian voyages, we must
picture him to ourselves as a University Professor—a Professor
with genius of a very uncommon kind—but still a man who has
been absorbed for nearly twenty years in details of teaching and
research. Important and noble as such a life may be, it is not
one which fits a man for playing an active part in practical
politics at a critical moment. Dion's invitation was the beginning
of what proved to be the tragedy of Plato's life.

To Dion and not to Plato must be assigned the initial blunder
of supposing that Dionysios the Younger was the kind of man
who could be trained as a philosopher king. In spite of his
ability and the noble qualities of his mind, Dion's conduct again
and again shows failure to judge character and a tendency to
cherish illusions which did more credit to his heart than to his
head, and it is hard to forgive him for dragging Plato into a
scheme foredoomed to failure by the fact that Dionysios was
an unpromising subject. Though not devoid of intelligence
nor of a certain amiability and desire for better things, the
young man was weak, vain, and self-indulgent; and it ought to
have been clear to Dion that his mind did not provide a foundation on which stability of character could be built. To guard
against any attempt at usurpation, his education had been
neglected and he had been kept in close confinement, where, as
Plutarch relates (*Dion*, 9), "through ignorance and want of other
employment, he amused himself with making little chariots,
candlesticks, wooden chairs and tables". At the time of his
father's death he must have been not less than twenty-eight years
old (Holm, II, pp. 156, 425).

The death of Dionysios with the legend attached to it by
Diodoros has been mentioned above. The following are the
essential parts of Plutarch's more trustworthy story (*Dion*, 6, 7;
translation from Langhorne with some alterations).

"In the last illness of Dionysios, when there seemed to be no
hope of his recovery, Dion would have applied to him on
behalf of the children of Aristomachê, but the physicians were

beforehand with him. They wanted to ingratiate themselves with his successor, and, as Timaios relates, when he asked for a sleeping dose, they gave him one so effectual that he awaked no more. However in the first council that was held when his son Dionysios came to the throne, Dion spoke with so much propriety on the state of affairs and on the measures that ought to be taken, that the rest appeared to be mere children in understanding.

"What alarmed them most was the steps he proposed to take with regard to the danger which threatened them from Carthage; for he offered either to go in person to Carthage and bring the war to an honourable conclusion, if the King wished for peace, or, if he were rather inclined for war, to fit out and maintain fifty triremes at his own expense....They spared no calumny that might enflame the young man's mind against him, representing that he certainly meant to make himself master by sea, and by that means to obtain the kingdom for his sister's children. ...They led the young and ill-educated king through every species of debauchery....Having once made a start, he continued to drink for ninety days in succession, during which the palace doors were closed against sober men and serious talk, and the court was a scene of drunkenness and buffoonery, revelry and riot."

Plutarch adds that, in spite of the general dislike of Dion, Dionysios continued to follow his advice in public affairs, and even began to listen to his counsels about the benefit which he would himself derive from a reform in his morals and from the study of philosophy under Plato. In time the young man's mind conceived a passionate craving to see and hear Plato, and invitations from Dion and Dionysios were sent to Athens.*

Plato's narrative of the doubts into which he was plunged by this invitation, of the hesitation with which it was accepted, and of his experiences at Syracuse, should be read as it stands (327 b 6–330 b 7, 332 c 7–333 a 5, 337 e 6–338 b 2). It requires

---

* Plato says definitely (327 d 7): ταῦτα Δίων ὀρθῶς διανοηθεὶς ἔπεισε μεταπέμπεσθαι Διονύσιον ἐμέ. It is not clear why Wilamowitz says (Pl. II, 285), "Dionysios hat ihn nicht eingeladen".

to be supplemented at two points. He passes over altogether his own reception at Syracuse and his first attempts to educate Dionysios; and he describes only in the most general terms the events which led to the deportation of Dion. Of the early incidents Plutarch's account is as follows:

"Such was the state of affairs when Plato came to Sicily. At first he was received with the greatest appearance of kindness, and he was conveyed from the trireme in one of the king's most splendid chariots.* Dionysios himself sacrificed to the Gods in acknowledgment of his safe arrival, and of the good fortune which had thus befallen his kingdom. The people had the greatest hopes of a speedy reformation. They observed an unusual decorum in the entertainments at court, and a sobriety in the conduct of the courtiers; while the king answered all to whom he gave audience in a very obliging manner. The desire of learning and the study of philosophy were become general, and the several apartments of the royal palace were like so many schools of geometricians, full of the dust in which the students draw their mathematical figures".

The only reference in Plato's Letters to this course of mathematical teaching is the angry retort of Dionysios about geometry, recorded in Ep. III (319 c 3). In the 7th Epistle he is silent on the subject,† and only dwells on the moral counsels given by himself and Dion. It would be wrong to suppose that he had any doubts about the wisdom of his own procedure. He probably felt that there was no chance of improving a mind so wholly untrained as that of Dionysios except by giving him a definite course of instruction, and that the young man's want of perseverance showed that his case was one of those hopeless ones to which he refers in Ep. VII, 340 d 6. He had had abundant

---

* Aelian (V.H. IV, 11) describes the landing, and makes Dionysios in person drive the chariot which conveyed Plato from the ship. He adds that, as a special mark of favour, Plato was allowed to enter into the presence of the tyrant without being searched. He is probably following Theopompos, his usual authority for Sicilian events of this period.

† There are indications that at one point a reference to it may have been removed. See Ep. VII, note 44.

experience of the teaching of adults; and the fact that he brought with him one of the best of his assistants, Xenokrates, shows that he came with the intention of giving systematic instruction to Dionysios and to other members of the court.

On the deportation of Dion Plutarch gives fuller details, which harmonise with Plato's short statement. Dion's leading opponent was the statesman and historian, Philistos, who from the first *coup d'état*, which led to the establishment of the tyranny, had been its most consistent supporter. He had, however, incurred the displeasure of the elder Dionysios, and had been sent abroad to his settlements in the Adriatic and detained there during the latter part of his reign. During his exile he composed the greater part of his history. The dates both of his banishment and of his recall are uncertain*; but he was at Syracuse quite early in the reign of the younger Dionysios, and taking an active part in the intrigues by which the young king soon began to be surrounded. He and the court party, which attached itself to him, viewed Plato's influence with alarm, and tried to bring it to an end by removing Dion.

Much of the management of affairs must have been left to him, while Dionysios was occupied with his mathematical studies, and charges that he was scheming to seize the monarchy for himself and his nephews were constantly whispered in the ears of the sovereign. At length, about four months after Plato's arrival, a letter addressed by Dion to the agents of Carthage, who were negotiating for a peace, fell into the hands of Dionysios. Dion urged them not to have their interview with Dionysios except in his presence, and promised his assistance in obtaining favourable terms. Dionysios showed the letter to

* Plutarch says that Philistos was recalled by Dionysios II on the suggestion of the court party, who wished his influence to counterbalance that of Plato (*Dion*, 11). It is more likely that the recall was an act of grace by the new king on his accession. For one of the most famous passages in the history of Philistos was his description of the funeral of Dionysios I, of which he was probably an eye-witness. The elaborate preparations for this would allow time for his return, if he was recalled soon after the accession. Diodoros (xv, 7) places the return of Philistos many years earlier; but this is one of his many mistakes in chronology.

Philistos, and acted on his advice. While walking alone with Dion by the wall of his castle near to the sea, he showed him the letter and accused him of conspiring with the Carthaginians against him. Then, refusing to listen to Dion's explanations, he forced him on board a small vessel and commanded the sailors to set him ashore in Italy (Plut. *Dion*, 14).*

For the later events of Plato's visit the autobiography is our best authority, and its narrative need not be repeated here. Two things come out clearly—the futility of the task on which he was engaged, and the uncomfortable position in which he was placed during the latter part of his stay at Syracuse. It must have been a relief when the engagements† of Dionysios obliged him to allow his visitor to return to his duties at Athens. It is clear that the two men parted on good terms. Plato must have recognised how important it was in Dion's interests, apart from other reasons, to maintain these friendly relations; and there was, no doubt, correspondence between them. The only specimen of this is the 13th Epistle. In my introductory remarks to this I have tried to show that it is a genuine document, and that its friendly tone gives no ground for suspicion. Apart from this letter we have no information about Plato's life during the five years between his two visits to the younger Dionysios. He was, no doubt, occupied with the work of his School and with the composition of some of the most important of his later dialogues. Dion was probably spending much of his time at Athens,‡ where he was hospitably entertained by Kallippos, and was on intimate terms with all the Platonic circle, especially with Plato's nephew, Speusippos.

* Diodoros (xvi, 6) gives a different account of the removal of Dion. He makes no mention of Plato's visit; but says that Dion's philosophy and great qualities brought on him suspicion as a man capable of overthrowing the tyranny, and that Dionysios resolved on putting him to death. Dion, however, managed to escape, first to friends in Sicily, and then to the Peloponnese. The expedition of Dion is described as if it occurred very shortly after his flight: the neglect of chronology is characteristic. See note on p. 23.

† For the war on which Dionysios was engaged see note on 338 a 4.

‡ See note on 346 b 3.

Plato started on his last journey to Sicily in the early part of
361 B.C.* The causes which led him to risk what he describes as
his third visit to Skylla and Charybdis (345 e) are stated at some
length both in the 3rd and in the 7th Epistles. In the 7th two
full pages of the text of Stephanus are devoted to a defence of
his decision; and the concluding sentence of the letter shows that
he attributed great importance to this point. What he says is
evidently intended for readers at Athens and in the Greek world
at large, rather than for the friends of Dion at Syracuse.

It is clear that Plato once more acted against his better
judgment in consenting to go, and that afterwards he bitterly
regretted the course which he was so anxious to defend. He
gives two reasons for his decision. One was the feeling that, if
there was any chance of the conversion of Dionysios to the
philosophic life, he must not miss the opportunity. The other
was the desire to do something to retrieve the fortunes of his
friend Dion. It is not easy for us—perhaps it was not easy for
him—to decide which of these had most weight with him. But
it cannot be right to say, as Ritter does (*N.U.* p. 377), that the
second was his only motive. He must have been also moved by the
pressure of Archytas and the Tarentines, whose wishes would be
strongly supported by Archedemos. We may perhaps guess that
he was one of the men who are much influenced by the desire
not to disappoint the hopes which others have formed about
them.

On this journey Plato was accompanied by his nephew
Speusippos, and by others whose names are not mentioned.
While he enjoyed the hospitality of Dionysios in his castle, they
were entertained in the city, presumably by friends of Dion.
Fifteen pages of the text of Stephanus are occupied with his
account of the relations between Dionysios and himself during
this visit; and nine of these are given to the philosophical side of
his enterprise. Evidently it is on this side that he is most
anxious to defend himself. His philosophy was by far the most

* Plutarch's narrative (*Dion*, 19) makes it clear that he arrived some
time before the eclipse of the sun, which took place on the 12th May,
361 B.C.

important thing in his life, and he wished to show that in his dealings with Dionysios he had been guided by the same principles as in his teaching at Athens.

This necessitated some explanation of the simplest first principles which underlay his teaching. There are two fundamental points on which he lays stress—first that the learner must have sound moral principles and be living a well-regulated life—and secondly that the teaching is not something which can be crammed from text-books, but involves long and laborious personal intercourse with a teacher. Plato was resolved, as soon as possible after his arrival, to put it to the test, whether there was any prospect of these principles being accepted and carried out by Dionysios. His account of the test proposed and of the interview in which he tried to apply it (340 b 3–344 d 2) should be compared with the shorter account of what is evidently the same interview in the 2nd Epistle (313 a 6–c 5). I have attempted in my Notes to make these two passages intelligible; but neither of them is very illuminating to a modern reader.

The fuller narrative, in Ep. VII, after starting to give an account of the interview, and describing how Plato's exposition was interrupted by the monarch, turns aside into a digression, of which the object is to show why philosophical teaching cannot be given by written treatises, and we are left without any information about the conclusion of the interview. From the shorter account it can be gathered that Plato tried in vain to make it clear to the monarch that he was over-rating his own understanding. Neither account enlightens us as to the nature of the mistaken views which were held by Dionysios and the teachers who had influenced him. A definite statement on this point would have done much towards clearing up the position. There are other sources, however, from which a conjecture on this point may be framed.

Plutarch (*Dion*, 19) tells us that Aristippos the Cyrenaic was, and apparently had for some time been, at the court of Dionysios. He was clearly a *persona grata* there, and we may infer that philosophic hedonism was a popular creed. This is borne out by a story which Athenaios (XII, 545 a) gives on the authority of

Aristoxenos, the musician, who had resided in Italy and must have conversed with contemporaries of Archytas. He says that among the envoys sent on one occasion to Archytas by Dionysios the Younger was a man called Polyarchos, a voluptuary, but conversant with philosophy. This man, in a discussion held in the garden of Archytas, upheld hedonistic principles in their most advanced form, maintaining that men ought to obey the dictates of nature and follow pleasure. This doctrine he supported by the fact that all men, when put into a position of absolute power, acted in this way, illustrating his view by the pains taken by the kings of Persia to provide themselves with a succession of novel pleasures, utilising for this purpose all the resources of their empire, and by the similar conduct, though on a less extensive scale, of Dionysios at Syracuse.

There are grounds for supposing that the hedonism which was fashionable at the court of Dionysios may have rested on a foundation of materialism, and that the views put forward by Dionysios himself were of this nature. The question which he sent to Plato by Archedemos περὶ τῆς τοῦ πρώτου φύσεως (312 d 7) is intelligible at once, if we suppose that he and others questioned Plato's view that in the order of things souls came before bodies, maintaining against him that bodies are the only realities. It is clear from Plato's *Sophist* (246 b) that a crude materialism of this kind was common at the time of his later visits to Sicily, and he represents it as familiar to the Eleatic Stranger from Magna Graecia. It is a creed adapted to a pleasure-seeking age. The 10th Book of the *Laws* shows how prevalent it was and how strongly the need for confuting it was felt by Plato, who had probably come into contact with this new gospel during his residence at Syracuse. In that portion of the *Sophist* which describes the opposition between the materialists and the εἰδῶν φίλοι we probably have a reminiscence of controversies at Syracuse between Sicilian or Italian materialists on the one hand and disciples of the Pythagorean school of Taras on the other. If Dionysios took the side of the materialists in such discussions, Plato's low opinion of his philosophy is sufficiently accounted for.

The remainder of Plato's narrative of this visit falls into two parts, the first of which may be dismissed briefly. It gives the story of his attempt to safeguard the interests of Dion, a very wealthy man, who owned lands and other property, bringing in large revenues. In a matter of this sort Plato was a child in the hands of Dionysios, who tricked him at every turn, and, after cajoling him by promises into staying the winter at Syracuse, sold Dion's estates, and kept the money for his own purposes. Plato was very sore about it, and treats the robbery of Dion as an affront to himself and as evidence that Dionysios felt no gratitude for his teaching (345 c 1–3).

The autobiography next passes to the mutiny of the body-guard, and from that to the concluding scenes of Plato's visit. The mutiny (348 a, b) was an alarming incident, and Dionysios attributed it to the intrigues of Herakleides. This man, who had been a friend of Dion, and a general of the forces of Dionysios, is, after Dion, the most important figure in the history of the next few years at Syracuse. He was, if we can trust Plutarch, a contentious mischief-maker, pursuing purely selfish objects, and untrustworthy as a subordinate or as a colleague.* It is probable that he was in command of the bodyguard, that the mutiny was fomented by him with a view to seizing the tyranny for himself, and that he was supported by his uncle Theodotes, an influential person in the court circle, and by Eurybios, who may have been a brother of Herakleides.

Herakleides was trying to escape punishment by flight, and his confederates wished to bring the influence of Plato to bear upon the monarch, in order to obtain lenient treatment for him. Plato was probably unaware of their real designs, and anxious only to secure the safety of a friend of Dion. But it was natural that Dionysios should be irritated by his interference.

The two interviews which Plato describes at this point (348 c–349 b) must have taken place after the eclipse of the sun of May 12th, 361 B.C.; for Plutarch's narrative (*Dion*, 19) shows that before that date there had been no quarrel between Plato

---

* Plutarch in his view of Herakleides is evidently following Timonides, an eye-witness of the occurrences, but prejudiced in favour of Dion.

and Dionysios. But they were evidently before the ten-days' festival of Demeter in October or thereabouts,* when Plato was sent to stay with his friend Archedemos outside the akropolis. They must be distinguished from the interview described in Ep. III, 319 a 2, which took place twenty days before Plato's departure, and in the presence, not of Theodotes and Eurybios, but of Archedemos and Aristokritos. (See Intr. Rem. to Ep. III.)

Plato was a placable man and it is probable that the semblance of friendly relations between him and the monarch was soon restored. But the vivid picture which he draws at 347 e 7 shows that the months which followed were a most galling experience for him. The story of the conclusion of his visit is told fully enough in his narrative (350 a–e), and need not be repeated. He probably left Syracuse in the spring of 360 B.C. and stayed with Archytas till the approach of the Olympic Games gave him the opportunity of travelling with other visitors to that festival, which took place in August 360 B.C.

It is not often in ancient history that events are described by the chief actors in them with the freshness and candour with which Plato in his 7th Epistle relates the incidents of his last visit to Syracuse and of his meeting with Dion at Olympia on his homeward journey. In the concluding scene (350 b 6) two points are brought out clearly, Dion's determination to embark on hostilities against Dionysios, and Plato's refusal to take part in them. The reasons which he gave to Dion were his own obligations to the tyrant, and his wish to reserve himself for the part of peacemaker, if opportunity offered. But he makes no secret of the fact that he was heartily sick of Sicily and its affairs.

§ III

DION'S EXPEDITION AND ITS RESULTS

Dion's expedition and the subsequent events, which led up to his murder, are vitally connected with the Platonic Epistles. The episode is interesting for the light which it throws on the strong

* It came at the beginning of the sowing season (Diod. Sic. v, 4, 5).

and weak points in the character of a remarkable man. Plutarch fortunately had good materials for the account given of it in his Life of Dion. He mentions three historians, whose works he evidently had before him, Ephoros, Theopompos and Timaios. Of these the two first were contemporaries of the events, and the third lived only a generation later. He also speaks more than once of Plato's Letters, and much of the early part of his narrative is coloured by reminiscences of the 7th Epistle.

Besides these sources he mentions letters written to Speusippos, the nephew of Plato, by Timonides the Leukadian. Timonides was one of the former pupils of the Academy who accompanied the expedition. His Letters, which are no longer extant, evidently contained reports of the doings of Dion's force. These probably began with his own arrival at Zakynthos, and ended at a point not long after the delivery of Syracuse from Nypsios. There is no reason to doubt their genuineness.* Their influence can be traced throughout Plutarch's narrative of the incidents which occurred round the person of Dion in the life-like character of the details, in the writer's strong animus against his hero's opponents, in his evident contempt for the Syracusans, and in the modest scale of the numbers which he gives for the forces engaged and their losses, which contrasts remarkably with the exaggerated figures of the other authorities. Plutarch's *Dion* is one of the best of his Lives, and it owes its excellence in some measure to the fact that the writer had before him the Platonic Epistles and the Letters of Timonides in addition to the narrative of the historians.

* Their genuineness has been assumed by most of the historians (Grote, Holm, Meyer, Bury); doubts have been expressed by C. Müller (*F.H.G.* vol. II), and more recently by R. Hackforth (*Camb. Anc. Hist.* VI, p. 281 n. 1). Susemihl (*Gr. Litt. in der al. Z.* II, p. 589 n. 34), while allowing that the question cannot be settled, considers it more probable that Timonides was a fictitious person. Howald (*Br. Pl.* p. 155) follows suit and thinks that the citations in all cases make it probable that the work was a "Briefroman". Biedenweg (*Plutarchs Quellen in den Lebensbeschreibungen des Dion und Timoleon*, Leipzig, 1884) makes out a strong case in favour of the letters, and tries to frame a probable idea of their contents. For a fuller statement of the evidence see the Note appended to this Section.

Dion had two personal grounds for attacking Dionysios; the monarch had appropriated his property, and had handed over his wife to another man.* But he justified his attack also by his intention to restore constitutional government at Syracuse and to re-establish the Greek States of Sicily, which the elder Dionysios had destroyed or left desolate. He was encouraged to take a bold line by Speusippos, who during his residence at Syracuse had learnt something of the temper of the citizens, and had formed the opinion that the position of Dionysios was not nearly so strong as people supposed. He assured Dion that his arrival in Sicily, even without an armed force, would be the signal for a rising against the tyrant.

Dion decided that it would be wiser to take with him a small force of picked mercenaries, well armed and equipped. Without a strong nucleus of that sort, he would have no chance against the tyrant's bodyguard. It was the age of mercenaries, who were professional fighting men; and a force of a little less than 800 carefully selected soldiers† was enlisted in the Peloponnese and assembled at the island of Zakynthos without being told their destination. Arms and armour for a further force of 2000 men and a good supply of stores were purchased; and, to convey all these, two large transports, one small one, and two thirty-oared galleys were brought to the same place.‡

* Her new husband was Timokrates, whom we shall see in charge of the city during the absence of Dionysios.

† This is Plutarch's figure, taken probably from Timonides. Diodoros first (xvi, 9) gives the number as 1000 men, with 5000 additional panoplies; but later on (xvi, 17) he describes Dion's picked men as more than 3000 in number. Aelian (*V.H.* iv, 8) gives 2000 mercenaries. We may safely follow Plutarch.

‡ Demosthenes, *Lept.* 62, speaking about two years after the event, described Dion as having come "with a merchant ship and a few soldiers" (πλοίῳ στρογγύλῳ καὶ στρατιώταις ὀλίγοις). This is the way in which an orator, wishing to minimise Dion's resources, would naturally speak of an expedition consisting of something a little short of 800 men, conveyed in two transports and some smaller craft. Even Demosthenes would hardly have spoken thus if there had been as many as 2000 mercenaries.

A thousand Syracusan exiles were scattered about among the States of Greece; but only thirty of them ventured to join Dion. He had with him also his brother Megakles, Kallippos, who had been his host at Athens, with his brother Philostratos, and three former students of the Academy, Timonides the Leukadian, whose letters have been mentioned, Eudemos the Kyprian, and Miltas the Thessalian. Eudemos lost his life in Sicily, and Aristotle, his friend and fellow-student, composed in his honour a dialogue on the Immortality of the Soul, of which fragments have survived. Miltas, we are told, was a prophet. No military expedition was complete without a prophet capable of expounding and interpreting omens, and Thessaly was the home of occult arts.

It was a small force with which to attack a monarch reputed to be the greatest power in the Greek world, whose personal bodyguard was a standing army of 10,000 men; and when the mercenaries were informed of their destination protests were raised against the expedition. But Dion had influential supporters and was able to persuade his troop of adventurers that their arrival would be followed by a general rising, and that their position would be that of leaders in a much larger force. Hopes also were probably held out of substantial rewards to be drawn from the treasures of Dionysios. The number of Dion's force, the daring nature of the enterprise, their sea voyage and landing, their rapid capture of the principal city of Sicily—all recall the expedition of Garibaldi and his Thousand. The parallel ceases, if we compare the components of the two forces. Garibaldi's followers were enthusiasts for liberty: Dion's men were professional soldiers.

Everything was now ready for a start. By sailing straight across the Ionian Sea they had a good chance of escaping the fleet of Dionysios, which would be awaiting their approach on the coast of Italy. The summer was well advanced, the moon was at the full, and the north wind, which blew at that season, would aid their course. Final sacrifices were offered to Apollo, the God whom Dion especially worshipped; and the whole force was entertained at a banquet, which was made impressive by the display of Dion's gold and silver plate.* While the feast was in progress the moon was eclipsed. This, we are told, caused no disturbance to the Athenians, who were familiar with its natural causes; but it was regarded as a dangerous omen by the rest of the force, until Miltas, the seer, persuaded them that what it portended was the downfall of the government of Dionysios.

The eclipse occurred on the evening of the 9th of August 357 B.C., and on the following day the expedition started. The winds were light, and it took them twelve days to cross the Ionian Sea. On the thirteenth day they were off Cape Pachynos, the south-eastern promontory of Sicily, and Pontos, their pilot, distrusting the weather, advised an immediate landing. Dion thought it would be dangerous to disembark so near to the city, and insisted on sailing to a more westerly point. While they were on their way, a strong north wind got up, and drove them far to the south, into the neighbourhood of the coast of Africa. Here they had a narrow escape from shipwreck on the rocky island of Kerkine, at the head of the Lesser Syrtes, and had to use their poles to keep their ships off the rocks. The gale abated; but it was followed by a calm, which was no less dangerous to their prospects. After some loss of time a land wind sprang up from the south, light at first, but gradually gaining strength. So they spread all sails, and, steering straight across the sea, on the fifth day they were off Heraklea Minoa on the south coast of Sicily.

Here Dion disembarked his men and stores, and received the welcome news that Dionysios had gone in person with eighty ships to await him off the coast of Italy. Minoa was about 115 miles from Syracuse and in Carthaginian territory; but the commander of the garrison, Synalos, was known to Dion, and gave him a friendly reception. Dion decided to march at once to Syracuse, leaving his stores till arrangements could be made for their transport. On the way his numbers were swollen by refugees from Akragas, Gela and Kamarina, who still haunted the neighbourhood of the ruined cities, and by Syracusans who resided in the rural districts. When he reached his last halting-

---

* The coins struck by Dion at Zakynthos (Freeman, IV, p. 247) are good evidence that he was well supplied with precious metals.

place, Akrai, eighteen miles from Syracuse, his followers numbered about 5000; but most of them had as yet no proper arms or armour.

At Akrai he learnt that Timokrates, who was in command in the absence of Dionysios, was occupying the slopes of Epipolae with a force of Campanian mercenaries, who had been provided with homes at Leontinoi, but had been brought in to Syracuse to guard the city. He sent out emissaries to spread among these men a rumour that his first attack was going to be on their settlements. On learning this they made off at once to protect their own possessions. Timokrates mounted a horse and fled, leaving the citizens in possession of the city.

Meanwhile Dion had made a night march, and at daybreak had reached the Anapos, the stream which flows across the flats about a mile from the city walls, and discharges its water into the Great Harbour (see Plan). Here a short halt was made, and Dion, crowning his helmet with a garland, offered a sacrifice to the rising sun. The omens were pronounced favourable, and all those round Dion garlanded their helmets. The column was then formed, Dion marching at its head, with his brother Megakles on one side of him and Kallippos on the other, and followed by a personal bodyguard of a hundred mercenaries. Behind these marched in order the rest of the force of regular soldiers under their officers, and after them the miscellaneous crowd which had attached itself to him. Plutarch gives the total number as 5000, which was probably the estimate of Timonides. Wordsworth reproduces it in his poem *Dion*:

Five thousand warriors—O the rapturous day!
Each crowned with flowers, and armed with spear and shield,
Or ruder weapon which their course might yield,
To Syracuse advance in bright array.

There was no one to bar their way. The bodyguard of Dionysios, of which there must have been a strong detachment in the citadel, were without a leader, and made no attempt to stop the column while it marched across the flats and up the slopes leading to the Temenitid Gate. Here they found the gates thrown open and the citizens of the better sort waiting in festal attire to receive them. As soon as Dion's force had entered the city, trumpets were blown and a proclamation made that Dion and Megakles had come to set free the Syracusans and the rest of the Sicilian Greeks. The new-comers then made a triumphal progress through the quarters of Neapolis and Achradina. Tables had been brought out into the streets, and bowls of wine set upon them; thanksgivings were offered and libations poured to the Gods, as the deliverers marched past, Dion's name receiving a share of the divine honours.* From the upper quarters of the city they moved to the Agora, where the citizens were summoned to the Assembly, the first free gathering which had been held in the city for forty-eight years. Here, not far from the gates of the citadel, Dion mounted on the sundial which had been put up by the elder Dionysios, and addressed the gathering, encouraging them to make a bold fight for freedom.

After his speech a resolution was carried that Dion and Megakles be appointed Generals with Full Powers (αὐτοκρά-τορες στρατηγοί). This was the title under which both Gelon and Dionysios had ruled. Anxious—perhaps over-anxious—to make it clear that he had no wish to continue the despotism, Dion proposed that twenty others should be appointed generals with them. The citizens jumped at this suggestion, and appointed ten of themselves and ten of the exiles who had returned with Dion.

The most urgent needs for the moment were arms for a citizen force, and some protection for the city against an assault by Dionysios on his return, which could not be long delayed.

---

* The mental attitude of the Sicilians was much the same in 1859, when Garibaldi arrived. Trevelyan (*Garibaldi and the Thousand*, p. 268), describing his march from Calatafini, says: "In the cornfields outside the town, men and women fell on their knees as he passed. Their primitive minds could not fail to attach some idea of supernatural power to any greatly admired object". Again (*ib.* p. 307), describing Garibaldi's appearance in Palermo: "When they saw sitting before them a stranger so beautiful, so kind, so strong to deliver and to slay, they felt as their remote ancestors felt when some God or hero was thought to have become the guest of man".

Arms were on their way from Minoa, and men were soon at work constructing a temporary wall across the low ground which intervened between the city and the citadel. On the seventh day after Dion's arrival Dionysios returned. He was master of the sea, and there was nothing to prevent his triremes from entering the inner harbour and discharging their crews in safety behind the defences of the citadel. On the same day wagons bringing Dion's military stores arrived from Minoa, and he was able to provide 2000 of the citizens with arms and armour.

Dionysios began by attempting negotiations, and commissioners were sent into the citadel to discuss terms with him. It was late in the day and no suspicions were aroused by the fact that the envoys were detained in the citadel for the night. But the intentions of Dionysios had been treacherous throughout, and at daybreak a strong force of his bodyguard, whose courage had been primed with drink, made a dash for the cross-wall.

The guards were taken by surprise, and the assailants had no difficulty in forcing their way through the temporary structure. The newly armed Syracusans lost their heads, and even the professional soldiers found it hard to hold their ground. Dion was soon on the scene, and put himself at the head of his men. A hand-to-hand struggle ensued, and he was in the thick of the fighting. It was one of those critical moments in which his finer qualities shone. At length he fell with a wound in the hand, and many broken javelins stuck fast in his shield. Dragged out of danger by his men, he mounted a horse, and rode into the city to rally the Syracusans and bring up reinforcements from his mercenaries, who were on guard at other points. Timonides, who had been put in command in Dion's absence, held his ground, and Dion, returning with fresh fighting men, was able to drive off the assailants, who retired into the citadel with considerable losses. On Dion's side there were seventy-four killed, most of them being, no doubt, Syracusans.

Dion's troops now set to work to repair and complete the cross-wall, while Dionysios attempted fresh overtures, which were again characterised by disregard of fair play. His messengers brought letters for Dion from his connections among the ladies of the court. These, which Dion insisted on having read to the Assembly, proved to contain entreaties to Dion for forbearance; but among them was one with the superscription, "From Hipparinos to his Father". The audience suggested that this letter from Dion's son should be treated as private; but over-anxious as usual to err on the side of generosity, Dion had it read with the others. It proved to be a letter from Dionysios himself, appealing to Dion's previous services to the tyranny, and urging him not to overthrow it, but rather to secure his own safety and that of his family and friends by seizing the chief power. Threats were added that, if he did not comply, vengeance would be taken on his relatives who were in the tyrant's hands. The document was cleverly framed so as to stir up in the popular minds those suspicions by which Dion was subsequently hampered.

When men's minds were thus prepared to transfer their favour to a rival, Herakleides arrived on the scene with seven triremes and three smaller craft. He had, as we have seen, during Plato's last visit to Syracuse, incurred the suspicion of Dionysios, and had made his escape with difficulty. He fled to the Peloponnese and joined Dion, with whom he had been on friendly terms in former days. But the two had quarrelled, and Herakleides had resolved to make an attempt against the tyrant independently.

Hasty action was a characteristic of the Syracusan Assembly, and Herakleides had a gift for winning popular favour, which Dion by his haughty manner soon forfeited. Without waiting to learn Dion's views the citizens passed a resolution appointing Herakleides to the command by sea. This was inconsistent with the authority given to Dion and his colleagues, and Dion made the Assembly rescind its resolution. Then, after remonstrating with Herakleides, he brought him before the Assembly, and with his usual excess of generosity not only appointed him admiral, but assigned to him the same bodyguard which had been allowed for himself.

Dionysios was still a formidable enemy, and so long as he held command on the sea and could bring in supplies under the protection of his navy, his position in Ortygia was impregnable.

A navy was therefore one of the first needs of the new government, and the ships of Herakleides were a useful nucleus for a larger force, which could be effectively manned by the Syracusan citizens, who were accustomed to maritime service. The fleet of Herakleides was soon brought up to a total of about sixty.

The crews of the new fleet, with the armed men who served on board, formed a strong party in the Assembly, which regarded the naval operations as more important than the land service. Herakleides used this party to foster opposition to Dion and ill-feeling towards his mercenary force. It was no doubt whispered generally that Dion could not be trusted, and that he was planning to seize the tyranny by the aid of these foreigners. Honourable as his intentions really were, there was probably a good deal in his personal bearing which gave support to this idea.

Dionysios also was trying to foster similar suspicions, and charges to this effect were openly made in the Assembly by an agitator named Sosis, who followed up his speeches by appearing in the Assembly with blood streaming from his head, and charged Dion's men with an attempt to murder him. Dion was able to show that the man was brother to one of the personal guards of Dionysios, that his wounds were self-inflicted, and that he had been employed to foment disorder in the city. Sosis was condemned to death; but the feelings of suspicion against Dion remained.

Plato's 3rd Epistle belongs to this period, and was evidently written for circulation in Syracuse at a time when Dionysios was still in possession of the citadel and was trying to foment disorder in the city. Dion had proclaimed himself champion of the Greek cities of Sicily which had been overthrown under the tyranny, and throughout the events which follow we hear of "the allies" acting as his steady supporters. Dionysios tried to undermine his position by circulating statements to the effect that he himself had fully intended to convert the tyranny into a constitutional monarchy and to re-establish the Greek cities of Sicily, but had been prevented from doing so by Dion and Plato. These in his 3rd Epistle, a pamphlet in the form of a letter to Dionysios, Plato attempts to disprove.

The new navy soon found work to do; for Philistos, the admiral of Dionysios, returned from the Adriatic, bringing with him a strong detachment of ships and some land forces; and the royal party began to be active both by land and by sea. But their operations had no success. Leontinoi, one of the few Greek cities of Sicily which was not in ruins, had taken advantage of Dion's arrival to revolt from Dionysios, and was now in league with the insurgents at Syracuse. Philistos tried to recover it by a night attack. He held a portion of the city for a few hours; but was driven out of it next day, when reinforcements arrived from Syracuse. The brave old man then attempted an engagement by sea, which began successfully, but ended in his defeat and capture. It was natural that so consistent a supporter of the tyranny should be singled out for special punishment. After savage outrages Philistos was beheaded, and his dead body was dragged through the city and thrown into the stone quarries.

The loss of his admiral was a severe blow to Dionysios, who was unable to fight his own battles. He made another attempt at negotiations, sending envoys to Dion with an offer to surrender to him the citadel with its contents, and to hand over the whole of his mercenary force with pay in advance for five months, on condition of being allowed to retire to Italy and retain his lands at Gyarta, a fertile region on the slopes of Etna. Dion referred the envoys to the Assembly, recommending that the offer be accepted, and this was obviously the wisest course. But the citizens had tasted blood in dealing with Philistos, and nothing short of similar vengeance on Dionysios would satisfy them; the envoys were driven away. Dionysios, if deficient in courage, was by no means wanting in cunning. A few ships were got ready in the Lesser Harbour; and, putting on board abundant treasures and a sufficient bodyguard, he selected a moment when a favourable breeze was blowing, and succeeded in eluding the guardships of Herakleides and making his escape to Italy, where he had safe quarters at Lokroi. His son, Apollokrates, was left in command of the force of mercenaries who held the citadel, and with him remained the rest of the royal family.

His escape was a blow to the popularity of Herakleides, who tried to regain favour by putting up a demagogue, Hippon, with proposals for a redistribution of lands. The measure was opposed by Dion and supported by Herakleides. It was carried in the Assembly, and followed by a further resolution that the pay of Dion's troops should be stopped, and that an election should be held for the appointment of fresh generals. When, after some delay, the election took place, twenty-five new generals were chosen, Dion's name being omitted and that of Herakleides included in the list. At the same time an attempt was made to detach Dion's mercenaries from him by an offer of citizenship. This they refused, and, mustering round Dion in marching order, insisted on his leading them away from the city.

They marched towards Leontinoi, which was about fifteen miles distant, and on the way, while crossing a stream, were overtaken and attacked by a force which the new government had hastily armed and despatched in pursuit. Dion's forbearance was now at an end; his men were highly trained soldiers, and a little rough handling from them sufficed to put the citizen force to flight. At Leontinoi he received a friendly reception, and, in order to gain something like a constitutional position for himself, he called an Assembly of the Sicilian States, whose restoration was one of the objects of his expedition. This body accepted him as their leader and condemned the action of the Syracusans.

Meanwhile the removal of Dion and his fighting men gave a fresh chance to Dionysios. He had still a strong force of mercenaries within the citadel, though for the moment it was closely blockaded by the navy of Herakleides; and it was not impossible to strike a blow which would put him once more in possession of the city. All he wanted was a capable commander. This he found in Nypsios, a Neapolitan soldier of fortune.

A relieving squadron of triremes under Nypsios, with abundant provisions on board, sailed from Lokroi. It arrived just in time; for the beleaguered garrison had come to the end of their food, and were on the point of capitulating. Sailing into the Great Harbour, Nypsios proceeded to disembark his men and stores at the landing-place by the Fountain of Arethusa (see Plan). The navy of Herakleides arrived on the scene and engaged the new-comers. They were not able to prevent Nypsios from landing his men and stores, but they got the better of his squadron of triremes, and carried off four of them in triumph.

This was a considerable naval victory, and called for public rejoicings. The rest of the day was devoted to banquets of the Sicilian type, and by nightfall most of the citizen troops were intoxicated. Nypsios could not have had a better opportunity. In the middle of the night a detachment of mercenaries, provided with ladders, made a dash for the temporary wall. This was soon in their hands, and the garrison issued from the citadel in force, intent on vengeance and plunder. Marching across the Agora they began a house-to-house attack on the lower parts of the town, which were soon suffering from all the horrors attendant on the sack of a captured city.

The city was a very large one, and at daybreak, while the barbarians were plundering the lower portions of it, an Assembly was hastily held in one of the upper quarters. It was clear that the only chance of averting a restoration of the tyranny was to bring back Dion with his professional soldiers. The knights,* supported by representatives of the allied States, were able with some difficulty to make the populace see this; and in the afternoon five knights with two of the allies mounted horses and rode at full speed to Leontinoi.

On their arrival they addressed themselves to Dion, who led them into the theatre, and bade them tell their story to his men. This they did, begging the soldiers to forget their own injuries and return before it was too late to save the city. Dion left it to his men to decide on their own course, but said that his duty was to return, and to be buried in the ruins of his native city, if unable to save it. Such an appeal could have only one result. The whole force begged Dion to lead them back at once to Syracuse. It was now evening, and Dion dismissed them with orders to get their supper and prepare for a night march.

Meanwhile in Syracuse the night brought a change of

* These were the wealthier citizens who served in the cavalry.

counsels. The barbarians had stopped their work of plunder at nightfall and retired to the citadel. The popular leaders, supported by Herakleides, persuaded the people that they could now hold their own without the aid of Dion, and a messenger was sent to tell him that his services were no longer needed. Not content with this, they closed the city gates to keep him out. At the same time the knights and allies sent their messenger urging him to press on. Dion halted his force six miles from Syracuse, and waited to see the course of events.

At daybreak the barbarians issued again from the citadel. Without stopping to plunder they now set fire to the lower quarters of the city, the conflagration being spread to more distant parts by means of burning arrows. Before long a large part of the city was in flames, and the inhabitants, as they fled from the burning houses, were cut down by the enemy. The citizen forces were helpless; Herakleides was wounded, and the defence once more became completely disorganised. The leading demagogues now took flight, and the brother of Herakleides with his uncle, Theodotes, came on his behalf to Dion, throwing themselves on his mercy, and begging him to take the command and do what he could to save the city. Dion at once put his force into motion, and they advanced at a run to the gates, which were now open to receive them.

Light-armed men were sent out to reassure those of the Syracusans who were still attempting resistance. Meanwhile as many hoplites as could be collected from the city were formed into compact columns, which were strengthened by distributing Dion's soldiers among them. These were sent to different points in the city to attack the barbarians. The fires which were raging in all parts made effective action difficult. But Dion had great qualities as a leader in moments of emergency: his personal courage inspired his men, and the orderly columns had the advantage over their numerous but scattered opponents. Before the day was over, the barbarians had been forced back, and driven once more with heavy losses into the citadel. Then all within the city set to work to extinguish the conflagration, a task which occupied them for the whole of the night.

Dion had thus for the second time been the saviour of his country, an achievement to which Plato (356 a 1) makes him appeal. If only he had had the same gifts for handling a political crisis which he had shown in dealing with the emergencies of war he would now have had the game in his hands. But he was wanting in the intuition which seizes on the right moments for severity and for generosity. The rest of his career is a series of failures leading up to a final tragedy.

The question which immediately confronted him was that of the punishment of those responsible for the recent disasters. His men demanded the execution of Herakleides and Theodotes, who were now in his hands. In the interests of public safety this step was clearly called for, and Timoleon, in Dion's place, would not have hesitated. But the two prisoners knew how to work on Dion's feelings: they acknowledged their fault, but begged him to give to them better treatment than he had received, and to show his superiority by forgiving men who had injured him. It was in vain that Dion's men entreated him not to listen to this appeal of mischievous scoundrels. He replied by expounding the teaching of the Academy on the control of anger and the duty of rendering good for evil.* The evil in human nature, he told them, is never so utterly bad that it cannot be overcome by goodness and kindness. Such views must have seemed madness to the mercenaries; but Dion acted on them and pardoned Herakleides and his uncle.

An Assembly was next held to appoint a new government. Herakleides came forward with a proposal that Dion be appointed General with Full Powers both by land and sea. This was received with angry murmurs from his own party and especially from the naval crowd. Dion yielded to the outcries and allowed the opposition to appoint Herakleides to the command by sea; but he once more brought himself into disfavour by compelling the Assembly to rescind its former resolution for a redistribution of lands. The antagonism between the rival leaders soon became more acute than ever. Of the operations by land and sea during the next few weeks we have only Plutarch's account, and it is not

* See note on Ep. VII, 351 c 6.

very enlightening.* The city seems to have been suffering from shortage of food supplies, and Herakleides was therefore sent with the fleet to Messana. While there he opened treacherous communications with Pharax,† a Spartan soldier of fortune now in command of the forces of Dionysios, who was trying to re-establish the monarch's authority in some of the outlying parts of Sicily.

Dion led a force into the interior to deal with Pharax, but had to hurry back on receipt of news that Herakleides was sailing from Messana to surprise and seize Syracuse. A night march with his cavalry brought him to the city in time, and Herakleides had to withdraw. He was now in open revolt. Plato's 4th Letter shows that he was in correspondence with friends in the Peloponnese, and Gaisylos now arrived, as accredited emissary from Sparta. The intention evidently was that he should play a part like that of Gylippos in the Athenian invasion. Dion was himself a citizen of Sparta, and declined to resign the leader-ship; but Gaisylos effected a temporary reconciliation between the rivals. Herakleides was pardoned and bound over by solemn oaths not to offend again.

The rebellious fleet was now disbanded. Its services were no longer required; for Apollokrates, whose provisions were exhausted, had been having trouble with his mercenaries, and came to terms with Dion. He was allowed to return to Italy with five triremes, taking with him his mother and sisters. His

---

* Ch. 48 of the Life of Dion is the last passage in which the personal touch of Timonides is clearly traceable. Biedenweg (*l.c.* p. 20) thinks that his letters were continued down to the murder of Herakleides. But Plutarch reports the murder in a rather perfunctory way, and his account of the operations against Pharax (ch. 49) would have more colour in it if it were taken from this source. Plato's complaint in Ep. IV of the absence of news is more intelligible if we suppose that the letters of Timonides had ceased some little time before the murder of Herakleides.

† For Pharax cf. Plut. *Timol.* 11, 4, and *Comp. Timol. et Aem. Paul.* 2. In both of these passages Pharax is mentioned as one of those who had disgusted the Sicilians with the intervention of foreigners. Theo-pompos (Fr. 188) mentions him as a Spartan who had adopted the profligate habits of the Sicilians.

departure and the opening of the gates of the citadel were convincing signs that the tyranny was now at an end. Whatever may be thought of the rest of Dion's career, he had performed something notable in completing, with resources which had at first been so insignificant, the overthrow of a power so firmly established. Plato was not exaggerating when he told him (Ep. IV, 320 d 3) that at this moment the eyes of all the world were fixed upon him.

Apollokrates had left behind him in the citadel Dion's sister, Aristomachê, his wife, Aretê, and his son, Hipparinos, a youth approaching manhood. As he approached the gates, these came out to meet him, his sister and son in front, his wife behind, hanging back shamefaced, and doubtful how she would be received after her transfer to another husband. Dion greeted his sister and son warmly; then Aristomachê led Aretê up to him and appealed to him to forgive one who had acted under compulsion. He was again true to his Academic principle of forgiveness, and took back Aretê to live with him as his wife.

The royal castle in Ortygia had no temptations for Dion, who continued to live in his own house as a private citizen. Plutarch says that he handed over the citadel to the citizens; but this can hardly be true; for they would have dismantled it without delay, and it is clear that Dion was responsible for the fact that the evil-looking fortress remained standing. It was demolished ten years later by Timoleon. During the interval it enabled four successive tyrants to rule over the unfortunate city. Dion probably felt that he might need both the citadel and a mercenary force to support the new constitution which he intended to establish.

The war was now at an end, and there was no longer any need for rulers with exceptional powers. If Dion intended to establish a constitutional government, this was clearly the moment for doing so. The problem was not an easy one. Syracuse was the largest city in the Greek world: its population had been artificially swollen by Dionysios I, who brought in large numbers of new citizens from the dismantled cities of Sicily and southern Italy, and conferred the citizenship on many liberated slaves.

The popular clamour now, as sixty years earlier after the victory over the Athenians, was for democracy. But with such a heterogeneous population there was little prospect of settled government under democratic forms. On the other hand there was no strong group of aristocratic families in whose hands power could be placed.

Dion had had abundant time to think, and ought to have been ready with his policy. He was not ready, and let it be known that he was going to send for commissioners from Corinth to draw up a new constitution. His political views rested on philosophical convictions, and he must be acquitted of any idea of seizing the tyranny for himself. Some idea of his intentions may be gathered from the constitutional monarchy which Plato in the 8th Epistle (355 e) makes him recommend to his friends after his death; only we must suppose that he would have been the titular sovereign himself, in place of the three kings who are there recommended.

For the time being he administered affairs personally with the aid of a Council (σύνεδριον) selected by himself.* It was natural that there should be opposition, and Herakleides, when invited to join the Council, refused to attend, and called on Dion to summon the Assembly. Some account of these difficulties must have reached Plato; for he wrote to Dion, appealing to him to re-establish harmonious relations with the rival leaders and to be more conciliatory in his manners (see Intr. Rem. to Ep. IV).

How long this period of friction lasted it is impossible to say, for Plutarch gives no dates. There was probably an interval of about a year between the surrender of the citadel and Dion's murder. The ill-feeling against Dion became stronger and was inflamed by his refusal to allow the tomb of Dionysios to be destroyed and his dead body to be outraged. At length his patience was exhausted; he listened to the persuasion of his friends and consented to the removal of Herakleides. There was no pretence of judicial proceedings, nor did Dion boldly take the

---

* Plut. *Dion*, 53. Diodoros (XVI, 31) speaks of him as στρατηγός at the time of his death; and it is probable that he continued to hold the post of στρατηγὸς αὐτοκράτωρ.

law into his own hands; the popular leader was assassinated. Dion gave him a military funeral with full honours, and himself delivered the funeral speech, excusing the murder on the ground of political necessity. Plutarch says that this was recognised by the people; but there were probably many malcontents, who found in the assassination a convincing proof that Dion's government was in fact a tyranny.*

The murder of Herakleides weighed on the mind of Dion, and he sank into a state of depression, which was increased by a tragedy of his own home life. His son, who had been restored to him after twelve years' separation, had had no proper bringing up, and had been encouraged in habits of vice by Dionysios. Dion put the young man under strict tutors, and attempted to reform his character. Here again he showed the same want of the gift for conciliation which hampered him in politics. The young man could not endure repression, and put an end to his life by throwing himself from the roof of the house.†

Dion's political difficulties were now aggravated by growing discontent in his own mercenary force. The main body of these professional soldiers would have been delighted to see Dion seize the position of tyrant for himself; and when it became clear that there was no chance of his doing so they were ready to give their support to a capable adventurer who could be put in his place. Such a man, if he could combine the position of popular leader with the command of the mercenary force, would have a good chance of success in an attempt to seize the tyranny. The temptation was too strong for Kallippos, the most prominent among the Athenians who had accompanied Dion, the friend who had entertained him at Athens, and had marched into Syracuse by his side. Plato, whose brief statement of the facts is entirely borne out by the narratives of Plutarch and Nepos, cannot bring himself to mention the name of Kallippos,‡ and is

* This is the view taken of it by Aristotle (*Rhet.* I, 12 1373 a 19), who considers Kallippos to have been "almost innocent" (ἐγγὺς τοῦ μὴ ἀδικεῖν) in his conspiracy against Dion.

† For further details see Intr. Rem. to Epp. VII and VIII.

‡ For the doubts about the names of Kallippos and his brother see Ep. VII, note 52.

careful to state that he and his brother, who acted with him, were not philosophers. But he was closely connected with the Academy group, and there can be little doubt that he had at one time been a member of the School. He was untroubled by scruples and now entered into communications with the leaders of the popular party. He obtained from them funds with which to secure the assistance of the disaffected among the Greek mercenaries, while they aggravated Dion's unpopularity in the city by spreading rumours that he was not only aiming at the tyranny for himself, but providing for its permanence by adopting Apollokrates, the son of Dionysios.

Dion's suspicions of these intrigues were lulled by Kallippos, who professed to be playing the part of spy and communicating with the malcontents among the bodyguard only in order to obtain information about their proceedings. Depression had made him lose interest in affairs, and perhaps he willingly closed his eyes. His wife and sister saw through the designs of Kallippos, and attempted to prevent them by making him go through the most solemn form of oath in the shrine of Demeter and Persephone. But education had freed him from any superstitious feeling about such ceremonies, and he even selected the day of the Korea, the great festival of Persephone, for his projected coup d'état.

When the day arrived, a small force of armed men, among whom was Kallippos, gathered round the house of Dion, while his brother, Philostratos, with another force was ready on board a trireme in the harbour, to carry away the conspirators if the enterprise failed. Dion had brought with him from Zakynthos some of the natives of that island, and these were sent unarmed to the house to ask for an interview with Dion. We may assume that they were searched before they were admitted. Dion was seated with several friends in a reception room. Some of the Zakynthians remained outside the room and secured the door, while the rest attacked Dion and tried to kill him by strangling. None of his friends came to his aid; some of them perhaps were in the conspiracy. Dion resisted desperately, and the murderers were unable to despatch him until one of the armed men outside the house passed in a sword through the window.

Of the events which followed Dion's murder our information is scanty and our informants not in complete harmony. Nepos (*Dion*, 10) says that Dion received a public funeral, and that there was a strong revulsion of popular feeling in his favour. Plutarch, on the other hand, states (*Dion*, 58) that for the moment Kallippos was a popular hero, that he obtained power over Syracuse and sent a despatch to the city of Athens; also (*ib.* 57) that he at once put into prison Dion's sister and his wife, that the wife was pregnant and bore a male child in prison, and that the women were able to persuade the guards to allow them to rear the child, Kallippos being occupied at the time with political difficulties.*

Diodoros (XVI, 31) confines himself to stating, under Ol. 106, 4, that in Sicily Dion the Strategos was murdered by some Zakynthian mercenaries employed by Kallippos, who succeeded to his power and ruled for thirteen months.

From these meagre sources we have to guess the probable course of events. The public funeral was probably a fact; Kallippos may have thought it wise to follow the precedent set by Dion after the murder of Herakleides. But for what follows Plutarch's account seems the more probable. The first step of Kallippos must have been to seize the citadel; and it was there, no doubt, that Dion's family were imprisoned. We may assume also that he was produced by the popular leaders before the Assembly, was hailed as a tyrannicide, and appointed to the post of Strategos Autokrator. His official letter to Athens would then be despatched. But his rule must very soon have been converted into an unmistakeable tyranny.

Of the later history of his thirteen months' reign our informa-

---

* After the expulsion of Kallippos Dion's family were released, and passed into the hands of one of his friends, Hiketas the Syracusan, who was persuaded by Dion's enemies to put the two women and the posthumous child on board a ship under pretence of sending them to the Peloponnese, and at sea they were murdered. The family of Dion was thus completely exterminated (Plutarch, *Dion*, 58).

tion is still more meagre. It falls in the interval between Plutarch's Lives of Dion and Timoleon, and the only fact to be gleaned from him is that Kallippos lost Syracuse while engaged in an expedition against Katana (*Dion*, 58).

Diodoros (XVI, 36), under Ol. 106, 4, 353 B.C., gives the bare statement: "In Syracuse civil strife occurred between the friends of Dion and of Kallippos. The friends of Dion were worsted and fled to Leontinoi. After some time Hipparinos, the son of Dionysios, sailed to Syracuse with a force, and Kallippos was defeated and driven out of the city. Hipparinos, after recovering his father's tyranny, reigned for two years".

Polyainos (*Strateg.* V, 4) gives a different story: "Hipparinos, being at Leontinoi, and perceiving that the city of Syracuse was undefended, because the citizens had marched to a certain place, marched from Leontinoi and seized the city of the Syracusans".

One more gleam of light comes from the fact that Eudemos, the friend of Aristotle who accompanied Dion, lost his life in one of the attacks on Kallippos which the Dionean party made from their refuge at Leontinoi. From the story told by Cicero (*de Div.* I, 25) it seems clear that the death of Eudemos must have occurred in 353 B.C.

From these materials we may guess that Kallippos had on his side the populace and its leaders. The friends of Dion would be supported, as before, by the knights and the allies; and at some date not mentioned they were strengthened by the co-operation of Dion's nephew, Hipparinos.* We are not told where he came from; but he had probably accompanied or followed his half-brother to Lokroi. The Dioneans then attempted a rising but were defeated and driven out. They took shelter, as Dion had done, at Leontinoi, and perhaps their connection with the allies may have secured for them the assistance of Katana. From these

* We are not told when Hipparinos began to co-operate with the Dioneans. But when Plato wrote the 8th Epistle, he evidently believed his correspondents to be in Syracuse and he had heard that Hipparinos was supporting them. If therefore, as I have supposed, Plato had not heard of the expulsion of Kallippos, Hipparinos must have joined the Dioneans before their retirement to Leontinoi. (See Intr. Rem. to Epp. VII and VIII.)

positions they probably made fresh attempts, by sea now as well as by land. Dionysios at Lokroi was perhaps co-operating with them behind the scenes and supplied them with ships. If Katana was their naval base, this would account for the march of Kallippos against that city. We may suppose that on his approach Hipparinos left Katana to its own resources and made a sudden descent with his ships on Syracuse, that he took the city by surprise and was able to open the gates to a supporting force which arrived by land from Leontinoi. This is only a conjectural reconstruction of the events; but it has the merit of providing a reason for the march of Kallippos against Katana, which is left unexplained by the narratives of Plutarch and Polyainos.

The expulsion of Kallippos was not followed by the establishment of a constitutional government. Hipparinos, as soon as he was master of the citadel, seized the supreme power for himself, and a new tyranny of the Dionysian dynasty followed, which lasted for nine years. Hipparinos, after reigning for two years, lost his life in a drunken brawl, and was succeeded by his brother Nysaios, who ruled for five years. Both men were worthless characters, to whom tyranny was merely a means of enjoying a life of unchecked self-indulgence. Nysaios was turned out by Dionysios, who re-established himself as tyrant in 346 B.C., and had a second reign of two years. None of these rulers gave settled government to the city, which sank into a deplorable condition; many of its citizens fled, and some of the streets were overgrown with grass. Tyrants were also ruling in those other Sicilian cities which Plato and Dion had been anxious to re-establish. Finally an appeal was made to Corinth, and the tyrannies of Syracuse and the other cities of the Sicilians were overthrown by Timoleon.* Democratic governments were established, and for a short time the land enjoyed rest.

It is usual to contrast the success of Timoleon with the

* Most of the tyrants met the usual fate of such usurpers. Dionysios was allowed to live in retirement at Corinth. His humbled position was illustrated by the usual crop of legends, and "Dionysios is at Corinth" became the Greek equivalent for "Pride has a fall". Cf. Cic. *ad Att.* IX, 9.

failure of Dion. As military leaders the two men had much in common, and both were singularly free from personal aims. In meeting the emergencies of politics Timoleon had the promptness and clear-headedness which Dion lacked, and in dealing with unscrupulous and dangerous adversaries he used those short and sharp methods which are called for in times of extreme disorder. He was free from the doctrinaire views of Dion, and secured contentment for the moment by giving to the Syracusans the democracy which the populace desired. But there was no permanence in the settlement which he effected; and twenty years after his death the city was groaning under the tyranny of Agathokles. There was a good deal in common between the Syracusans of this date and the fifteenth-century Milanese. What was said by Machiavelli of Milan after the death of Filippo Visconti was no less true of Syracuse after the removal of Dionysios—she was so corrupt that nothing could make her free.

The rapid succession of changes at Syracuse during the forty years which followed the overthrow of the tyranny by Dion bears out Plato's estimate of the instability of forms of government in a State in which unchecked self-indulgence prevails and moral laws have lost their restraining power (326 d). Plato and Dion aimed at the permanent well-being of the State, but believed that this could only be secured by laying a foundation of sound morals. Constitutional reform was for them a means of securing moral reform. In their political philosophy they had something of the fervour of religious leaders, and for a parallel to the kind of community at which they aimed we must turn to the government of Geneva under Calvin. The new constitution was to be drafted by men who themselves lived the simple life in the old-fashioned style of the Dorian States (336 c 6), and would legislate with a view to enforcing a similar life on the citizens. Such legislation had, no doubt, often been a subject of discussion between Plato and Dion, and Dion clung to these aims with the tenacity of a religious enthusiast, when it ought to have been clear to him that the machinery by which they might have been carried out was no longer in existence. His failure in practical politics was due partly to features in his character, which have been pointed out in this narrative, but partly, and in no small measure, to his fidelity to ideals which under the circumstances were not attainable.

Note on the Letters of Timonides

Reference has been made above to the suspicions cast by some critics on the lost letters of Timonides. The grounds for believing that this work really was what it professed to be call for a fuller statement. In what follows I owe a good deal to Biedenweg's *Dissertation* (*v. sup.* note on p. 30).

Plutarch refers twice to Timonides as an authority for facts. In ch. 31 he gives Timonides as his authority for the words, "To his father from Hipparinos". "Timaios", he adds, "says that Dion's son was called Aretaios from his mother, Aretê. But we should place more confidence in Timonides, the friend and fellow-soldier of Dion." Here the whole scene evidently comes from Timonides, Timaios being only brought in as an authority for the name Aretaios.

Again in ch. 36, when describing the death of Philistos, Plutarch says, "Ephoros states that when his ship was captured he killed himself; but Timonides, who was present from the first at these events in company with Dion and wrote about them to Speusippos the philosopher, relates (ἱστορεῖ) that Philistos was taken alive when his ship had run aground, etc."—here follows a description of the slaying of Philistos and the maltreatment of his corpse. Plutarch prefers the story told by Timonides both to the statement of Ephoros and to the more sensational narrative of Timaios, which he next gives.

The only other mention of the letters of Timonides in antiquity occurs in the list of the works of Speusippos (Diog. Laert. IV, 5), where it is stated that "Simonides wrote to him the narrative (ἱστορίαν) in which he had arranged the achievements of Dion and Bion". It is clear that "Simonides" is here a mere mistake (probably of a scribe) for "Timonides", and the name of "Bion" also is probably due to a corruption in the MSS. This passage bears out the view that the letters were of the nature of the despatches of a war correspondent, and that there were several of them. Though called ἱστορίαι by Diogenes Laertius, and quoted by Plutarch with the verb ἱστορεῖ, the Letters must have been preserved as an adjunct to the works of Speusippos, a philosopher. The writings of philosophers were not used as sources by historians; and this accounts for the fact that, like the Platonic Epistles, the Letters of Timonides were unknown to Diodoros and to Nepos.

Plutarch's account of Dion's expedition and of the events which followed his return to Sicily bears the marks which we should expect to find in a narrative based largely on such despatches. It may be said that Plutarch was deceived, and that the features which he has faithfully reproduced may have been merely the inventions of a clever writer of fiction.* The historical novel has made such devices familiar in the present day. But Greek literature gives us no parallel group of imaginary letters so true to its historical setting and so rich in convincing detail and characteristic action, as the Letters of Timonides must clearly have been. Such a work could only have been produced by a writer of genius, and would have had successful imitators. In the Letters of Chion we have a fair specimen of the kind of work which the Greek writer of epistolary fiction produced. The narrative is dull, lifeless and mechanical. The writer had a good subject in the murder of the tyrant, Klearchos, by two pupils of Plato's Academy; but he has missed the opportunities which his material offered for producing a convincing story, and he makes no attempt at historical accuracy.†

* This is the view adopted by Susemihl and Howald in the works cited above (note on p. 30). Howald, when rejecting the testimony of Timonides about the name of Hipparinos (*Dion*, ch. 35), describes the Letters attributed to him as "ein Briefroman", adding, "Das machen auch die sonstigen Zitate aus diesem Werke durchaus wahrscheinlich". But he does not justify this verdict by specifying anything which looks like fiction, and he would find it difficult to do so.

† For the story see Grote, ch. 98, and for some remarks on the Letters see Wilamowitz (*Pl.* 1, 705), who considers that the work belonged to Roman imperial times, and points out the writer's want of historical knowledge and departures from chronological order, but considers the letters well written.

Plutarch's narrative offers abundant proof that the despatches of Timonides were of a widely different character. Their influence can be traced from about the middle of his 22nd to the end of his 48th chapter. In the 22nd he describes the mustering of Dion's force at Zakynthos, and mentions that it included three members of the Academy, Eudemos the Kyprian, Timonides the Leukadian, and Miltas the seer, a Thessalian. These three probably joined the expedition at Zakynthos, where Dion made some stay. Timonides under these circumstances would not think it necessary to mention at this point those members of the Academy who had accompanied Dion from Athens. This explains the absence here of any reference to Kallippos as a member of the force. The presence of Eudemos is brought into the region of fact by the evidence of Aristotle, to which reference has been made above; and there is no reason to doubt that Timonides and Miltas were equally real characters.

A fair idea of the extent of Plutarch's debt to Timonides may be gained by comparing his narrative with that of Diodoros. The latter certainly drew his material from Ephoros in his account of the death of Philistos (XVI, 16), and probably did so throughout. According to his story Dion, in order to escape death at the hands of Dionysios, took flight from Syracuse, accompanied by Herakleides and Megakles, sailed to Corinth, and there forthwith collected the force with which he returned. From Corinth the force sails to Zakynthos. Herakleides, who is Dion's second in command, is left behind at Zakynthos with some triremes and ships of burden. Dion sails to Sicily, and lands at Minoa. No details are given either of the stay at Zakynthos or of the sea voyage. It follows that all the incidents related by Plutarch as taking place at Zakynthos and on the way to Sicily, which so evidently form the continuous narrative of one authority, come from another source, and it is a fair inference from their character that the source is Timonides rather than Timaios.

The incidents have all the marks of the personal experiences of an eye-witness in close attendance upon Dion, and have the support of positive evidence in the date of the eclipse, and of probability in the character and duration of the sea voyage and the details of the storm. The narrative of the voyage is a parallel, though on a smaller scale, of that which the companion of Paul of Tarsus has given of their voyage from Caesarea to Puteoli, and is no more likely to be a work of imagination.

We may next compare the narratives of the two historians in a portion of the story where both give details, their account of Dion's landing at Heraklea Minoa, the march to Syracuse, and the entry into the city. A summary has been given above of Plutarch's description of these events, but it does not contain all his details. For the complete story see Plutarch, *Dion*, 25–29.

In the story told by Diodoros the main outlines are the same, but the differences of detail are considerable. He gives the name of the Carthaginian commander at Minoa as Paralos instead of Synalos. He omits the collision between Dion's men and the garrison and Dion's proposal to halt there in order that his men may rest. The panoplies (5000 in number instead of 2000) are handed over to the Carthaginians, as in Plutarch, to be forwarded in wagons, and Dion starts. On the way he persuades the Akragantines, the Geloans, and some of the Sicani and Sicels from the interior, to support him in the war of liberation. Plutarch's precise detail about the 200 men from Eknomos does not appear. But armed men from all sides join Dion, and the force of soldiers is swollen to 20,000. Others are summoned from the cities of Italy and from Messana, and all come eagerly and in haste.

On the borders of the Syracusan territory Dion is met by a large number of unarmed Syracusans, to some of whom he distributes his 5000 panoplies: the carts have apparently caught him up; but we are not told of their arrival. The rest of the newcomers get such weapons as they can. An Assembly is now held, and Dion and Megakles are appointed Generals with Full Powers. Immediately after the Assembly, Dion sets his force in order and leads it to the city. Meeting with no opposition, he passes inside, and marches down through Achradina to the Agora. His force of soldiers has by this time increased to 50,000, just ten times the number given by Plutarch. They are all garlanded, and Dion and Megakles march at their head. A lengthy passage follows, describing the joy of the citizens.

In Plutarch's narrative the only additions to Dion's forces are 200 Akragantines from Eknomos, some men from Gela and Kamarina, and unarmed Syracusans from the rural districts. His force, when he enters the city, numbers only 5000 men, most of whom are insufficiently armed. The carts do not rejoin him till the seventh day after his arrival. The Assembly is held after his entry into the city: Dion addresses it from the sundial, and on his proposal twenty additional generals are appointed to share the government with himself and Megakles. Other new details are the encampment at Akrai, the march onwards before dawn, the crossing of the Anapos, and the sacrifice at sunrise. The undefended state of the city is explained by the flight of Timokrates, and the gate by which Dion entered is named. The reception given to him by the upper classes in their holiday attire, and the vengeance taken by the mob on the secret agents of the tyranny, are also new features. Dion's entry into the city and march through Achradina are described with more colour; Kallippos appears along with Dion and Megakles at the head of the column. On the whole comparison there can be no doubt that Plutarch, though he may have had Ephoros before him, is still following the same authority which he used for the voyage.

Similar features reappear in Plutarch's narrative, wherever he is dealing with incidents at which Timonides was present. They come out strongly in the battle scenes. But the art of imparting life to these was familiar to historians; and two other sections deserve mention: (1) the appeal made by the Syracusans to Dion and his men after their retirement to Leontinoi—the ride of the emissaries, their reception on arrival, and the discussion in the theatre which followed; and (2) the scene at Syracuse after the recovery of the city from Nypsios, when Dion in the presence of his men had to decide on the fate of Herakleides and Theodotes. Neither of these is at all likely to have been the work of a writer who had not genuine materials before him. The first is not unworthy of a place beside the pages in which Thucydides describes how the Athenians reversed their sentence on the Mytileneans.

58   INTRODUCTION

Three other points may be mentioned, which are characteristic
of the sections in the Life which are inspired by Timonides.

(1) The writer is, as might be expected, inclined to dwell on
the prowess of Dion's men, which he contrasts with the incapacity and cowardice of the Syracusans. One instance of this,
out of many, is the account given of the surprise of Dion's cross-
wall by the bodyguard. The Syracusans are panic-stricken, and
disaster is only averted by the courage and presence of mind of
Dion's men, while the final repulse of the barbarians is only
brought about by a fresh detachment of these led down from the
city by Dion. In the account of Diodoros all those engaged on
Dion's side are spoken of indiscriminately as "the Syracusans",
and the fighting is described as an engagement between two
compact masses of men struggling at close quarters, with incidents natural to such an encounter.

(2) The writer dwells on incidents which bring out the incapacity of the Syracusans for political life, their sudden
changes of attitude and their readiness to be swayed by agi-
tators. This is shown by the way in which they listen to the story
of Sosis (*Dion*, 34), by the postponement of the Assembly for
fifteen days on account of thunderstorms and its dispersal by the
irruption of the runaway bull (*ib.* 38), and in particular by their
ingratitude to Dion.

(3) A strong prejudice is shown throughout against Herakleides and Dion's other enemies, who are described as κακοὶ καὶ
βάσκανοι ἄνθρωποι (*ib.* 47). Herakleides himself, who is
characterised as δυσμεταχείριστον καὶ διεφθαρμένον ὑπὸ φθόνου
καὶ πονηρίας (*ib.* 48), appears throughout the latter part of the
narrative as an unscrupulous leader of the popular party,
gaining his ends by pandering to the mob. This is in striking
contrast to the account of Nepos, who, following probably
Timaios, represents Herakleides as the leader of the nobles
(*Dion*, 6).

A good deal more might be said; but these indications are
sufficient to establish the fact that Plutarch's debt to Timonides
is a large one. This does not mean that he is likely to have
reproduced individual passages as they stood in his source. That

was not his method. The way in which he uses the Platonic Epistles makes it probable that, when he is taking material from other authorities, his language is his own, with occasional reminiscences of his source. But it is beyond doubt that he took over much material from the despatches of the Leukadian, and most improbable that these were anything else but the reports of a witness who took part in the events.

§ IV

THE QUESTION OF GENUINENESS

The history of criticism is mainly the history of error.
THOMAS HARDY.

More than one vexed question is at issue in the controversy on the genuineness of the Platonic Epistles. It has its bearing on the trustworthiness of ancient documents generally, the character of Plato and the nature of his religious and philosophical convictions, the truth of certain matters of fact in Greek history, and the value which should be assigned to the "ipse dixit" of some critics of note. It shows how much easier it is to assault than to defend, and how readily, even among the learned, established views yield to a noisy and brilliant attack. Karsten's Dissertation* still deserves reading as a specimen of all that should be avoided by the fair-minded critic. He saw mistakes in fact where none existed, and the peculiarities of style which he treated as proof of forgery are now recognised as evidence of genuineness. His slashing attack was, however, one of the principal causes of a swing of the pendulum so decisive that for several decades no scholar could have maintained the genuineness of the Epistles without imperilling his reputation.

The external evidence in their favour is good as far as it goes; but it does not go far enough. The book, in the form in which we

* Karsten, H. T., *De Epistolis quae feruntur Platonicis*, Utrecht, 1864. A typical instance of Karsten's methods is his positive statement (p. 24) that in Ep. xi the context makes it clear (*argumentum clamat*) that the Sokrates mentioned cannot be Sokrates the Younger. There is no justification for this piece of bluff.

now have it, was certainly in existence when the Life of Plato, which bears the name of Diogenes Laertius, was written (c. A.D. 100); for the author not only gives correctly the number of the letters as thirteen, but mentions the names of the persons to whom they are addressed, with the single exception that he substitutes Aristodemos for Aristodoros.*

Plutarch (c. A.D. 90), in his Life of Dion, has several references to the letters which are all verifiable in our collection. Lucian (c. A.D. 150) quotes from the 3rd Epistle as a document which must be treated with respect.† Cicero was familiar with the Epistles: he quotes a long passage from the 7th, which he describes as "praeclara epistula Platonis ad Dionis propinquos" (*Tusc. Disp.* v, 35), and twice cites Ep. IX, which seems to have been a favourite with him. His own judgment on the genuineness of a Greek work may not be of great value; for he evidently accepted as genuine the Letters of Anacharsis. But it is clear that the book in its present form was in his day accepted as a classic at Athens and by the cultivated world generally.

The external evidence carries the Epistles back to a point two centuries earlier than Cicero. Diogenes Laertius (III, 61), after giving his first classification of Plato's works, in which the Epistles are placed under the subhead ἠθικὸς λόγος, continues as follows: "Some, among whom is Aristophanes the Grammarian, arrange the Dialogues in trilogies, and they put first the one in which the *Republic* comes first, with the *Timaeus* and *Critias*, second the *Sophistes*, *Politicus*, and *Cratylus*, third the *Laws*, *Minos*, and *Epinomis*, fourth the *Theaetetus*, *Euthyphron*, and *Apology*, fifth the *Crito*, *Phaedo*, and *Epistles*; the other works they mention one by one, in no particular order".

Aristophanes the Grammarian was Librarian of the Alexandrine Library, and was born about 260 B.C. We have no information as to the principle on which these trilogies were classified; but the passage proves that a collection of Platonic letters was extant at a date not long after the middle of the third century B.C., that it was accepted as part of the genuine works of

* Diog. Laert. III, 61.
† Lucian, de lap. in sal. ch. 4.

Plato, and stood on the same footing as two of the most admired of the Dialogues. It is most unlikely that in the period between Cicero and Aristophanes any important change can have been made in a work of this kind, which must have been familiar to readers both at Athens and Alexandria.

The external evidence, therefore, makes it reasonably certain that the collection in its present form was in existence, and regarded as genuine, within about a century of the death of Plato. But it carries us no farther, and leaves it still possible that all or some of the letters may be the work of some other hand than his. For among the works included in the trilogies is the *Minos*, the contents of which make its genuineness unlikely. If we had the list of Aristophanes complete, we should probably find in it all the works which appear in the tetralogies of Thrasylus, some of which, as the *Theages* and the *Second Alcibiades*, are certainly apocryphal.* Grote's view, that we are obliged by the evidence to accept as genuine all that has come to us in the tetralogies, can only be regarded as an eccentricity on the part of a man whose judgment was generally sound.

There is no more external evidence as to the early history of the text of Plato's works. We may regard it as certain that in the time of Aristophanes the Alexandrine Library had a copy of them which was considered to be complete. But we have no right to assume that a complete copy was obtained from Athens in the earliest days of the Library. What is actually done in such cases is not always what we should expect to be done. We might expect that an Aristotelian like Demetrios of Phaleron would have seen to it that Alexandria had a complete copy of the works of Aristotle. But the history of the text of Aristotle makes it

---

* Diogenes Laertius (III, 66), after describing the critical marks used by the commentators on Plato, adds τὰ μὲν σημεῖα ταῦτα καὶ τὰ βιβλία τοσαῦτα· ἅπερ, Ἀντίγονός φησιν ὁ Καρύστιος ἐν τῷ περὶ Ζήνωνος νεωστὶ ἐκδοθέντα εἴ τις ἤθελε διαγνῶναι μισθὸν ἐτέλει τοῖς κεκτημένοις. It is not quite clear how much of this comes from Antigonos. He certainly said that the circulation of collected editions was something recent. May we infer that he specified the works included in the collected edition and that their number corresponded to that included in the tetralogies? If so, there is evidence for the view given above as probable.

unlikely that this was done. We may safely infer that the most admired and popular works of both authors were put into the new Library; but a generation or more may have elapsed from the foundation of the Library before its collection of Plato's works was made complete.

As to what may have happened to the text of Plato's works at Athens during this interval, and during the generation or more which preceded it, we can only conjecture; and once again it must be remembered that what men do often differs from what they may be reasonably expected to do. We may treat it as certain that his works were preserved in his School, and treated with reverence. The works themselves, as they stand to-day, are sufficient proof of this. The text of the *Laws* affords evidence that unrevised passages have been allowed to stand, as they were left by the author, without being edited or corrected. But though we may be sure that the genuine works of the Master have not been extensively tampered with, it is not impossible that other works, composed by his associates or successors, have been attached to the School copy of the Corpus Platonicum. The name of the author did not usually appear in the interior of a papyrus roll, and the distinction of authorship may have been lost sight of even in the School itself, and much more when the works were circulated outside.

What would such supplementary works most probably be? It is probable that the composition of dialogues in the Platonic manner was a form of exercise practised by students of the Academy in its early days. One would expect that some specimens of these should be preserved at the School; and this is the probable origin of the collection of "Spuria" (περὶ δικαίου and the rest), which is appended to the Platonic Canon, and of apocryphal works like the *Minos* and *Theages*, which have found their way into it. The best of these may have been used for the earlier studies of pupils. It is natural that there should cease to be any very definite line between genuine dialogues and other Platonic writings used in this way. But can it be regarded as likely that exercises in the Academy ever took the form of imaginary letters from Plato? In schools of rhetoric, as we shall see, such exercises had become common about three centuries later, and they may have been in use as early as the third century B.C.; but they were quite outside the work of the Academy.

There is, however, no positive evidence in support of our assumption of the early existence of the Epistles at the Academy; and we have therefore no right to dismiss as *prima facie* impossible the view that they originated elsewhere, e.g. as exercises in rhetorical schools. This was in fact the view of the earlier critics, Karsten and others, who condemned the whole collection.

Such critics, and with them the more recent scholars who condemn individual letters, like the 3rd, as the product of schools of rhetoric, may fairly be asked, to what schools of rhetoric they refer, and what works produced in them are at all comparable to the Platonic Epistles. What do we know about the Greek schools of rhetoric of the third century and the closing years of the fourth century B.C.? Very little. The main body of the extensive Greek prose literature which was produced between the death of Demosthenes and the beginning of our era has been lost, and is only known to us in fragments. We have a good deal of information, largely from Roman sources, about the Greek teachers of rhetoric of the first and second centuries B.C., but not much about the rhetorical schools of the third century. Specimens of their work, no doubt, survive among the spurious speeches which have been included in the works of Demosthenes and other orators. But it is mere bluff on the part of critics to assume that there is a *prima facie* probability that such works as the more important of the Platonic Epistles originated in rhetorical schools.

What we can be reasonably sure of is that those who produced such exercises worked with models before them, and followed recognised rules as to form and order. In the treatise of Demetrius on Style, a work which probably belongs to the first century B.C. or A.D., the epistolary style is considered in a passage of some length (§§ 223–235), and in a short treatise by the same author twenty-one types of letters are classified under their appropriate headings, as "Friendly Letter", "Letter of Introduction", "Letter of Abuse", etc., with specimens of each;* but the author speaks of his classification as a novelty. In the second century of our era the "letter" had taken its place as one of the most popular forms of Greek literature, and during the Byzantine period collections of letters helped, along with prose fiction, to meet the demand for light reading, either imaginative or edifying. They are of the most varying quality, ranging from the charm of Alkiphron to the mechanical frigidity of the Letters of Chion and the puerilities of those ascribed to Hippokrates. Many of them are the merest scraps intended to cater for a public which wanted something of the nature of *Tit-Bits*.

Several of these collections, like the Letters of Chion and those of Themistokles, are narratives of the nature of historical novels in letter form, the "Briefroman". Others are made up of imaginary letters from real characters, but not combined into a story; such are Alkiphron's letters from Glykera to Demetrios Poliorketes and from Leontion to Epikouros. Most of the collections do not bear the name of any author and came to be regarded by the more foolish of modern readers as the genuine correspondence of the imaginary writers. Bentley, when in his Dissertation he dissipated this error, was careful to distinguish from the mass of later fictitious letters the thirteen Platonic Epistles, which he accepted as genuine. He defended at some length the 13th Epistle, the only one which had been attacked at that date (see Notes, Intr. Rem. to Ep XIII).†

Some of the nineteenth-century critics, as Sauppe and Susemihl, accounted for the Platonic Epistles as something in the nature of a "Briefroman". But it is now generally recognised that they must belong to a date not far removed from the death of Plato; and there is no evidence that at that date either the composition of letters was studied in rhetorical schools, or that the "Brief-

---

* Hercher, *Epist. Gr.* p. 1.

† "Back to Bentley" is the keynote of some excellent remarks by Apelt in the Introduction to his Translation of the Epistles. Of the collections dealt with by Bentley the "Sokratic Epistles" is the only one which has much bearing on the question now under discussion. See the Note at the end of this Section.

roman" existed as a literary form.* New literary forms are not invented by forgers; and those who attack the Platonic Epistles must not only produce evidence that they are not likely to be the work of Plato, but must also have some reasonable theory to account for the existence of such remarkable documents.

It is worth while to consider what evidence we have with regard to Greek letters in the fourth and third centuries before Christ. For the fourth century we have nothing† extant which has any claim to be considered genuine except the Platonic Epistles and the Letters of Isokrates.‡ About the genuineness of the second of these two collections there ought to be no doubt. Jebb's verdict is decisively in their favour; and on the evidence of style it is difficult to see how any careful student of Isokrates can have any other opinion. Seven of them are of the nature of pamphlets rather than letters, and should be compared with the 3rd, 7th and 8th Platonic Epistles, which belong to about the same period. We may assume that these pamphlet-letters were published, and that each writer knew what had been written by the other. The differences between those of Plato and those of Isokrates are characteristic of the two men.

* If the "Briefroman" had become popular in the time of Cicero, references to it must have occurred in his works. He quotes the Letters of Anacharsis; but they are a mere collection of letters of good advice, telling no story. They are, no doubt, the sort of thing out of which the "Briefroman" developed. Cicero's mention of them is an indication that if the other more remarkable collections of letters, such as the Sokratic Epistles or the Letters of Phalaris, had been extant in his day, references to them would have been found in his works and those of other well-informed Romans.

† I have not mentioned the six letters ascribed to Demosthenes. The evidence of style is as strongly against these as it is in favour of those of Isokrates. They seem to have been extant in the time of Cicero, who apparently refers to the 5th letter (*Brutus*, 31, 121). They are perhaps as early as the third century B.C., and are the sort of letters which would probably have been produced in a rhetorical school of that date. The longer ones should be compared with those Platonic Epistles which have been supposed by critics to owe their origin to the schools of rhetoric.

‡ For a fuller account of these see Jebb, *Attic Orators*, I, pp. 238 ff.

The 3rd and 4th letters of Isokrates, to Philip and Antipater respectively, are not pamphlets, but personal letters. Of the 4th Jebb says, "Alone of the nine letters this has the ease of private friendship". It shares this characteristic with the 13th Platonic Epistle; it is worth noting that both are letters of introduction. Of private correspondence between individuals, when not called for by some special reason, there was probably not much at this period. Letter-writing as an occupation or amusement had not become fashionable.*

Besides these two collections there is satisfactory evidence that some few other genuine fourth-century letters, now no longer extant, were well known in antiquity. Diogenes Laertius mentions a collection of letters from Aristotle to correspondents whose names he gives, and letters from Speusippos to Dion, Dionysios, and Philip. Athenaios also (XI, 507 e) quotes from a letter of Speusippos to Philip, reminding the king of the services rendered to him in early life by Plato; and Plutarch (*Adul.* ch. 29) quotes from a letter of Speusippos to Dion. Neither of these quotations is to be found in the letters purporting to be from Speusippos to Philip and Dion in the extant collection of Sokratic Epistles. That collection is undoubtedly of late origin, and the letters quoted by Plutarch and Athenaios may have been genuine documents. But nothing more can be said about them. Another collection of fourth-century letters which was probably genuine, the Letters of Timonides to Speusippos, has been dealt with above (Note to Section III). They were of the nature of despatches from a war correspondent rather than personal letters.

The Letters of Aristotle require further notice on account of the frequent mention of them in ancient authors. A collection of all the passages referring to or quoting from them will be

---

* The fragments of the Letters of Epikouros show that in the middle of the third century B.C. the intimate personal letter was becoming fashionable. It was natural that it should come into being along with the New Comedy. The Letters of Theopompos mentioned by Dionys. Hal. (*Ep. ad Pomp.* §§ 782, 786) were evidently pamphlets, and were probably modelled on those of Isokrates.

found in Rose's edition of the Fragments of Aristotle (1886), pp. 411–21. There is some doubt about their number.* Diogenes Laertius mentions twenty besides letters of Philip and to the Selymbrians, whatever these may have been. Hesychius also mentions twenty letters. The list of Ptolemy gives the number twenty, and, though the text leaves it doubtful whether he meant twenty letters or twenty books of letters, we shall probably be right in assuming that he meant twenty letters. Of those mentioned separately in the list of Diogenes Laertius four were to Alexander, nine to Antipater, and one each to other correspondents, Mentor, Ariston, Olympias, etc. All these were probably of the type which would now be called semi-official. If the collection had come down to us, it would probably be found to have much in common with the Platonic Epistles. This is fully borne out by the judgments of the ancient critics quoted by Rose (*l. c.* p. 411). Demetrios, in his remarks on the epistolary style referred to above, says (περὶ ἑρμ. § 234): "Letters addressed to cities or kings should be in a somewhat elevated style; for they must be made to suit the characters to whom they are addressed. But, though elevated, they must not take the form of a treatise rather than a letter, like those of Aristotle to Alexander and the letter of Plato to the friends of Dion".

Simplicius, whose opinion is worth considering, says of Aristotle (*in Categ.* f. 2, ed. Bas. 1551): "The style of his letters, which reproduces attractively the conversational discourse suitable to a letter, shows conclusively that he could express himself clearly. And none of those who have been compared with Aristotle equal him in the epistolary style".

Photios, whose judgment is perhaps less valuable, makes the following comparison between the two collections (*Epist.* 207): "Plato's letters fall short equally of the eloquence of Demos-

---

* The six letters which bear the name of Aristotle in Hercher's *Epistolographi* hardly deserve mention. The first five of them are letters of advice, containing the twaddle usually found in letters of this type in the other late collections. The 6th is perhaps earlier. It is a short one of four lines, in answer to a similar one from Alexander. The pair are quoted by Aulus Gellius (20, 5) and referred to by Plutarch (*Alex.* 7). They are not likely to be genuine.

thenes and of the epistolary style. But those of Aristotle, though more eloquent than his other writings, are not equal even to those of Plato ".

Ammonios, proleg. in Ar. cat. (p. 36 b 32 Br.), says of Aristotle: " In his Epistles he seems to have successfully hit the right style for letters, which ought to be concise and clear, and free from all difficulty of construction and phrase ".

From these expressions of opinion it may be inferred that the two collections had a good deal of resemblance in form and character, that they were carefully studied and compared by professional critics, who were dealing with their own language and qualified to express an opinion on style, and that neither of them gave rise to suspicions of its genuineness.

It was worth while to dwell for a little on the Letters of Aristotle, because one of the theories put forward during the most sceptical years of the nineteenth century was that they were genuine, and were the model on which the Platonic Epistles and other epistolary forgeries were copied. It was something to recognise that forgeries of this sort could hardly have come into existence without some model to copy from. But a sense of humour should have prevented the formulation of a theory which carried faith in the unknown and suspicion of the known to such lengths. The theory has since been abandoned by its author.* But it is not out of place to recall the past judgments of critics whose "ipse dixit" carries great weight.

So far all that we have shown is that there is no such *prima facie* case against the Epistles as there would be if we had a mass of similar literature of the same date which could be proved to have issued from schools of rhetoric or philosophy. The disappearance of most of the prose literature which followed the death of Aristotle has left us without much evidence on either side. But such information as we have makes it highly improbable that forgeries of this type were produced at or about the date to which the Platonic Epistles must certainly belong.

---

* This theory was put forward by U. von Wilamowitz-Moellendorff (*Antig. v. Karyst.* p. 151 note 15). It was approved as a probable view by F. Susemihl (*Gr. Litt. in der al. Z.* pp. 579, 580).

We have to consider, not merely the Greek style and the knowledge of detail which they show, but also the successful assumption of the character of the supposed writer, which all the more
important letters reveal. If they are not genuine, we can only
account for their existence by crediting their author with a
dramatic power which is not likely to have been found at that
age except in a writer of original genius. In our day the historical
novel has made devices familiar which were unknown in the
fourth and third centuries before Christ. Those who think it
likely that such a work as the 3rd Platonic Epistle issued from
a school of rhetoric at that period, or was produced by an
unknown rhetorician, show a want of literary perception which is
remarkable in scholars of taste and ability.

But while it is *prima facie* improbable that the more important
of the Platonic Epistles are forgeries, it is neither impossible nor
improbable that such a collection of letters may have been left
behind by Plato himself. The state in which we have received
the writings both of Plato and of Isokrates makes it likely that
both of them, in their old age, collected their works with a view
to their preservation. It is natural that they should have attached
to these collections copies of their pamphlet-letters. It is also
natural that to these they should have added copies of some of
the more important of their private letters, most of which, as
we have seen, would be of the semi-official type. This accounts
for all of the nine letters of Isokrates, and for seven of those of
Plato, the 2nd, 3rd, 4th, 6th, 7th, 8th and 13th.

There is nothing wildly improbable in the supposition that
Plato himself may have attached to his collection other shorter
letters of which he happened to have copies. No positive proof
can be given that the shorter letters, the 5th, 9th, 10th, 11th and
12th, are not intrusions by another hand. At a later date short
letters to or from philosophers were fabricated in large numbers,
and several are preserved by Diogenes Laertius. Among these
very poor productions are two which have evidently been
written for the express purpose of filling up gaps in the collection
of Platonic Epistles. In Ep. VII Plato, when relating the conclusion of his third visit to Sicily, says that Archytas sent a

thirty-oared galley with an emissary to Dionysios, praying for his release. The biographer reproduces a short colourless document which professes to be the actual letter written by Archytas (Diog. Laert. III, 22). Again, the 12th Platonic Epistle is an answer to a letter from Archytas, and in his Life of Archytas (VIII, 4) Diogenes quotes our 12th Epistle, and with it gives another commonplace scrap, which professes to be the letter to which it is a reply. These two letters from Archytas were probably not composed by the author of the biographies, but taken by him from some collection of fictitious letters; and it is worth noting that, though evidently written as amplifications of our collection, they have not found their way into it. They are an indication that the collection, as we have it, was preserved against those intrusions of fictitious documents, which are common in some other works of the same period, e.g. the speeches of orators.

If we suppose that the collection arose in this haphazard way, the fact that it is arranged in no sort of order calls for no explanation. We are still left with the serious difficulty presented by the 1st Epistle, which was quite obviously not written by Plato. Its presence in the collection seems likely to remain an unsolved problem. I have dealt with it in the Notes. It is unfortunate that, in its present position, it must have prejudiced many readers against the letters which follow it. The 12th letter also, though its contents present no insuperable obstacle, suffers from a *prima facie* prejudice owing to the note condemning it, which is attached to it in some of the MSS. This also may be reserved for discussion in the Notes.*

Putting these two aside, we may now turn to the question whether the rest present internal evidence which obliges us *prima facie* to refuse to accept them as genuine. Most of them possess strongly marked characteristics, which at once put them on a different footing from the fictitious documents which

* I have not thought it necessary to make any reference to the five additional letters which C. F. Hermann, from various sources and with no authority, added to the Platonic Epistles in his edition of the text of Plato (Teubner: Leipzig).

make up the greater part of the "Epistolographi Graeci". The question hotly contested among critics is whether these characteristics are what we should expect to find in letters written by Plato. Jowett, after many years devoted to the study of Plato, said of the Epistles: "The final conclusion is that neither the Seventh nor any other of them, when carefully analysed, can be imagined to have proceeded from the hand or mind of Plato" (Preface to 3rd edn. of Translation of Plato).

Here we have the sceptical attitude in the extreme form in which it was held almost universally in Germany and England at the time when Jowett wrote. It may be traced to three causes: (1) personal impressions of Plato as a man; (2) misapprehensions as to the nature of his philosophical work and teaching; (3) the apparent absence of independent evidence for his visits to Sicily. I will deal briefly with each of these points.

(1) Plato's mind was one of such astonishing genius that a prolonged study of his works almost forces the reader to put him on a pedestal by himself. It is forgotten that in private life he must have had some of those weaknesses to which all human minds are liable—that there may have been sides to his character which were not allowed to obtrude themselves in his published works, but which he would not have felt called on to suppress in a private and personal letter, and which even in a pamphlet intended for a wider public might force themselves to the front, when he was writing about himself under the influence of strong emotion.

Most readers of the Dialogues would allow that they reveal little or nothing about the nature of the writer except the fact that his remarkable powers were accompanied by an equally remarkable reticence about himself. In this they resemble the plays of Shakespeare. Both men had the dramatic gift, and along with it the power, characteristic of genius, which enables a man to lose himself for the time being in absorption with the object on which his mind is working. It is only when we get to Plato's latest work, the *Laws*, that one is occasionally conscious of something in the nature of self-revelation; it can hardly be doubted that the real Plato is sometimes speaking to us in the person of the Athenian Stranger. But this is a feature which has no parallel in the earlier Dialogues.

Now it is not an exaggeration to say that the 7th Epistle is one of the most remarkable pieces of self-revelation to be found in ancient literature:* as a psychological study it stands almost alone. There is some reticence with regard to names and events. The story of the Athenian Revolution is told without mentioning a single name except that of Sokrates, and the names of Dion's murderers are suppressed. But with regard to his own mental history, Plato, if the letter is his work, has passed from the extreme of reticence to a frankness for a parallel to which we must go to Rousseau or Augustine; and features are revealed which give a shock to those to whom Plato is a figure on a pedestal.

But if the letter is not Plato's work, what probable or possible author can be found for it? Are we to ascribe it to a friend or to a foe? As an honest attempt on the part of Plato to tell the truth about himself, the work is intelligible. But it is not the kind of work which any friend or admirer would have composed to defend his memory. On the other hand it contains much which makes it impossible to regard it as the work of a clever sophist who wished to hold Plato's character up to contempt. Such a highly dramatic fragment of autobiography might have been thought out by an Athenian Browning, if we can suppose such a writer to have been capable of maintaining throughout so long a work a style so unusual as that which this letter shares with Plato's *Laws*. But the supposition is so improbable that it does not call for discussion.

After all, the character which the letter reveals is not one which is at all impossible, or unlikely to have been combined with great artistic and philosophical gifts. The writer evidently has a considerable sense of his own importance, and a tendency towards egoism. He is acutely sensitive, and occasionally shows something like fretfulness. Are these things altogether un-common in men of genius? At the same time he shows strong religious feelings, loyalty to his friends, unwillingness to injure

* The saying of Demetrios (περὶ ἑρμ. § 227), σχεδὸν γὰρ εἰκόνα ἕκαστος τῆς ἑαυτοῦ ψυχῆς γράφει τὴν ἐπιστολήν, was probably suggested by Plato's Letters, which he mentions almost immediately after it.

even an unworthy person like Dionysios, a passion for truth, devotion to philosophy as the one serious business of life, and an anxiety to save souls (see 339 e) to which, except in Sokrates, it is not easy in that age to find a parallel. These things are surely not un-Platonic; nor is it perhaps wholly fancy to feel that the mind at the back of the 7th Epistle is the same as that which speaks to us from the mouth of the Athenian Stranger in the *Laws*.

(2) But it is not merely the character revealed by the letter which has been regarded as un-Platonic. The philosophy, of which the writer talks at some length, has been said to be not that of Plato. Such a feeling was natural on the part of those who believed that Plato taught a sort of Hegelian idealism. To such readers it came as a shock when they were told that all that was necessary in the way of metaphysics could be put so briefly that there was no risk of any one forgetting who had once mastered it;* that philosophy cannot be learnt from books, and that the writer would not think of enshrining his philosophical teaching in a written treatise; that the highest truths are apprehended by a flash of intuition, which passes from the mind of the teacher to that of the learner; that only souls akin to the subject can hope to attain this enlightenment; that the path of approach is a life, not only of study, but of self-denial and abstinence; and, most unwelcome tenet of all to the classical scholar, that the preliminary studies are largely mathematical.

An attempt has been made in the Notes to show in detail that the philosophy of which we get glimpses in the 7th and other Epistles is that which was actually taught in the School of Plato. I will only add here that, if the philosophy of the Letters is all wrong, the critics of antiquity, who were familiar with the Academy and its teaching, would certainly have pointed out the discrepancy.

(3) Scepticism has not been content with denying the Platonic authorship of the Letters; it has transferred to legend the whole

* Cf. 341 e 3, 344 e 1; and compare the Cambridge Platonist, John Smith, *Select Discourses*, p. 12, "Truth is not, I fear, so voluminous, nor swells into such a mighty bulk as our books do".

story of Plato's visits to Sicily. Jowett, after the remark about the Epistles quoted above, continues as follows:

"The other testimonies to the voyages to Sicily and the court of Dionysios are all of them later by several centuries than the events to which they refer. No extant writer mentions them older than Cicero and Cornelius Nepos. It does not seem impossible that so attractive a theme as the meeting of a philosopher and a tyrant, once imagined by the genius of a sophist, may have passed into a romance which became famous in Hellas and the world. It may have created one of the mists of history, like the Trojan war or the legend of Arthur, which we are unable to penetrate....If we agree with Karsten that they [i.e. the Letters] are the forgery of some rhetorician or sophist, we cannot agree with him in supposing that they are of any historical value, the rather as there is no early independent testimony by which they are supported or with which they can be compared".

Here we have a similar attitude to that of those who, influenced by the absence of independent testimonies, question the historicity of the death of Christ. None of the historians has adopted this view, and it might have been passed over here were it not that for some years prior to 1929 it was put forward in the *Encyclopædia Britannica* as a view generally adopted by the learned. In the case of Plato the absence of early independent testimony may fairly be ascribed to the loss of works such as the Histories of Philistos, Timaios, Ephoros and Theopompos, and the Letters of Timonides and Speusippos. The Lives written by Plutarch and Nepos furnish abundant evidence that, if we had this lost literature before us, it would corroborate the main facts, as they relate them. Further indications in the same direction are scattered about in the works of Athenaios, Aelian, Diogenes Laertius and other by-paths of ancient literature. Nor is it even conceivable that any writer of antiquity could have constructed such a fiction without coming to grief again and again in matters of fact.

Unfortunately Jowett was misled by Karsten into the belief that the writer of the Epistles had come to grief in several places. His suspicions were no doubt enhanced by the fact that Diodoros, in his notices of events belonging to the reign of Dionysios the Younger, makes no mention of the visits of Plato. This ought not to be a matter for surprise. The references to Sicily in that historian, which are fairly full throughout the reign of the elder Dionysios, become very meagre after his death. His chronology for Sicilian affairs omits altogether the ten years which follow the banishment of Dion, and he records Dion's return as if his absence had been one of a few months only. In the years which follow, the only Sicilian events which he relates with any fullness are some of the military operations of Dion. In one of the much fuller passages devoted by him to the reign of the elder Dionysios the visit of Plato to the court of that monarch is recorded. The visits to his son would, no doubt, have been mentioned also if that reign had been dealt with in a less summary fashion.

No more need be said here about the 7th Epistle. The only serious historical difficulty in it is dealt with in the Notes. In view of the decisive swing of the pendulum in its favour which has taken place in recent years, its genuineness might perhaps have been taken for granted. But scepticism with regard to it, though moribund, is not altogether dead: for in a review of J. Souilhé's edition of the Epistles in the *Classical Review* for May 1927 it is once more singled out for attack on the ground of style. This aspect of the letter will be referred to in a note attached to this Section.

Remarks on the genuineness of each of the other letters will be found in the Notes. All modern editors except Apelt are agreed that the 1st Epistle is not the work of Plato, and most of them allow that some doubt attaches to the 12th, though its genuineness, which is maintained in this edition, is also supported by A. E. Taylor and F. Novotný. The view that the rest of the collection are genuine letters of Plato has undoubtedly been gaining ground in recent years. It was consistently maintained by Grote in an age of universal doubt, and more recently endorsed by E. Meyer, whose short but weighty remarks, scattered about Volume v of his *History of Antiquity*, deserve attention. Among modern writers this view has been ably supported by H. Raeder, J. Burnet, and A. E. Taylor, and in the editions of O. Apelt, F. Novotný and W. Andreae. On the other hand the opinion that other spurious letters, besides the 1st and 12th, have found their way into the collection by the side of genuine ones still has supporters whose names carry weight. It is instructive to tabulate the views of the more recent of these critics, which illustrate how widely personal impressions vary on a question of this kind.

	Accepted	*Rejected*	*Doubtful*
R. Adam, 1906	VII	All the rest.	
C. Ritter, 1910	III, VII, VIII	I, II, V, VI, IX, X, XI, XII, XIII	IV
R. Hackforth, 1913	III, IV, VII, VIII, XIII	I, II, V, VI, XII	IX, X, XI
U. von Wilamowitz-Moellendorff, 1920	VI, VII, VIII	I, II, III, IV, V, IX, X, XII, XIII	XI
E. Howald, 1923	VI, VII, VIII	All the rest.	
L. A. Post, 1925	II, III, IV, VI, VII, VIII, X, XI, XIII	I, V, IX, XII	
J. Souilhé, 1926	VII, VIII	All the rest.	
R. G. Bury, 1929	VII, VIII	All the rest.	
G. C. Field, 1930	All except I, II, XII	I, II, XII	

To these may be added two earlier names, R. F. Unger (*Philologus*, N.F. IV, p. 191, 1891), who accepted Ep. XIII and rejected the rest, and A. Brinkmann (*Rhein. Mus.* LXVI, p. 266), who defended Ep. VI and rejected the rest, a view which was formerly held also by Wilamowitz.

Those who attempt to follow the vagaries of higher criticism will not be surprised at these divergences of opinion. There are few critics whose opinion on the genuineness of doubtful works, especially prose works in a foreign or ancient language, is worth much, when it has nothing to rest on except style and general impression. The best judges would probably be the most unwilling to express, on such grounds as these, a decisive opinion on documents so short as the 4th, 5th, 9th, 10th, 11th and 12th letters. Such works must be judged, in some measure at least, by the company in which they appear.

The disagreement between the two critics whose names stand, perhaps, the highest, C. Ritter and U. von Wilamowitz-Moellendorff, deserves special attention. Ritter accepts Ep. III as written by Plato, and IV as a genuine document, but more probably the work of Speusippos than of Plato; II, VI and XIII he assigns, on the evidence of style, to one and the same forger. Wilamowitz assigns VI to Plato,* and condemns the group made up of II, III and IV as "jämmerlichen Machwerken", ascribing them to the same hand, that of a forger imitating the style of VII; while he assigns XIII to another forger who makes no attempt to imitate the style of Plato. Such disagreements among the eminent ought to inspire caution with regard to the higher criticism of the moment, and to suggest a doubt whether the attacks on any of these five letters are justified. It ought to be possible to arrive at something like certainty with regard to documents of such length as the 2nd, 3rd and 13th letters. I have attempted in the Notes to show that the objections urged against these are groundless. The 6th also may fairly be considered to provide sufficient proof of its own genuineness. Those who accept these, in addition to the 7th and 8th, will probably feel that the others, except the 1st and perhaps the 12th, may with some likelihood be regarded as the work of Plato.†

But at present the question is still *sub judice*, and the controversy has been carried on with some acrimony. It is difficult to be tolerant of those who believe either less or more than ourselves; and it is not possible to examine the views of others with any thoroughness without mentioning their names. Some of those against whose opinions I have argued are scholars of eminence, living and dead, and I should be sorry if anything said here seems to suggest depreciation of men whose names are deservedly held in reverence. But it is better to point out errors which have led the world seriously astray. Few critics now doubt that the 7th Epistle was written by Plato, that, as literature, it is not unworthy of his great name, and that the view

---

* Of Ep. VI he says (*Pl.* II, p. 281): "Er trägt den Stempel von Platons unnachahmlicher Altersstyl und ist ein kostbares Dokument seiner Denkart". The contrast between this view and Ritter's condemnation of the letter (*N.U.* p. 373) is startling.

† A short but enlightening discussion of the question will be found in A. E. Taylor's *Plato: the Man and his Work*, pp. 15, 16. See also the Appendix to his second edition, pp. 541 ff.

taken of it by what passed for higher criticism in England and Germany sixty years ago was one of those temporary aberrations to which the human mind is liable.

Another generation may see a change of views with regard to the other letters similar to that which has occurred in the case of the 7th and 8th. I cannot expect that my judgment in such a matter will carry any weight. But surely more attention should have been paid by the iconoclasts to the fact that the Epistles were read without suspicion by the Greek writers on style, Demetrios and others, who have referred to them, that Plutarch knew them intimately and treated them as a classic without feeling any doubt, and that a sceptic like Lucian quotes them with respect. Allusion has already been made to the views of Cicero and of Bentley. Cicero admired the 7th Epistle, was fond of the 9th, and evidently had no suspicion of the others. He had studied Plato under the best Greek teachers, and was a good judge of a letter. Bentley was prepared to pull down any idol: and no other scholar has had an equal knowledge of Greek epistolary literature. Richards puts him out of court by saying, "Bentley accepted the letters, but the question had not then been raised" (*Platonica*, p. 272). The *Dissertation* ought to have shown him that Bentley would have been the first to raise it, if there had been solid grounds for doing so.

Another critic, whose views on this question should carry scarcely less weight than those of Bentley, is the poet Gray, whose notes on Plato,* written without any idea of publication, were the result of many years of wide and independent study of Greek literature. He approaches the Epistles with an open mind, condemns the 1st, thinks that the oath in the 6th may be a forgery, and that some of the paragraphs at the end of the 13th may have been inserted by an idle sophist, who was an enemy to Plato's character. But he expresses no doubt about the rest, and brings much learning to bear on the historical questions to which they give rise. Gray's literary perception was very sensitive, and his judgment deserves attention as that of a man of taste, uninfluenced by any current of contemporary fashion.

* They will be found in vol. IV of E. Gosse's edition of the *Works* of Gray, London, 1906.

Note I: On the Sokratic Epistles

The Sokratic Epistles are a collection of thirty-seven letters which, though from different correspondents, form a single group, and may be regarded as a fair specimen of one type of the Greek " Briefroman ". They do not form a narrative dealing with a single story, but are intended to give a picture of the doings and views of one group of philosophers, or friends of philosophers, who were all connected, directly or indirectly, with Sokrates.

The collection is described by Bentley in his *Dissertations upon the Epistles of Phalaris*, etc. (vol. II, p. 189 of Dyce's edition of the *Works* of Bentley) and more recently and fully by W. Obens (*Qua aetate Socratis et Socraticorum epistulae, quae dicuntur, scriptae sint*, Münster, 1912). The text has been published by L. Köhler (*Philologus*, Suppl. Band xx, Heft II) with a translation and notes. The contents of some of the letters have been discussed at some length by C. Ritter (*N.U.* pp. 379 ff.). I have not thought it necessary to give references for every instance in which my remarks have been drawn from or anticipated by these writers. Monographs on the subject, which I have not been able to consult, have also been published by O. Schering (Greifswald, 1917), and by F. Paulu (Vienna, 1924).

The collection may be divided into six groups:

(1) Letters 1–7 b.* Eight letters from Sokrates to various correspondents: to Archelaos, King of Macedon, giving reasons for declining an invitation to visit him; to an unnamed correspondent giving a discourse on the uselessness of wealth; to one of the exiles at Thebes giving news of Athens under the rule of the Thirty. These three are very lengthy. Of the five shorter letters two are to Xenophon, one giving advice about his expedition into Asia, and the other asking him to aid Chairephon who has been sent as ambassador to the Peloponnese; one is written from Potidaea to an unnamed correspondent at Athens introducing Mnason, an exile from Amphipolis; and one informs

* The numbers are those of Hercher's *Epistolographi Graeci*.

Plato very briefly of his reasons for refusing Kriton's offer to help him to escape from prison. All these are obviously fictitious. Sokrates left no written works, and no letters to or from him are quoted by any author of antiquity. They are made up of materials drawn mainly from the Dialogues of Plato, Xenophon and Aischines of Sphettos. (For the author's debt to the last of these see Dittmar, *Aischines of Sphettos*, pp. 63 f., 92 f., 194 ff., 210, 243, 284 ff., 307.)

(2) Letters 8–13 and 29. Nos. 8–13 are six short letters in pairs to and from Aristippos when resident at the court of the younger Dionysios at Syracuse—his correspondents being Antisthenes the Cynic, Aischines of Sphettos, and Simon the philosophical cobbler. These are intended to be amusing. No. 29 is a long letter from Aristippos at Syracuse to his daughter Aretê at Kyrene. Diogenes Laertius, who gives a list of the works of Antisthenes and Aischines, makes no mention among them of any letters. He does mention a letter from Aristippos to his daughter; and in this case our author may possibly have drawn details from the original letter. But the original, if genuine, can hardly have been, like No. 29, in Attic Greek. For the other five letters the materials were probably taken from dialogues then extant. A dialogue by Phaidon was named after Simon (Diog. Laert. II, 9), and this was probably the source from which later writers drew their information about him (see paper by Wilamowitz in *Hermes*, XIV, p. 187): but it is not necessary, as some critics have done, to dismiss Simon as a purely fictitious personage.

(3) Letters 14–17. Four letters from various correspondents, dealing for the most part with the trial and death of Sokrates. One of them, No. 14, is a long one intended perhaps to be from Aischines, and is a good specimen of the kind of narrative which the later sophists constructed from materials offered by the earlier literature. Another, No. 17, gives the legend of the punishment of the accusers of Sokrates, which became current some years after his death. No. 15 contains a quotation from the 2nd Platonic Epistle. Since that letter dates itself as written not less than thirty-five years after the supposed date of No. 15,

it is clear that the author of the Sokratic Epistles made no
secret of the fact that his work was fictitious. (See Bentley,
l. c. p. 203.)

(4) Letters 18–22. A group of letters from or connected with
Xenophon. Two are invitations to friends to visit him on his
estate; one is a friendly letter to Xanthippê, the widow of
Sokrates; one is to the Theban friends of Sokrates, Simmias and
Kebes, describing his progress in the composition of his
Memorabilia; and one is a short letter from either Simmias or
Kebes to a friend at Athens.

(5) Letters 23–28. A group of letters centring round Plato's
journeys; viz. (23) from Aischines to Phaidon giving an account
of his own reception by Dionysios at Syracuse and of interviews
with the monarch in which Plato and Aristippos took part;
(24) from Plato to a correspondent in Syracuse, perhaps
Dionysios, describing his own intention of living a life of
seclusion like Timon—the writer was evidently acquainted with
the 1st Platonic Epistle; (25) from Plato to Dionysios introducing Krinis; (26) from Plato to friends at Syracuse praising
them for their loyalty to Dionysios and urging them to continue
in the same course—a letter of advice, resembling the 10th
Platonic Epistle; (27) from Phaidros, who has heard that Plato
contemplates a long journey and begs not to be deserted by him;
(28) from an unnamed correspondent who, having heard that
Plato is in Egypt, writes to him making a great display of his
own knowledge of all that is to be seen there.

(6) Letters 29–37. A group of letters to or from Speusippos
illustrating the connection of the Academy, first with Macedon
and then with Syracuse, and the relations between Speusippos,
Xenokrates, Dion and Dionysios. The most important is No. 30,
a long letter from Speusippos to Philip of Macedon, criticising in
detail the speech of Isokrates to Philip (Isok. *Or.* v). No. 31
professes to be a letter of advice from Plato to Philip. Nos. 32
and 33 are from Speusippos to Xenokrates describing his own
bad health and asking him to come and take charge of the work
of the Academy. No. 34 is the answer of Xenokrates, who in
language borrowed partly from the 4th Platonic Epistle declines

on the ground that he wishes to devote himself to philosophy. No. 35 is a letter of forty-two lines from Speusippos to Dion, written in lighter vein to accompany a more serious letter, which is not included in the collection. No. 36 is from Dionysios to Speusippos. The writer is evidently familiar with the contents of No. 35, to which he makes spiteful retorts. The text of Nos. 35 and 36 has suffered considerably, and that of No. 37 is so corrupt that nothing can be said about its contents.

There is no reason to doubt that this collection of letters forms a single work, put together by one author. It must belong to a time when collections of imaginary letters had become a favourite form of light literature, and cannot possibly be dated earlier than the beginning of the Christian era. When the letters of Alkiphron were written, in the latter part of the first century A.D., this literary form was fully established, but was probably still a novelty.

The Greek prose writers of the second and third centuries after Christ, the second Sophistic Period, were, most of them, orators or rhetoricians, who travelled about, delivering speeches in the great cities of the Hellenistic world. They lived largely in an artificial and imaginary world, which they had constructed out of literary materials, drawn from the Dialogues of Plato, Xenophon, Aischines and other literary sources. They used these in a way which may be compared with the use made of the Bible by Milton in his *Paradise Lost* and *Samson Agonistes*.

The Sokratic Epistles are full of indications that they belong to this period. Bentley evidently assigned them to this date, and Obens has made a full collection of evidences that they belong to a date not earlier than the second century A.D.

One important piece of external evidence has been alluded to, viz. that Diogenes Laertius makes no mention of letters in the lists which he gives of the works of Antisthenes and Aischines. If any collection of letters of these writers had been extant as early as the first century A.D., they must almost certainly have appeared in his lists.

Another is furnished by the story in the 1st letter (§ 9) about the flight of Sokrates and others from the battle of Delium

(424 B.C.). This is told to illustrate the guidance which Sokrates received from his "divine sign", and is a good specimen of the legends about him which became current after his death. The same story is told more briefly by Cicero (de Div. I, 123) with the information that it was taken from the work on omens by the Stoic Antipater. It is also told by Plutarch (D.D. Sokr. 581 d) but with differences of detail which show that he must have taken it from another source. It is a fair inference that Plutarch and Cicero, if they had known of a letter purporting to be written by Sokrates himself on the subject, would have mentioned it. Plutarch, who was writing a treatise on the "Divine Sign", could not have failed to do so.

The probability that the letters belong to a date not earlier than the first century of our era is fully borne out by internal evidence. The Greek style is that of the prose authors of that date. Obens has made an extensive collection of instances illustrating the vocabulary, the order of words, and the uses of prepositions and particles. The evidence of vocabulary is striking. After reducing the list given by Obens by cutting out cases in which the difference is one of form and spelling, I find it still shows sixty-five instances of words and uses of words which belong to the later prose writers, though some are found earlier in poetry. Some of these are words which became extremely common, as καταστρατηγεῖν (to outwit), προκοπή (progress), αἵρεσις (a sect of philosophers). There are other features characteristic of the Atticist revival of the first century A.D. which are not likely to be found in works written during the three preceding centuries, as the use of the dual, and the frequent use of the middle voice, both of which were artificially revived by the Atticists.

The contents of the letters point to the same conclusion. They contain much that is purely legendary. The Delium incident is one instance. Another is furnished by Letter XVII, which gives in its fullest form the myth of the punishment inflicted by the Athenians on the accusers of Sokrates. The writer, a friend of Sokrates who had fled from Athens after his death, has been encouraged to return by a change in public opinion, the cause of which he relates to another friend of Sokrates in the island of Chios. Communication between Athens and Chios was easy enough under the Roman Empire, but difficult at the supposed date of the letter, four or five hundred years earlier. The Athenians, the writer says, have now waked up, and brought to trial and put to death Anytos and Meletos, the accusers of Sokrates. After the death of Sokrates the Athenians soon began to miss him, and this feeling was brought to a head by the incident of the Spartan youth. This young man had been so attracted by what he had heard about Sokrates that he came to Athens to make his acquaintance. On his arrival, while still outside the gates, he learned that Sokrates had been put to death. He was so overcome by grief at the news, that he would not enter the city, but, enquiring where the grave of Sokrates was, he spent the night by it, weeping. In the morning, after kissing the grave, he started on his journey home. The Athenians were moved to repentance by the contrast between their own conduct and that of this young man.

No contemporary writer mentions this prosecution of the accusers of Sokrates. Anytos was a prominent person at Athens, and, if he had been punished in this way, some allusion to the fact would certainly have been made, either by the historians, or in the Dialogues of Plato and Xenophon. The whole incident is pure fiction. Later generations began to feel that poetical justice required that punishment should fall on the heads of the accusers of such a man as Sokrates, and a story providing this was in time forthcoming (see Dittmar, l.c. p. 63).

In other cases the letters give fiction blended, not always skilfully, with fact. Xenophon's estate in the Peloponnese is transferred from its proper situation in Elis to Lakonia; and his son, Gryllos, who, as a young man, was killed at the battle of Mantinea, 362 B.C., is spoken of as having been a boy at Athens at the time of the trial of Sokrates in 399 B.C. Among other points indicating a late origin for the letters may be mentioned the omission of the third accuser of Sokrates; the fiction, in Letter XXIX, that he had a second wife Myrto; the allusions (IX, 3, and XIII, 2) to big beards as a mark of philosophers;

and the allegorical explanation of the myth of Bellerophon (1, 11, 12).

C. Ritter (*l.c.*) has tried to state a case for assigning an earlier origin to some of the letters of the last group. He is attracted by the idea that some of these may be genuine letters of Speusippos, and, though he finally decides that there is not sufficient evidence to justify this view, he thinks that they may be made up from material taken from the genuine letters, which were extant in antiquity, and are quoted by Plutarch and Athenaios, besides appearing in the list of the works of Speusippos given by Diogenes Laertius.

The most important of them, No. 30, the long letter devoted to a criticism of the 5th Speech of Isokrates, may be by a different hand from the others; for it contains fewer instances of hiatus. But the nature of its contents makes it unlikely that it belongs to a date considerably earlier. It has its parallel in the criticisms of Plato in the speech of Aelius Aristides "On behalf of the Four". The letter and the speech both show the same attempt to display extensive historical knowledge, and they probably belong to the same age and school. Ritter discusses at length the peculiarities of No. 35, a letter addressed to Dion, and No. 36, the reply to it, in which the writer is clearly assuming the personality of the younger Dionysios. He attributes too great importance to the difficulty caused by the fact that Dionysios is acquainted with the contents of a letter not addressed to him. Such a difficulty would not have been felt by one of the authors of these epistolary romances. The writer may have taken some particulars from the Letters of Speusippos which were extant in his day; but it is most unlikely that letters, which actually passed between Athens and Syracuse, were filled with the trivialities which we have in these two epistles. Parallels for most of the details in them can be found in the works of Athenaios, and there is no reason to doubt that all their contents could have been drawn from sources readily accessible to a writer of the second Sophistic Age.

To sum up—with the Sokratic Epistles before us we can form a fair idea of what the Platonic Epistles would have been, if they had been produced in the schools of rhetoric, to which some of them are still assigned by critics. Both in matter and style the two works present a striking contrast, and this in spite of the fact that the author of the Sokratic Epistles evidently had the Platonic Epistles before him and has borrowed freely from them. The later work is largely made up of padding of the kind which comes easiest to the letter-writer, good advice and moralising in general terms. Legends are introduced which were the inventions of a later age, facts are freely altered, intervals of time are ignored, and the attempts at humour are unworthy of the persons to whom they are attributed. In the Platonic Epistles we are moving in a real world; the narrative gives the facts as they are known from other sources; the writer is grappling, or attempting to grapple, with serious political questions and often brings a scene before us with remarkable dramatic power.

Note II: On the Literary Style of the Epistles

By style I here denote actual language and phraseology, not those vaguer impressions by which we seem to discern the personality of a writer behind his composition. The subject falls into four divisions: (1) Choice of words; (2) Order of words; (3) Structure of sentences; (4) Mannerisms.

In a collection of letters, written for different purposes at different periods of a man's life, uniformity of style is not to be expected. In pamphlets like the 3rd, 7th and 8th Epistles we may expect to find, if they are genuine, a style resembling that of the published works which belong to the same period of the writer's life; and we may look for a similar style in the more formal of the shorter letters, as for instance the 6th. But in an intimate personal letter like the 13th, in which the writer is manifestly trying to be informal, we must be prepared for something different.

The 6th, 7th and 8th letters belong, if genuine, to the later years of Plato's life, when he was occupied with his last great work, the *Laws*; and the stylistic features in common between these three letters and the *Laws* with its short supplement, the

*Epinomis,** are so striking that they stare the reader in the face. In the 3rd letter, another pamphlet separated from the 7th by two or three years only, similar features present themselves. The 2nd, a personal letter, but occupied with serious subjects, and coming about four years before the 3rd in date, shows, with one important exception, similar features. In the 13th, which precedes the 2nd by about five years, and is a studiously informal personal letter, these special features are absent. I shall confine myself to giving illustrations of some of the more important points under the four heads mentioned above. For further details the reader is referred to Raeder (*Rhein. Mus.* LXI, pp. 441 ff.) and to R. Hackforth's monograph (*The Authorship of the Platonic Epistles*, Manchester, 1913).†

(1) VOCABULARY

Raeder starts his examination of the vocabulary with a list of 98 words which are found in the *Epistles* and do not occur elsewhere in Plato's works. This figure looks more formidable than it is. Plato had an enormous vocabulary and was fond of coining new words. Each of the Dialogues contains words not found in any of the others. There are 93 such words in the *Theaitetos*, 99 in the *Sophist*, and over 1000 in the *Laws*. Of the 98 words in Raeder's list, seven are marked by him as not found elsewhere in Greek literature, and four more might perhaps have been marked in the same way. Some of these, as ξεναπατία, ἀκοινωνία, εὐπαράκλητοι, were perhaps coined by Plato; the non-occurrence of the others in extant literature may be due to mere accident. Among the remaining words a few would not be

---

* For the style of the *Epinomis* I may perhaps refer to my edition of the dialogue (Clar. Press), Intr. v. Almost all the features of style which are there dealt with might have been illustrated equally well from the 7th Epistle. The two works correspond so closely that a careful student is not likely to ascribe them to different authors.

† Raeder makes the unfortunate mistake of trying to date the shorter letters by numerical occurrences of stylistic features. Ritter makes great play with this in his attacks on Raeder (*N.U.* pp. 347 ff., 418 ff.). In spite of this, and of other weaknesses pointed out by Hackforth, Raeder's collection of the features of style is useful, and affords good evidence of the genuineness of the more important letters.

likely to occur out of their present context, e.g. συσφαιρισταί, στραγγουρία, πολιανομεῖν; a few are poetical words, such as Plato was always fond of introducing, c.g. ξενοφόνος, but the large majority are words used by contemporary prose authors for which no apology is necessary. The important question is whether among the remainder there is any considerable sprinkling of words of which the use in prose is confined to late writers.

The later writers, from Polybios onwards, added largely to the vocabulary of Greek prose. A few of the new words were required to denote new things, institutions, or ideas; but the greater number were introduced in order to give either heightened colour or more definiteness to the language. Heightened colour was obtained by borrowing from the poets, definiteness by using, in place of the simple words, compounds, which the Greek language formed with the same facility as the German. Among the 98 words I find only nine of which the use in prose appears to be confined to later authors, viz. in Ep. VII, ἀναφλέγω, ἀνοσιουργία, αὐτόκλητος, ἐπιχρώννυμι, ἰσόνομος, παρακοή, παράκουσμα; in Ep. III, λυκοφιλία; in Ep. XIII, προσαγγέλλω. The absence of earlier instances of the last of these must be the result of pure accident. None of the nine are tell-tale words such as those we find in the Sokratic Epistles, e.g. αἵρεσις, προκοπή, καταστρατηγεῖν, which became very common in later times and might fairly be taken as indicating a later authorship. The list therefore as a whole is valuable, not for what it contains, but for what it does not contain. It go to prove that the vocabulary of the Epistles contains nothing inconsistent with Plato's authorship of them. A writer of the generation which followed the conquests of Alexander would almost certainly have betrayed himself.

Raeder next gives a list of 245 words in the Epistles which are found in Plato's other writings, but are either not found, or only rarely found, with the same meaning elsewhere. Such a list ought to provide evidence of that which most readers of the Epistles must have felt, that their vocabulary is Platonic. Unfortunately it contains words which are of fairly frequent occurrence in other fourth-century prose writers, and Hackforth has shown that it ought to be cut down to 126 words which may fairly be described as distinctively Platonic, and among these he selects 38 as characteristic of the later Dialogues. Using these figures, he argues that there is a clear lexical affinity between the later Dialogues and Epp. III, VII and VIII. To this conclusion he might have added, on the evidence of his own figures, that the 2nd Epistle shows a similar lexical affinity, though not so strongly marked.

It is not safe to infer more than this. In the case of documents so short as the Epistles, any attempt to tabulate statistics of vocabulary with a view to calculating averages and using the results to arrange the letters in order of time must break down completely. The evidence however goes to show that under the head of vocabulary there is nothing that can be urged against any of the letters, and a good deal in favour of four of the five longer and more important ones.

(2) ORDER OF WORDS

It may be urged that it is easy to imitate peculiarities of vocabulary, and that their presence does not go far as a proof of genuineness. This is true, though in practice the imitator or parodist rarely fails to betray himself in his attempts to reproduce an author's vocabulary. Peculiarities in the order of words are less easy to reproduce. The deviations from normal order in the Epistles may be considered under three heads: (a) Hyperbaton; (b) The avoidance of hiatus; (c) The clausula or conclusion of a sentence.

(a) Greek writers of prose were anxious to impart to their style a distinction similar to that of poetry. One device used for this object was that of hyperbaton or departures from the natural order of words, such as we get in poetry. These are found in other prose authors; but Plato, who was himself a poet, was specially fond of them. Instances from his Dialogues generally have been collected in Riddell's *Digest of Platonic Idioms*, pp. 236 ff. The habit grew on Plato with advancing years, and some of the more daring instances, which belong to the later Dialogues, will be found quoted in my *Epinomis*, pp. 51, 53. The following instances show that in this feature the style of the 3rd, 7th, and 8th letters corresponds to that of the later Dialogues:

Ep. III, 318 a 2: πρὸς δὲ τούτοις ᾤμην δεῖν τὰ κατ' ἐνιαυτὸν ἕκαστον εἰωθότα αὐτῷ κομίζεσθαι καὶ μᾶλλον ἐγὼ ἔτι καὶ οὐχ ἧττον ἐμοῦ παραγενομένου πέμπεσθαι (where ἐγὼ belongs to ᾤμην).

Ep. III, 318 e 6: σχεδὸν δ' εἰς λόγον ὁ λόγος ἥκει μοι συνεχὴς τῷ νύνδη γενόμενος, περὶ οὗ μοι τὸ δεύτερον ἀπολογητέον ἔφην εἶναι (where σχεδόν belongs to συνεχής and the antecedent to οὗ is λόγον).

Ep. VII, 325 c 5: τοσούτῳ χαλεπώτερον ἐφαίνετο ὀρθῶς εἶναί μοι τὰ πολιτικὰ διοικεῖν (where ὀρθῶς belongs to διοικεῖν).

Ep. VII, 351 a 4: διανοοῖτ' ἂν εὐεργετῶν ἐν δυνάμει καὶ τιμαῖσιν γενέσθαι τὰ μέγιστα ἐν ταῖς μεγίσταις (where τὰ μέγιστα belongs to εὐεργετῶν and ταῖς μεγίσταις to δυνάμει καὶ τιμαῖσιν).

Ep. VIII, 353 a 3: νῦν ὑμῖν καὶ τοῖς πολεμίοις σχεδόν, ἐξ οὗπερ γέγονεν ὁ πόλεμος, συγγένεια ἄρχει μία διὰ τέλους (where σχεδόν belongs to διὰ τέλους).

One of Plato's forms of hyperbaton is the misplacing of τε, like Horace's transposition of *que* in "Insanum te omnes pueri clamentque puellae", *Sat.* II, 3; cf. *Ep.* VII, 337 a 6 with *Laws*, 884 a 5. This also belongs to the style of poetry.

(*b*) The avoidance of hiatus between successive words, except in cases where it was regarded as legitimate, was brought into fashion at Athens under the influence of the School of Isokrates about 360 B.C., and it is possible to date prose works by it in the same way as the prose works of English authors of the last two or three decades can be distinguished from those of the Victorians, by their more careful avoidance of the split infinitive. Men had recently discovered that "oft the ear the open vowel tires", and a strong reaction against the hiatus set in. The fashion of avoiding it was at its height during Plato's later life, and was carried to an extreme in his works of that period. The following table, adapted from Raeder, shows the proportion between the instances of illegitimate hiatus and the number of pages in five of the earlier and five of the later Dialogues of Plato, and in the five longer Epistles arranged in their order of time. The other eight Epistles are omitted as too short for the application of such a test.

Title of work	Pages in Didot text	Instances of illegitimate hiatus per page
Lysis	14·9	45·9
Apology	19·7	38·7
Gorgias	61·6	35·7
Phaidon	49·2	40·9
Republic	193·7	35·2
Sophistes	39·6	0·6
Politikos	43·2	0·4
Timaios	53·0	1·1
Philebos	43·2	3·7
Laws	236·8	5·8
Ep. XIII	2·9	29·6
,, II	3·4	27·3
,, III	3·4	2·9
,, VII	20·0	9·2
,, VIII	3·9	8·7

These figures speak for themselves, and show that in their treatment of hiatus the Epistles, like the Dialogues, fall into two groups. In one of these, which contains earlier and informal letters, viz. XIII and II, there is little or no attempt to avoid illegitimate hiatus. In the other, which contains later or more formal letters, viz. III, VII, VIII, it is avoided in a way too systematic to be the result of accident. Which is the more likely hypothesis with regard to this difference—that it is the natural result of the different date and circumstances to which the letters, as genuine compositions by Plato, belong, or that it has been produced by the carefully maintained artifice of a forger?

Raeder laid himself open to attack by using hiatus statistics to prove the date of the shorter letters, and Ritter's position is sound when he lays it down that such statistics only have value for the five longer letters. He has no difficulty in showing that all sorts of strange consequences can be proved for the longer letters, if they are cut up into lengths equal to the shorter ones, and that the attempt to date the beginning of Plato's avoidance of the hiatus by the figures shown in the 5th Epistle is absurd.

But his arguments do not touch the fact that the hiatus statistics of the five longer letters are what we should expect to find if they were all written by Plato, but are difficult to account for if all, or any of them, were the work of a forger.

(c) The clausula, or grouping of syllables at the end of a sentence, is another point which received increasing attention from the teachers of rhetoric during the fourth century. Plato's earlier Dialogues show very little study of it, but his later writings show a growing preference for certain groupings. Aristotle lays it down (*Rhet.* III 8, 1409 a) that the most effective opening for a sentence is the 1st Paeon (– ᵕ ᵕ ᵕ), and the most effective conclusion the 4th Paeon (ᵕ ᵕ ᵕ –). See the note on Demetrios περὶ ἑρμ. § 39, by W. R. Roberts, who refers to the Paeonic character of Aristotle's work on the Athenian Constitution. Plato's growing preference for clausulae of certain types has been dealt with by L. Billig, "Clausulae and Platonic Chronology", *Journ. of Phil.* XXXV, No. 70, who tabulates results, and shows that the Dialogues fall into two groups, an earlier one in which no special attention is paid to the clausula, and a later one in which certain types of clausula are preferred. Billig has also tabulated results for the more important of the Epistles, which correspond closely to those of the Dialogues. His tables give figures for several types of clausulae, but to simplify matters I shall confine myself to the 4th Paeon. Billig's percentages for sentences ending with this foot in five of the later Dialogues and in the five longer Epistles are as follows: *Timaios* 12·0, *Politikos* 14·2, *Philebos* 17·1, *Laws* 19·0, *Epinomis* 25·6, Ep. II 13·0, Ep. III 10·0, Ep. VII 18·6, Ep. VIII 14·7, Ep. XIII 4·7. It will be seen that in the earlier and informal 13th letter the ends of the sentences are left to take care of themselves, while in the later ones there is a systematic attempt to end with an impressive arrangement of syllables, and the figures correspond with remarkable closeness to those of the later Dialogues. The late group in this case includes the 2nd Epistle; but there is nothing unnatural in the fact that Plato should have begun attending to his clausulae before he started systematically avoiding hiatus. Here again the

facts explain themselves if we believe all the five letters to have
been written by Plato, but are not easy to explain if one or more
of them were forged.

(3) STRUCTURE OF SENTENCES

The most noteworthy point here is the prevalence of intentional
irregularities. In the 7th Epistle long unwieldy sentences
abound; and the writer sometimes seems to lose his way.
Similar sentences are common in the *Laws*; and it is not likely
that Plato really lost his way. A typical instance is the passage
which begins with ὁρῶν δήπου, 324 d 7. Here we are looking
forward to a verb in the first person, but have to wait some time
for it: in the interval we have, inserted parenthetically, two
detached sentences with principal and subordinate clauses, each
independent of the main principal sentence and of one another:
ultimately ὁρῶν is repeated by καθορῶν, and we get the conclusion of our main principal sentence. "Huiusmodi anacoluthis
scatet epistola", says Karsten; and he diagnoses the cause
rightly, when he adds that the writer, "dum gratam affectat
negligentiam, mutilat periodos".

Again and again in the *Laws*, *Epinomis* and Epistles, we are
confronted with what may be called a studied informality. One
form in which this shows itself is that of changes of construction in the course of a sentence. These are sometimes so slight as
to be scarcely noticeable, sometimes so abrupt as to defy all
rules of grammar. For a striking instance see the long sentence
330 d 5–331 a 5, with the note it.

The commonest type of such irregularities is the nominativus
pendens. It was familiar to the Greeks in poetry, and Plato was
a poet before he wrote prose. The instance in 324 d, described
above, is a mild one, because the nominative does ultimately get
its verb. There are others where, as in 333 b 7 and 344 b 3, the
construction is entirely changed, and the verb never comes.

Sometimes a change of construction occurs in connection with
reported speech or thoughts in oratio obliqua; e.g. Ep. II,
313 b 3, οὐ μὴν ἄλλῳ γε ποτ' ἔφην ἐντυχηκέναι τοῦθ' ηὑρηκότι,
ἀλλὰ ἡ πολλή μοι πραγματεία περὶ τοῦτ' εἴη. Hackforth calls

this a harsh anacoluthon, and considers that it is "very possibly copied from Ep. VII, 328 a 2". But the two passages have nothing in common except the change of construction. Imitation seems to be out of the question: but if they were written by the same hand the resemblance is just what we should expect. In these two instances the change is from infinitive to optative. Sometimes, as at 326 d 3 and 328 c 7, it is from optative to infinitive. In both cases the writer's object is to suggest an informal, conversational, manner.

The extraordinary thing is that Karsten should not have been aware of this feature of Plato's later writings, and that others, who must have known better, did not point out that his criticisms should not be taken too seriously.

A more interesting question is, why Plato drifted more and more into this way of writing in his later years. An anacoluthic style has an attraction for elderly men of powerful mind: they expect others to make the same jumps of thought as themselves. It appears in the later works of Shakespeare and Milton. A good instance is *Par. Lost*, IX, 921 ff.:

> *Bold deed thou hast presumed, adventurous Eve,*
> *And peril great provoked, who thus hast dared,*
> *Had it been only coveting to eye*
> *That sacred food, sacred to abstinence,*
> *Much more to taste it, under ban to touch.**

Plato's preference for such sentences may have been enhanced by another reason. Is it not possible that the excessive regularity of Isokrates reacted on him, and made him cultivate a different style? To surpass Isokrates in his own style was hardly possible, nor was it a style which harmonised with the character and thought of Plato. But a study of the works of the two men shows that each was a good deal in the mind of the other; and just as one suspects that some of the violent irregularities of Browning may be due to a desire, conscious or unconscious, to produce something strikingly different from the smoothness of Tennyson, so it seems not impossible that Plato was attracted by the idea of producing work which would appeal to those who were getting

---

* Punctuated as in Newton's edition of 1790.

tired of the harmonies of Isokrates, and to whom a little mutilation of periods would be acceptable. Where there is no grammatical irregularity, there is often a studied neglect of the usual conventions of literary prose. A good instance will be found in the fourteen lines which begin at ταῦτα Δίων, 327 d 7. Karsten complains of the "languida iunctura" of this passage, in which we have ἐδεῖτο followed soon by another ἐδεῖτο, and λέγων repeated first by καταλέγων and then by another λέγων.

Among minor irregularities may be noted a loose use of the relative pronoun, reminding one of Mrs Gamp's "which", to which attention has been drawn in the notes on 317 e 4 and 323 c 2, and the tendency to tack on a phrase or clause as a sort of afterthought, as τὰ δὲ διέφθαρται in 344 a 1.

Where there is no grammatical irregularity there is sometimes an irregularity of thought, an attempt to take the reader by surprise and say something different from what he expects. This irritates some readers, who put it down to perversity on the author's part; but it attracts attention, and makes those think, who are capable of thought. Here again Karsten helps us by pointing out passages which have aroused his suspicions by features which are really indications of the hand of Plato; e.g. παρεκάλουν εὐθὺς ὡς ἐπὶ προσήκοντα πράγματά με, 324 d 2, where it would have been more obvious to say παρεκάλουν με ὡς προσήκοντα ἐπὶ τὰ πράγματα, and πονηρῶν καὶ πολλῶν instead of πολλῶν καὶ πονηρῶν, or again ἀρετὴν περὶ πλείονος ἡδονῆς ἠγαπηκώς, where instead of saying either ἀρετὴν πλέον ἡδονῆς ἠγαπηκώς, or ἀρετὴν περὶ πλείονος ἡδονῆς ποιούμενος, the writer gives a sort of combination of the two. Karsten notes a similar tendency in the matter of the narrative: in 327 e we are led to expect that we shall get Dion's letter in full, but we only get one sentence of it. Just the same thing occurs with the letter of Dionysios in 339 b.

(4) MANNERISMS
These have been fully treated by Hackforth, and a few instances here will suffice:

(a) Pleonasms and tautologous phrases, e.g. 324 b 1, ἦν

ἔσχον δόξαν...Συρακοσίους οἴεσθαι δεῖν ἐλευθέρους εἶναι; cf. 353 d 2, 315 b 1, 2, 324 b 3, 327 a 4, 338 c 7.

A striking case is the superfluous δεῖ, e.g. 328 b 8, δεῖν πειρατέον εἶναι; 352 a 3, ἀναγκαῖον εἶναι ἔδοξέ μοι ῥηθῆναι δεῖν; cf. 352 d 1, 2. This is a typical colloquialism, or, as England calls it, a conversational superfluity. For the numerous instances of similar redundancy in the *Laws* see Hackforth's Appendix.

(*b*) Circumlocutions, e.g. the use of periphrastic tenses, as in 326 a 4, τὰ γὰρ τῶν νόμων σχεδὸν ἀνιάτως ἔχοντά ἐστιν. These are sometimes formed with the verb συμβαίνω in the sense "turns out to be"; e.g. 327 c, ἀμήχανον ἂν μακαριότητι συμβῆναι γενόμενον; cf. 328 a 7, 339 c 3, 347 e 6, 349 a 5.

Another form of circumlocution is seen in the peculiar uses of the preposition περί; e.g. 327 b 6, τοῦ θανάτου τοῦ περὶ Διονύσιον γενόμενον (= the death of Dionysios); 316 c 5, πολλῆς ἀπειρίας οὔσης περί σε (there being on your part much inexperience); 350 e 1, Σωκράτης ἐστιν περὶ ἀσθένειαν (Sokrates is suffering from ill-health).

(*c*) A tendency to modify or soften down statements. A typical instance is the constantly recurring σχεδόν. As in the later Dialogues the phrase σχεδόν τι has given way almost completely to the simple σχεδόν, which occurs twenty-two times (as against two instances of σχεδόν τι). The average per page is the same as that given by the 122 instances in the *Laws*. The following are typical instances, and show that we are dealing with a pure colloquialism: 314 a 2, σχεδὸν οὐκ ἔστιν τούτων καταγελαστότερα ἀκούσματα; 324 a 4, σχεδὸν οὐκ εἰκάζων ἀλλ᾽ ὡς εἰδὼς σαφῶς εἴποιμ᾽ ἄν; 324 e 1, ὃν ἐγὼ σχεδὸν οὐκ ἂν αἰσχυνοίμην εἰπὼν δικαιότατον εἶναι τῶν τότε.

The unwieldy and anacoluthic sentences, described above, appear mainly in the 7th Epistle, but the other irregularities and mannerisms which have been illustrated here are distributed about the 2nd, 3rd, 6th and 8th letters, as well as the 7th, and go to show that all these are the work of the same hand.

LETTER I

Plato (?) *to* Dionysios. Welfare[1]*

After spending so long a time at your court and being trusted   309 a
more than all others in the administration of the government, I
was bearing patiently all the onus of ill-repute, while you and
your friends received all the benefits. For I knew that none of
your severer measures would be thought to have been done with
my approval, since all who took part with me in your government   b
are there as witnesses in my favour, and I made great efforts on
behalf of many of them, saving them from severe punishment.
But after keeping your city safe on several occasions, when I administered the government with full powers,[2] I received a dis-
missal too insulting even for a beggar, whom you were ordering
to sail away and begone after spending so long a time among you.
For my part, I shall for the future regulate my conduct in a way
which takes me farther from the society of men;[3] and thou, "great
monarch as thou art, shalt live alone".

The fine present of gold, which came from your hand for my   c
travelling expenses, is returned to you herewith by the hand of
Baccheios, the bearer of this letter. Such a sum was not sufficient
for the cost of my journey, nor was it worthy of my manner of life
in general: it reflects the greatest discredit on you as giver and
not much less on me as receiver: therefore I decline it. It is clear
that to give or receive such a sum makes no difference to you—
so[4] take it and show to some other of your associates the same
favour which you have shown to me. For my part, I have had
enough of your favours; and I may suitably quote the verse   d
of Euripides, that some day, when a change of fortune befalls
you—

Thou'lt pray that such a man were standing by thee.

I should like to remind you that[5] most of the other tragic

* The numbers refer to Notes.

poets, when they bring in a monarch receiving his death-blow from a regicide, make him cry out:

310a   *Unhappy me!*
                    Deserted by my friends I'm brought to ruin.[6]

But none has represented him as brought to ruin by want of gold.

The following piece of poetry also "to men of sense seems not to be amiss":[7]

'Tis not fine gold that is the most precious thing in the desperate life
    of mortals;
Nor do adamant and couches wrought with silver, flashing on the
    eyes, bring assurance in comparison with a man;
Nor do fields of broad earth teeming with fertility give support,
So sure as the united thought and counsel of men of worth.

b   Farewell; and, that you may be happier in your treatment of others, learn that you have made a great mistake in your treatment of me.[8]

LETTER II

Plato *to* Dionysios. Welfare

I hear from Archedemos that you think it right that not only I, but my associates, should refrain from doing or saying anything

c   disparaging to you; Dion alone you regard as an exception. Your making Dion an exception signifies that I have no influence over my associates.—Well, if I had had influence over anyone, especially Dion and yourself, more good, so I say, would have resulted to all of us and to the rest of the Greeks. But as it is, my power[1] consists only in showing myself obedient to my own teaching.

I say this because there is no truth in the statements which have been made to you by Kratistolos and Polyxenos,[2] one of

d   whom is said to have stated that at the Olympic Games he heard many of my associates speaking evil of you. Perhaps he has quicker ears than I have. I certainly heard nothing of the sort.

In future when anyone makes statements of this kind about any of us, the proper course for you, in my opinion, is this, to write and make enquiries from me. I shall be neither afraid nor ashamed to tell you the truth.

The3 present state of relations between you and me is as follows: There is perhaps not a single Greek to whom we are not 310 e well-known persons; there is no secret about our intercourse, and you may be sure that there will be no secret about it in the time to come. This follows from the character of those who have known about it, and from the fact that it has gone to considerable lengths and has not been a thing done in a corner. What then have I to say at the present moment? I will tell you, beginning at the beginning.

Wisdom and great power are naturally fitted for union with one another.4 These two are always pursuing, seeking for, and coming into touch with, one another. And, moreover, men delight in talking about the instances of this and hearing them from others, both in conversation and poetry.5 For instance 311 a when men speak of Hiero6 and Pausanias the Lacedaemonian, they delight in bringing up their intercourse with Simonides, with details of his conduct and sayings. So also they celebrate Periandros of Corinth with Thales of Miletos, Pericles with Anaxagoras, and Cyrus as ruler with Croesus and Solon as wise men.

The poets again, imitating these instances, couple Kreon with Teiresias, Minos with Polyidos,7 Agamemnon with Nestor, b Odysseus and Palamedes; and, as it seems to me, the earliest of mankind linked together in the same way Prometheus8 with Zeus. And in some cases they represent these associates as at enmity with one another, in others as friends, in others as sometimes at enmity and sometimes friends, or agreeing on some subjects and disagreeing on others. All this I say to make c it clear that, when we are dead, the history of our doings will not be buried in oblivion. We must, therefore, make that history our concern. For, I think, we cannot help being concerned with futurity, because there appears to be a natural law by which the most slavish and abject of mankind pay no attention to it, while the best men use every effort to be well spoken of in the future. I regard this very fact as an indication that the dead have some perception of what is going on here. For the best spirits have a presentiment that this is the case, while the worst deny it; and the presentiments of godlike men are more worthy of trust than those of the ungodly.9

311 d

I think too that those men of the past whom I have mentioned, if they had the chance of amending the details of their own intercourse, would strive hard to make their history more honourable than it now is. You and I now, by the grace of God,10 have the chance to amend in word and deed anything that has been amiss in our previous intercourse. For11 as regards the true philosophy I maintain that if we attain to excellence, men will think and speak of it better, but if our standard is a low one, the result will be just the opposite. And indeed, if we devote ourselves to this pursuit, our occupation will be of all others the most godly, and most ungodly if we neglect it.

e

Let me tell you how this ought to be done and what justice demands. I came to Sicily with the reputation of being highly distinguished among those engaged in philosophy, and my desire in visiting Syracuse was to make you a fellow-witness in order that I might get philosophy honoured by the people as a whole. The attempt did not lead to a favourable result.12 I do not attribute this failure to the cause which many would assign to it, but to your apparent want of confidence in me. You wanted, as it seemed, to send me away and send for others, and to raise the question what my system was, distrusting me, as I think. This gave rise to loud comments on the part of many to the effect that you thought little of me and had given yourself over heart and soul to other views. This has been a matter of general talk.

312 a

b

Now, as to what it is right for you to do next, listen, and you will have an answer also to your own question what the relations between you and me ought to be. If you despise philosophy altogether, have nothing more to do with it. If you have received from others or found out for yourself better teaching than that given by me, honour that teaching. If, however, my teaching

really satisfies you, you should honour me above others.[13]
The position now is the same as it was at the start; you must give
the lead, and I will follow. Honour me, and I will honour you.   312c
If you do not honour me, there will be no move on my part.
Moreover in honouring me, and taking the lead in this, you will
be thought to be honouring philosophy; and the very fact that
you made trial of others as well as of me will bring you credit
with many as a man of philosophic mind. Honour from me,
unless preceded by honour from you, will be put down to the
worship and pursuit of wealth, and we know that this gives a
man an ill-name with everyone. To put the matter in one word:
marks of honour will bring credit to both of us, if given by you,   d
disgrace to both, if given by me. Enough of this.

Your sphere[14] is not right. Archedemos will explain this to
you when he comes. Also on this other question, which is
deeper and more sacred than that, he must explain to you very
fully the difficulty with regard to which you have sent enquiries.
For, as he states, you say that you have not received full enough
teaching on the nature of "that which is first".[15] Here I must
speak in riddles, in order that, if to my tablets "in folds of sea or
land[16] mischance befall" he that readeth may not understand.
The truth is this: All things stand in relation to the King[17] of all,   e
all things are for His sake, and He is the cause of all that is
beautiful. The things that are second are related to a second, and
the things that are third to a third.

With regard to these existences, the human soul craves to
learn what qualities[18] they have, looking for things akin to
itself, none of which has real sufficiency. Now with regard to the   313a
King and the existences which I mentioned, there is nothing of
that nature (i.e. nothing anthropomorphic). So after this the
soul says: "But what sort of thing is it?" It is this question, O
son of Dionysios and Doris, or rather the travail of the soul
engendered by it, which is the cause of all the mischief, and
unless a man can free himself from this, he will never attain to
the truth.

In your talk with me in the garden under the laurels,[19] you
said that you had grasped this truth for yourself, and that this

313 b   was your own discovery. I said that if this was your view of
the matter, you would thereby have relieved me of much
discourse. However, I said that I had never met with anyone
before who had made this discovery, and that the greater part
of my labours were devoted to elucidating this point.²⁰ You
perhaps had heard this point dealt with by someone, or possibly
had jumped at it by some happy providence, and afterwards in
the idea that you had a firm grasp of it, you did not make the
proofs of it secure;²¹ but your conception of it is a fluctuating

c   one, moving now this way, now another way, in the region of the
apparent, whereas the fundamental truth is really nothing of that
kind. You are not the only person to whom this has happened.
I can assure you that no one heard of it from me for the first
time without going through just the same experience. Some
have more trouble, some less, in accomplishing their final
release; but hardly anyone does so without considerable difficulty.

In view of these past and present experiences, I think I may
say that we have found out the answer to your question what the
relations between us should be. For, since you are putting my
teaching to the test in your intercourse with others, comparing it
with the teaching of others and studying it, as it is in itself, these

d   truths, if the test is a decisive one, will now become a part of
your nature, and you will become at home with them and with
us. How can this, and all that I have said, be realised? You
acted quite rightly in sending Archedemos on the present
occasion. When he has returned to you and informed you of my
answers, further difficulties will perhaps assail you in the
future. You will then, if you are wise, send Archedemos to me
once more, and he, like a trader²² travelling between us, will
return to you again. If you do this two or three times, and give a

e   fair trial to the instructions which I send to you, I shall be much
surprised if your present difficulties do not assume an aspect
quite different to that which they now have. Be of good heart
and do this, both of you. For you will never send, and Archedemos will never bring back merchandise that is fairer and dearer
to heaven than this.

But be on your guard lest these communications fall into the 314ª
hands of uninstructed persons. For I suppose there is nothing
which, when heard by the world in general, sounds more
ridiculous than these doctrines,[23] while to those who are properly
gifted by nature, there is nothing which seems more wonderful
and more full of divine inspiration. And if they are often
repeated and continually listened to for many years, by dint of
much endeavour they are at length purified as gold in the
furnace. Let me tell you what is a remarkable thing in this
teaching.[24] There are men, and a considerable number of them,
who have listened to it—men with good capacity for learning   b
and remembering and for applying every test of criticism to it—
who, quite late in life, after fully thirty years devoted to study,
say that only now what had formerly appeared to them most
incredible became most convincing and clear, while that which
formerly seemed convincing, now seemed just the reverse.
Bear this in mind and have a care lest at some time in the future
you may have to regret things now put forth in an inadequate
form.

The best safeguard is to avoid writing and to commit things to
memory. For when a thing has once been committed to writing,
it is impossible to prevent it from gaining publicity. It is for   c
this reason that I myself have never written anything on these
subjects.[25] There is not, and there never will be a written treatise
of Plato's. Those that are called his are really the teaching of
Socrates restored to youth and beauty.

Farewell; be guided by my advice, and begin now by burning
this letter when you have read it through several times.[26] Enough
of this.[27]

With regard to Polyxenos,[28] you express surprise that I sent   d
him to you. But about him, as well as about Lykophron and the
others who are with you, I say just what I have always said—
that in dialectic you are far superior to them, both in natural
gifts and in logical method. There is not one of them who is
willing to be proved wrong, as some consider themselves to be;
but they are all convinced against their will. And, indeed, I
think that you have been extremely kind in your treatment of

them, and your presents to them. So much for them—too much, considering what they are. If you are making use of
314e   Philistion, continue to do so by all means.[29] But if it is possible, lend him to Speusippos, and send him here. Speusippos also makes this request of you, and Philistion also promised me that, if you would let him go, he would gladly come to Athens. You did well in granting the release of the man who was in the stone quarries.[30] It is easy for you to grant also his request with regard to his servants and with regard to Hegesippos, the son of
315a   Ariston. For you sent word to me that if anyone wronged either him or those others, and you perceived it, you would not pass it over.

It is worth while also to let you know the truth about Lysikleides. Of all those who have come from Sicily to Athens, he is the only one who has never changed his attitude in speaking of the intercourse between you and me. He has always something good to say, and always puts the best interpretation on the facts.

LETTER III

"Plato wishes joy to Dionysios"[1]—Suppose I started with this
b   greeting, should I be making a right choice of the best form of address? Or is it better to follow my usual practice and write "welfare", as I habitually do in my letters to friends? I do not forget that you addressed even the God of Delphi[2] with the same flattering formula, so it was reported by those who were consulting the oracle at the time—bidding him, so they say— "Rejoice and preserve for the monarch his life of pleasure unceasing".

c   But for my part I could never in my greeting to a man bid him to rejoice, much less a God. Not a God—because I should be bidding him do something contrary to his nature; for the divine nature is something far removed from pleasure and pain. And not a man—because pleasure and pain usually do him hurt, engendering in his soul incapacity for learning, forgetfulness,

folly and pride. Let this suffice with regard to my formula of
greeting. Read it, and take it in whatever spirit you like to take it.

It[3] is a matter of general report that you told some of those who
came as envoys to you that, on one occasion, when I heard you   315 d
announce your intention of re-establishing the Greek cities of
Sicily and of relieving the Syracusans by converting your
despotism into a limited monarchy, I prevented you, as you say,
from doing these things, though you were most anxious to do
them, while now I am instructing[4] Dion to do the very same
things, and we two by means of your own ideas are trying to
take your sovereignty from you. You know best whether you are   e
likely to be benefited by these assertions. But you are certainly
wronging me by saying what is just the opposite of the facts.
Enough bad feeling against me was inspired by Philistides[5] and
many others in the minds of the mercenaries and populace of
Syracuse, because I remained in the akropolis, and those outside, if any error was committed, threw all the blame on me,
saying that you obeyed me in everything. Now you yourself
know very well that, even at the beginning of my visit, when I   316 a
thought that I might accomplish something, I took very little
active part voluntarily in your political measures. I interested
myself in a quiet way in some minor matters and especially in the
preambles[6] of your laws—I do not include the additions made by
yourself and others. For I am told that my preambles were subsequently patched by some of you. The authorship of the
different parts will be readily recognised by competent judges of
my character. To resume: as I said before, I do not want any
more ill-feeling to be inspired among the Syracusans and any
others whom you try to influence by these statements. What I
want much rather is to make my defence against the ill-feeling of   b
those earlier days, and against that of to-day, which has followed
it, and which is growing in dimensions and violence. I must,
therefore, make two separate defences against two separate
points. First I must prove that I was right in shrinking from
any partnership with you in State affairs, and secondly, with
regard to your statement that I stood in the way of your intentions to re-establish the Greek States, I must prove that the

advice and prevention which you allege did not come from me.
316c Listen now first to the origin of the first charges which I
mentioned.

I came to Syracuse on the invitation of you and of Dion. Dion
was a man whose worth I had proved, and with whom I had had
friendly relations of long standing; he was also a man who had
reached the mature years of middle age, qualifications which any
man not altogether devoid of intelligence must certainly possess,[7]
if he is to form an opinion on matters of such importance as
those which were in your hands. You, on the other hand, were
extremely young and suffered greatly from want of experience[8]
d on those matters which most called for experience. You were
also quite unknown to me. After this, and brought about by
some man, god, or unlucky accident co-operating with you,
came the removal of Dion. You were then left to stand alone.

Do you really think that there was any partnership in State
affairs at that time between you and myself, after I had lost my
wise partner and saw my foolish partner left in the hands of a
large train of unscrupulous associates, not ruling, though you
fancied you were ruling, but being ruled by men of that stamp?
In such a position what course was I to take? Was I not forced to
take the course which I took, to give a wide berth for the future
e to State affairs, trying to avoid the misrepresentations which
arise from jealousies, and at the same time to leave no stone unturned to bring about a full reconciliation between you two,
estranged as you were and at enmity with one another? On this
point even you will be my witness, that I never ceased striving
for that one object. Finally after much difficulty an agreement
317a was arrived at between us that, since you and your people were
occupied with a war,[9] I should sail for home; and that on the
conclusion of peace, Dion and I should come back to Syracuse
and that you should invite us. This is the history of my first
visit to Sicily and of my safe return home.

On[10] the conclusion of peace, you invited me a second time,
not however in accordance with your agreement, but you wrote
to me to come alone, and said that you would send for Dion
subsequently. For this reason I did not come, and for the

moment had Dion against me as well as you. For he thought it
better that I should go and comply with your orders. A year   317 b
after this a trireme arrived with letters from you and among the
contents of the letters the first thing was that, if I would come,
Dion's affairs would all be settled in accordance with my wishes,
but, if I did not come, just the opposite would happen. I am
really ashamed to say how many letters then came from you, and
from others in Italy and Sicily on your behalf, and to how many   c
of my friends and acquaintances—letters all urging me to go and
begging me at all costs to comply with your wishes. Well, all my
friends with one voice, led by Dion, gave their verdict that it was
my duty to sail, and not to be faint-hearted. I pleaded my age,
and, with regard to you, laid stress on the fact that you would not
be able to hold your own against those who misrepresented[11] us
and were anxious for a rupture between us. For I saw then, as
I see now, that great accumulations of wealth in the hands of
individuals as well as of sovereigns usually tend to produce, in   d
proportion to their growth, more numerous and more powerful
retinues of mischief-makers and flatterers bringing ruin and
disgrace in their train. There is nothing worse than this in all
the brood of evils begotten by wealth and other forms of
personal power.

However, I put on one side all other considerations, and
returned, feeling that it was not right that any of my friends
should be able to say that want of enterprise on my part had
brought upon them wholesale ruin which might have been   e
averted. After my return—well, you know the whole story of
what subsequently happened—I naturally requested, in accordance with the agreement contained in your letters, first that
you should bring back Dion, attaching him to you by a bond of
union[12] which I specified; and if you had taken my advice with
regard to this, the result, so far as I can form a conjecture, would
most likely have been better than it has been for you and for
Syracuse, and for the rest of the Greek States. In the next place
I requested that Dion's personal property should be put in the   318 a
hands of his own family and not administered by those adminis-
trators whom you know of. In addition to this, I thought that

the revenues of his own property, which it was the practice to remit to him every year, ought to be sent, not less, but all the more after my arrival.

Having[13] failed to obtain any of these requests, I asked leave to depart. You then tried to persuade me to stay till the end of the year, saying that you would sell the whole of Dion's property, and send half the proceeds to Corinth, and leave the remainder on the spot for his son. I could mention many promises which you made and did not carry out; but they are so numerous that I pass them over. Well, you sold all Dion's property without obtaining his consent, though you said you would not sell without his consent, and then, my good friend, you put the finishing stroke in the most brilliant way to all your promises. For you hit on an expedient which was neither honourable nor pretty, nor just, nor fitting—that of frightening me, as though I were in the dark about what was being done at the moment, in order that I too might not attempt to get the money remitted. For when you banished Herakleides (unjustly, as the Syracusans held, and as I held), because I joined with Theodotes and Eurybios in begging you not to banish him, you laid hold of this as a sufficient pretext, and said that it had long been evident that I cared nothing for you, but only for Dion and Dion's friends and connections, and that since Theodotes and Herakleides, connections of Dion, were under a cloud, I was leaving no stone unturned to save them from punishment.

So much for the supposed partnership[14] between you and me in State affairs; and, if you saw any other instance of opposition to you on my part, you are right in supposing that all such cases were due to the same cause. And you need not be surprised at it; for bad indeed, and justly bad, would be the opinion formed of me by anyone of intelligence, if, when my old friend and ally, a man not worse than you—to put it mildly—had been brought by you to an unfortunate plight, I had been seduced by the greatness of your position as sovereign ruler, to forsake him and prefer you, his oppressor, and do whatever you dictated—with the motive, obviously, of filling my own pocket: for no one could have supposed that there could be any other motive for my

318 b

c

d

e

change of attitude, if I had changed. So much for these facts,
which by your action led to the wolf-and-sheep friendship[15] and
absence of real partnership between us.

And[16] now my narrative, in almost direct continuation of what
I was just saying, has brought me to that point on which I said
that I had to make my second defence. Please give me your best 319a
attention and see if I deviate at all from the truth. For I say that
it was in the garden in the presence of Archedemos and Aristokritos about twenty days before my departure homeward from
Syracuse that you made the statement[17] which you have been
making recently laying to my charge that I cared more for
Herakleides and all the rest than for you. And you asked me in
their presence, if I remembered, on my first arrival, bidding you
to re-establish the Greek cities. I acknowledged that I re- b
membered it, and that it still seemed to me to be the best thing
to do. I must now, Dionysios, relate what was said next after
this. I then asked you whether this was the only advice that I
had given you, or whether there was anything else besides.
You answered me very wrathfully and in taunting style, as you
fancied—with the result that what you then said in insult[18] has
now proved to be waking fact; you said, with a very forced
smile, if my memory serves me right, "You used to bid me to do c
all these things, after I had received instruction, or not to do
them at all". I said that you had remembered excellently.
"Well", you continued, "did you mean instruction in geometry
or what?" To this I did not make the retort which naturally
occurred to me, fearing lest, for one small word, when it came to
my expected departure, I might find my path barred and no
sea-room for me.[19]

To resume, let me say what is the real reason of all this narrative. Do not misrepresent me by saying that I prevented you
from re-establishing the Greek cities which had been destroyed
by the barbarians, and from relieving the Syracusans by d
establishing a limited monarchy in place of a tyranny. For there
is no falsehood which you could utter which is less in keeping
with my character than these; and, in addition to what I have
said, I could, if there were a competent tribunal, submit for

examination still more convincing proofs that I urged you to take these steps and that you were unwilling; and surely it is not difficult to say in plain words that these were the best steps, if

319e they were taken, for you and for the Syracusans and for all the Greeks of Sicily. But my good friend, if you, who said these things, now deny that you said them, I have got my deserts.[20] But if you plead guilty to having said them, the next step for you is to reflect that Stesichoros[21] was a wise man, and, imitating his recantation, to retract your falsehoods and tell the truth.

LETTER IV

Plato *to* Dion the Syracusan. Welfare.

320a I suppose that throughout this eventful time my hearty sympathy with the results accomplished has been manifest, and my great anxiety to further their accomplishment, and this for no reason more than love of honour directed to noble objects.

b For I think it just, that those who are truly men of worth and who act up to their character should obtain the recognition which they deserve.[1]

What you have done up to the present time, by the grace of God,[2] is excellent; but the greatest struggle is still to come. To excel in courage, speed and strength, is a matter within the power of other men; but when it comes to truthfulness, justice,

c greatness of character and the grace of bearing which is appropriate to these qualities, anyone will agree that those who claim to make these things their ideals must be expected to rise above the level of other men in them. Now what I am driving at is obvious enough; but for all that, we ought to keep on reminding ourselves that more even than men surpass children[3] ought other men to be surpassed by the—you know of course who I mean. We must therefore show clearly that we really are the sort of men we profess to be, especially as, by the grace of God, it will be easy to do so.

For other men are under a necessity to travel far afield, if they   320 d
intend to be known. But your present position is such that,
though it may seem rather tall talk to say so, the eyes of all the
world are fixed on one place, and, in that place, chiefly upon
you. As therefore the observed of all observers, try to put
into the shade⁴ the famous Lycurgus, and Cyrus, and any other
of those eminent for character and statesmanship; and all the
more, because it is the talk of many people and of almost all   e
Athens that there is a great prospect that, after the fall⁵ of
Dionysios, the cause will be brought to ruin by the ambition of
yourself, Herakleides, Theodotes and the other notables. Let us
hope that no one will show such symptoms; but, if anyone does
so, do you play the part of physician, and then you may all move
forward to the right goal.

Perhaps it seems absurd to you that I should say these things,   321 a
when you yourself are no stranger to them. But in the theatre⁶
I see that the performers are cheered on by children—to say
nothing of friends, whom, as well-wishers, a man expects to be
active in encouraging him. Therefore put forth all of you your
best powers, and if you are in need of anything, write to me
about it.

The position here is much the same as it was when you were
with us. Also write us word what you have done and are doing,   b
since, though we hear much, we know nothing. At the present
time letters from Theodotes and Herakleides have come to
Lacedaemon and Aegina, while we, as I have said, though we
hear much about local affairs,⁷ know nothing. Remember too
that you are thought by some people a little wanting in gracious-
ness. Do not lose sight of the fact that it is by complacency
towards men that effective action becomes possible, and that a   c
haughty temper⁸ has isolation as its fellow-lodger. Farewell.

LETTER V

Plato *to* Perdikkas. Welfare.

321 c   In accordance with the instructions in your letter, I have advised Euphraios to study your affairs and devote his time to them. Advice is due from friend to friend, and is, as the proverb tells us, a sacred duty:[1] I am therefore bound to offer it on the points which you mention and on the use which you should now
d   make of Euphraios. For he is a man who can be useful to you in many things, and the most important of these is something of which you stand in need at present, partly because of your youth, and partly because there are not many who can advise the young about it.

Forms of government, just like animals, have each their own peculiar voice;[2] democracy has one, oligarchy another, monarchy
e   another. Many men would say that they know these voices, but, with the exception of a few rare characters, they are very far from discerning them aright. Now that form of government, whatsoever it be, which speaks with its own voice to gods and men, and makes its acts harmonise truly with its voice, thrives and enjoys security; but that which imitates the voice of another is brought to ruin. It is in this matter that Euphraios is most likely to be useful to you, though in other matters also he is a
322 a   man of courage. For I think that, of those who are in your society, he is the most likely to discover the proper speech of monarchy. If therefore you use him for this end, you will secure your own advantage, and will confer the greatest benefit on him.

If any, hearing this, remarks, "Plato, as it seems, professes to know the interests of democracy; but, though it is open to him to speak to the people and offer them the best advice, he has never once got up and opened his lips", please reply[3] as follows:
b   "Plato was born late in his country's history, and found the democracy grown old and accustomed by his predecessors to many forms of action quite different from what he would advise.

For nothing would have pleased him more than to have offered advice to the people as to a father, if he had not believed that he would have been running useless risks where there was no prospect of doing good. I think that he would have dealt with the advising of me in the same way. If my condition seemed to be incurable, he would leave me to my own devices, and not attempt to offer any advice with regard to me or my affairs". 322 c Good luck to you.

LETTER VI

Plato *to* Hermeias, Erastos *and* Koriskos. Welfare.

It seems to me that one of the Gods, of his good will, is preparing for you good fortune in abundance, if you receive it aright. For you are living as near neighbours among yourselves, and you have wants of such a kind that you can render the greatest services one to the other. To Hermeias on the one hand, neither horses[1] in numbers, nor allied forces of other kinds, nor additional supplies of money, would be a greater source of strength for all purposes than the possession of trustworthy friends of sound character. To Erastos and Koriskos, on the other hand, I say, old man though I am,[2] that in addition to that noble wisdom which comes from the study of ideal forms, they require a wisdom which is on its guard against evil and unjust men and a protecting power of some sort. For they want experience, having spent a great part of their lives with us who are quiet and inoffensive people. For this reason I say that they need this additional help in order that they may not be compelled to neglect that true wisdom and to devote too much of their attention to this human wisdom required by the force of circumstances. This latter power Hermeias seems to have gained, both by his natural gifts, so far as I can judge without personal knowledge of him, and by the skill which comes from experience.

What then is my message? To you, Hermeias, having had more personal knowledge than you of Erastos and Koriskos, I

d

e

323 a

say, declare and testify, that you will not easily find characters more worthy of confidence than those of these neighbours of yours. I urge you to attach yourself by every just means to these men, and to treat this as a matter of the first importance. Koriskos and Erastos on their part I urge to attach themselves to

323 b Hermeias, and to try by these mutual attachments to form one knot of friendship. And if any of you seem to be loosening this knot—for human ties are not always permanent—write to me and my friends here a letter stating the cause of complaint. For I think that the words which come from us here will, by the power of justice and reverence, if the rupture be not a great one, prove more effective than any spell in reuniting3 and binding you together again into your previous state of friendship and

c partnership, with regard to which4 if all, both we and you, act as philosophers, so far as we are able and our several fortunes permit, what I now foretell will be found true. Of the other case—if we do not act so—I will say nothing.5 For I confine my prophecy to words of good omen, and I say that, God willing, we shall do everything that is good in this matter.

This letter you must all three read, if possible, all together, if not, in parties of two, as often as you can meet together for the purpose; and you must make an agreement and enactment

d binding upon you, as it is right, taking an oath,6 half in play and half in earnest, with an earnestness free from pedantry, and a playfulness that is sister to earnestness, and swearing by the God who rules all things present and to come, and by the Father and Lord of that ruler and cause, whom, if we are true philosophers, we shall all know clearly, so far as this is within the power of men favoured by heaven.

LETTER VII

Plato *to* the relatives and friends of Dion. Welfare.

You write to me that I must consider your views the same as those of Dion, and you urge me to aid your cause so far as I can in word and deed. My answer is that, if you have the same opinion and desire as he had, I consent to aid your cause; but if not, I shall think more than once about it. Now what his purpose and desire was, I can inform you from no mere conjecture but from positive knowledge. For when I made my first visit to Sicily, being then about forty years old, Dion was of the same age as Hipparinos[1] is now, and the opinion which he then formed was that which he always retained, I mean the belief that the Syracusans ought to be free and governed by the best laws. So it is no matter for surprise if some God[2] should make Hipparinos adopt the same opinion as Dion about forms of government. But it is well worth while that you should all, old as well as young, hear the way in which this opinion was formed, and I will attempt to give you an account of it from the beginning. For the present is a suitable opportunity.

In[3] my youth I went through the same experience as many other men. I fancied that if, early in life, I became my own master, I should at once embark on a political career. And I found myself confronted with the following occurrences in the public affairs of my own city. The existing constitution being generally condemned, a revolution took place, and fifty-one[4] men came to the front as rulers of the revolutionary government, namely eleven in the city and ten in the Peiraeus—each of these bodies being in charge of the market and municipal matters—while thirty were appointed rulers with full powers over public affairs as a whole. Some of these were relatives[5] and acquaintances of mine, and they at once invited me to share in their doings, as something to which I had a claim. The effect on me was not surprising in the case of a young man. I considered that they would, of course, so manage the State as to bring men out

324 a

b

c

d

of a bad way of life into a good one.[6] So I watched them very
closely to see what they would do.

And seeing, as I did, that in quite a short time they made the
former government seem by comparison something precious as
gold[7]—for among other things they tried to send a friend

324 e   of mine, the aged Sokrates, whom I should scarcely scruple
to describe as the most upright man of that day,[8] with some

325 a   other persons to carry off one of the citizens by force to
execution, in order that, whether he wished it, or not, he might
share the guilt of their conduct; but he would not obey them,
risking all consequences in preference to becoming a partner in
their iniquitous deeds—seeing all these things and others of the
same kind on a considerable scale, I disapproved of their
proceedings, and withdrew from any connection with the abuses
of the time.

Not[9] long after that a revolution terminated the power of the
thirty and the form of government as it then was. And once
more, though with more hesitation, I began to be moved by the

b   desire to take part in public and political affairs. Well, even in the
new government, unsettled as it was, events occurred which one
would naturally view with disapproval; and it was not surprising
that in a period of revolution excessive penalties were inflicted by
some persons on political opponents, though those who had
returned from exile at that time showed very considerable
forbearance. But once more it happened that some of those in
power[10] brought my friend Sokrates, whom I have mentioned,

c   to trial before a court of law, laying a most iniquitous charge
against him and one most inappropriate in his case: for it was on a
charge of impiety that some of them prosecuted and others
condemned and executed the very man who would not partici-
pate in the iniquitous arrest of one of the friends of the party
then in exile,[11] at the time when they themselves were in exile
and misfortune.

As I observed these incidents and the men engaged in public
affairs, the laws too and the customs, the more closely I examined
them and the farther I advanced in life, the more difficult it

d   seemed to me to handle public affairs aright.[12] For it was not

possible to be active in politics without friends and trustworthy
supporters; and to find these ready to my hand was not an easy
matter, since public affairs at Athens were not carried on in
accordance with the manners and practices of our fathers; nor
was there any ready method by which I could make new friends.
The laws too, written and unwritten, were being altered for the
worse, and the evil was growing with startling rapidity.[13] The
result was that, though at first I had been full of a strong im-
pulse towards political life, as I looked at the course of affairs and   325 e
saw them being swept in all directions by contending currents,
my head finally began to swim; and, though I did not stop
looking to see if there was any likelihood of improvement in
these symptoms and in the general course of public life, I   326 a
postponed action till a suitable opportunity should arise. Finally
it became clear to me with regard to all existing communities,
that they were one and all misgoverned. For their laws have
got into a state that is almost incurable, except by some extraordinary reform with good luck to support it. And I was
forced[14] to say, when praising true philosophy, that it is by this
that men are enabled to see what justice in public and private
life really is. Therefore, I said, there will be no cessation of evils
for the sons of men, till either those who are pursuing a right and   b
true philosophy receive sovereign power in the States, or those
in power in the States by some dispensation of providence
become true philosophers.

With these thoughts in my mind I came to Italy and Sicily on
my first visit. My first impressions on arrival[15] were those of
strong disapproval—disapproval of the kind of life which was
there called the life of happiness, stuffed full as it was with the
banquets of the Italian Greeks and Syracusans, who ate to
repletion twice every day, and were never without a partner for
the night; and disapproval of the habits which this manner of   c
life produces. For with these habits formed early in life, no
man under heaven could possibly attain to wisdom—human
nature is not capable of such an extraordinary combination.
Temperance also is out of the question for such a man; and the
same applies to virtue generally. No city could remain in a state

of tranquillity under any laws whatsoever, when men think it
right to squander all their property in extravagant excesses, and
consider it a duty to be idle in everything else except eating and
drinking and the laborious prosecution of debauchery. It
follows necessarily that the constitutions of such cities must be
constantly changing, tyrannies, oligarchies and democracies
succeeding one another, while those who hold the power cannot
so much as endure the name of any form of government which
maintains justice and equality of rights.

With[16] a mind full of these thoughts, on the top of my
previous convictions, I crossed over to Syracuse—led there
perhaps by chance—but it really looks as if some higher power[17]
was even then planning to lay a foundation for all that has now
come to pass with regard to Dion and Syracuse—and for further
troubles too, I fear, unless you listen to the advice which is now
for the second time offered by me. What do I mean by saying
that my arrival in Sicily at that moment proved to be the foundation on which all the sequel rests? I was brought into close
intercourse with Dion who was then a young man, and explained
to him my views as to the ideals at which men should aim,
advising him to carry them out in practice. In doing this I seem
to have been unaware that I was, in a fashion, without knowing
it, contriving the overthrow of the tyranny which subsequently
took place. For Dion, who rapidly assimilated my teaching as he
did all forms of knowledge, listened to me with an eagerness
which I had never seen equalled in any young man, and resolved
to live for the future in a better way than the majority of Italian
and Sicilian Greeks, having set his affection on virtue in preference to pleasure and self-indulgence. The result was that
until the death of Dionysios[18] he lived in a way which rendered
him somewhat unpopular among those whose manner of life
was that which is usual in the courts of despots.

After that event he came to the conclusion that this conviction, which he himself had gained under the influence of good
teaching, was not likely to be confined to himself. Indeed he saw
it being actually implanted in other minds—not many perhaps,
but certainly in some; and he thought that, with the aid of the

Gods, Dionysios might perhaps become one of these,[19] and that, if such a thing did come to pass, the result would be a life of unspeakable happiness both for himself and for the rest of the Syracusans. Further, he thought it essential that I should come to Syracuse by all manner of means[20] and with the utmost possible speed to be his partner in these plans, remembering in 327 d his own case how readily intercourse with me had produced in him a longing for the noblest and best life. And if it should produce a similar effect on Dionysios, as his aim was that it should, he had great hope that, without bloodshed, loss of life, and those disastrous events which have now taken place, he would be able to introduce the true life of happiness throughout the whole territory.[21]

Holding these sound views, Dion persuaded Dionysios to send for me; he also wrote himself entreating me to come by all manner of means and with the utmost possible speed, before e certain other persons coming in contact with Dionysios should turn him aside into some way of life other than the best. What he said, though perhaps it is rather long to repeat, was as follows: "What opportunities", he said, "shall we wait for, greater than those now offered to us by Providence?" And[22] he described 328 a the Syracusan empire in Italy and Sicily, his own influential position in it, and the youth of Dionysios and how strongly his desire was directed towards philosophy and education. His own nephews[23] and relatives, he said, would be readily attracted towards the principles and manner of life described by me, and would be most influential in attracting Dionysios in the same direction, so that, now if ever, we should see the accomplishment of every hope that the same persons might actually become both philosophers and the rulers of great States. These were b the appeals addressed to me and much more to the same effect.

My own opinion, so far as the young men[24] were concerned, and the probable line which their conduct would take, was full of apprehension—for young men are quick in forming desires, which often take directions conflicting with one another. But I knew that the character of Dion's mind was naturally a stable one and had also the advantage of somewhat advanced years.

Therefore I pondered the matter and was in two minds as to whether I ought to listen to entreaties and go, or how I ought to act; and finally the scale turned in favour of the view that,[25] if

328 c   ever anyone was to try to carry out in practice my ideas about laws and constitutions, now was the time for making the attempt; for if only I could fully convince one man, I should have secured thereby the accomplishment of all good things.

With these views and thus nerved to the task, I sailed from home, not in the spirit which some imagined, but principally through a feeling of shame with regard to myself, lest I might some day appear to myself wholly and solely a mere man of words,[26] one who would never of his own will lay his hand to any act. Also there was reason to think that I should be betraying

d   first and foremost my friendship and comradeship with Dion, who in very truth was in a position of considerable danger. If therefore anything should happen to him, or if he were banished by Dionysios and his other enemies and coming to us as exile addressed this question to me:[27] "Plato, I have come to you as a fugitive, not for want of hoplites,[28] nor because I had no cavalry for defence against my enemies, but for want of words and power of persuasion, which I knew to be a special gift of yours, enabling you to lead young men into the path of goodness and justice, and to establish in every case relations of friendship and

e   comradeship among them. It is for the want of this assistance on your part that I have left Syracuse and am here now. And the disgrace attaching to your treatment of me is a small matter. But philosophy[29]—whose praises you are always singing, while you say she is held in dishonour by the rest of mankind—must we not say that philosophy along with me has now been betrayed,

329 a   so far as your action was concerned? Had I been living at Megara, you would certainly have come to give me your aid towards the objects for which I asked it; or you would have thought yourself the most contemptible of mankind. But as it is, do you think that you will escape the reputation of cowardice by making excuses about the distance of the journey, the length of the sea voyage, and the amount of labour involved? Far from it". To reproaches of this kind what creditable reply could I have made? Surely none.

I took my departure therefore, acting, so far as a man can act,   329 b
in obedience to reason and justice, and for these reasons leaving
my own occupations, which were certainly not discreditable
ones, to put myself under a tyranny which did not seem likely to
harmonise with my teaching or with myself. By my departure I
secured my own freedom from the displeasure of Zeus Xenios,[30]
and made myself clear of any charge on the part of philosophy,
which would have been exposed to detraction, if any disgrace
had come upon me for faint-heartedness and cowardice.

On my arrival,[31] to cut a long story short, I found the court of
Dionysios full of intrigues and of attempts to create in the   c
sovereign ill-feeling against Dion. I combated these as far as I
could, but with very little success; and in the fourth month or
thereabouts, charging Dion with conspiracy to seize the throne,
Dionysios put him on board a small boat and expelled him from
Syracuse with ignominy. All of us who were Dion's friends
were afraid that he might take vengeance on one or other of us
as an accomplice in Dion's conspiracy. With regard to me there
was even a rumour current in Syracuse that I had been put to
death by Dionysios as the cause of all that had occurred.   d
Perceiving that we were all in this state of mind and appre-
hending that our fears might lead to some serious consequence,
he now tried to win all of us over by kindness: me[32] in particular
he encouraged, bidding me be of good cheer and entreating me
on all grounds to remain. For my flight from him was not likely
to redound to his credit, but my staying might do so. Therefore
he made a great pretence of entreating me. And we know that
the entreaties of sovereigns are mixed with compulsion. So to   e
secure his object he proceeded to render my departure impossible, bringing me into the akropolis, and establishing me in
quarters from which not a single ship's captain would have taken
me away against the will of Dionysios,[33] nor indeed without a
special messenger sent by him to order my removal. Nor was
there a single merchant, or a single official in charge of points of
departure from the country, who would have allowed me to
depart unaccompanied, and would not have promptly seized me
and taken me back to Dionysios, especially since a statement had

now been circulated contradicting the previous rumours and giving out that Dionysios was becoming extraordinarily attached to Plato. What were the facts about this attachment? I must tell the truth. As time went on, and as intercourse made him acquainted with my disposition and character, he did become more and more attached to me, and wished me to praise him more than I praised Dion, and to look upon him as more specially my friend than Dion,34 and he was extraordinarily eager about this sort of thing. But when confronted with the one way in which this might have been done, if it was to be done at all, he shrank from coming into close and intimate relations with me as a pupil and listener to my discourses on philosophy, fearing the danger suggested by mischief-makers, that he might be ensnared, and so Dion would prove to have accomplished all his object. I endured all this patiently, retaining the purpose with which I had come and the hope that he might come to desire the philosophic life. But his resistance prevailed against me.35

The time of my first visit to Sicily and my stay there was taken up with all these incidents. On a later occasion I left home and again came on an urgent summons from Dionysios. But before giving the motives and particulars of my conduct then and showing how suitable and right it was, I must first, in order that I may not treat as the main point what is only a side issue, give you my advice as to what your acts should be in the present position of affairs; afterwards, to satisfy those who put the question36 why I came a second time, I will deal fully with the facts about my second visit; what I have now to say is this.

He who advises a sick man,37 whose manner of life is prejudicial to health, is clearly bound first of all to change his patient's manner of life, and if the patient is willing to obey him, he may go on to give him other advice. But if he is not willing, I shall consider one who declines to advise such a patient to be a man and a physician, and one who gives in to him to be unmanly and unprofessional. In the same way with regard to a State, whether it be under a single ruler or more than one, if, while the government is being carried on methodically and in a

right course, it asks advice about any details of policy, it is the   330 e
part of a wise man to advise such people. But when men are
travelling altogether outside the path of right government and
flatly refuse to move in the right path, and start by giving notice
to their adviser that he must leave the government alone and
make no change in it under penalty of death—if such men[38]   331 a
should order their counsellors to pander to their wishes and
desires and to advise them in what way their object may most
readily and easily be once for all accomplished, I should consider as unmanly one who accepts the duty of giving such forms
of advice, and one who refuses it to be a true man.

Holding these views, whenever anyone consults me about any
of the weightiest matters affecting his own life, as for instance
the acquisition of property or the proper treatment of body or   b
mind, if it seems to me that his daily life rests on any system, or
if he seems likely to listen to advice about the things on which
he consults me, I advise him with readiness, and do not content
myself with giving him a merely perfunctory answer.[39] But if a
man does not consult me at all, or evidently does not intend to
follow my advice, I do not take the initiative in advising such a
man, and will not use compulsion to him, even if he be my own
son. I would advise a slave under such circumstances, and would
use compulsion to him if he were unwilling. To a father or   c
mother I do not think that piety allows one to offer compulsion,[40]
unless they are suffering from an attack of insanity; and if they
are following any regular habits of life which please them but do
not please me, I would not offend them by offering useless
advice, nor would I flatter them or truckle to them, providing
them with the means of satisfying desires which I myself would
sooner die than cherish. The wise man should go through life
with the same attitude of mind towards his country. If she
should appear to him to be following a policy which is not a   d
good one, he should say so, provided that his words are not
likely either to fall on deaf ears or to lead to the loss of his own
life. But force[41] against his native land he should not use in
order to bring about a change of constitution, when it is not
possible for the best constitution to be introduced without

driving men into exile or putting them to death; he should keep quiet and offer up prayers for his own welfare and for that of his country.

These are the principles in accordance with which I should advise you, as also, jointly with Dion, I advised Dionysios, bidding him in the first place to live his daily life in a way that would make him as far as possible master of himself and able to gain faithful friends and supporters, in order that he might not have the same experience as his father. For his father, having taken under his rule many great cities of Sicily which had been utterly destroyed by the barbarians, was not able to found them afresh and to establish in them trustworthy governments carried on by his own supporters, either by men who had no ties of blood with him, or by his brothers whom he had brought up when they were younger, and had raised from humble station to high office and from poverty to immense wealth. Not one of these was he able to work upon by persuasion, instruction, services and ties of kindred, so as to make him a partner in his rule; and he showed himself inferior to Darius[42] with a sevenfold inferiority. For Darius did not put his trust in brothers or in men whom he had brought up, but only in his confederates in the overthrow of the Mede and Eunuch; and to these he assigned portions of his empire, seven in number, each of them greater than all Sicily; and they were faithful to him and did not attack either him or one another. Thus he showed a pattern of what the good lawgiver and king ought to be; for he drew up laws by which he has secured the Persian empire in safety down to the present time.

Again, to give another instance, the Athenians took under their rule very many cities not founded by themselves, which had been hard hit[43] by the barbarians but were still in existence and maintained their rule over these for seventy years, because they had in each of them men whom they could trust. But Dionysios, who had gathered the whole of Sicily into a single city,[44] and was so clever that he trusted no one, only secured his own safety with great difficulty. For he was badly off for trustworthy friends; and there is no surer criterion of virtue and

331 e

332 a

b

c

vice than this, whether a man is or is not destitute of such friends.

This[45] then was the advice which Dion and I gave to Dionysios, since owing to the bringing up which he had received from his 332 d father he had had no advantages in the way of education or of suitable lessons, in the first place... ; and in the second place that, after starting in this way, he should make friends of others among his connections who were of the same age and were in sympathy with his pursuit of virtue, but above all that he should be in harmony with himself; for this it was of which he was remarkably in need. This we did not say in plain words, for that would not have been safe; but in covert language we maintained that every man in this way would save both himself and those whom he was leading, and if he did not follow this path, he e would do just the opposite of this. And after proceeding on the course which we described, and making himself a wise and temperate man, if he were then to found again the cities of Sicily which had been laid waste, and bind them together by laws and constitutions, so as to be loyal to him and to one another in their resistance to the attacks of the barbarians, he would, we told him, make his father's empire not merely double what it was 333 a but many times greater. For, if these things were done, his way would be clear to a more complete subjugation of the Carthaginians than that which befel them in Gelon's time, whereas in our own day his father had followed the opposite course of levying a tribute[46] for the barbarians. This was the language and these the exhortations given by us, the conspirators against Dionysios according to the charges circulated from various sources—charges which, prevailing as they did with Dionysios, caused the expulsion of Dion and reduced me to a state of apprehension. But when—to summarise great events which happened in no great time—Dion returned from the Pelopon- b nese and Athens, his advice to Dionysios took the form of action.[47]

To proceed—when Dion had twice over[48] delivered the city and restored it to the citizens, the Syracusans went through the same changes of feeling towards him as Dionysios had gone through, when Dion attempted first to educate him and train him to be a sovereign worthy of supreme power and, when that was done, to be his coadjutor in all the details of his career. Dionysios listened[49] to those who circulated slanders to the

333 c effect that Dion was aiming at the tyranny in all the steps which he took at that time, his intention being that Dionysios, when his mind had fallen under the spell of culture, should neglect the government and leave it in his hands, and that he should then appropriate it for himself and treacherously depose Dionysios. These slanders were victorious on that occasion; they were so once more when circulated among the Syracusans, winning a victory which took an extraordinary course and proved disgraceful to its authors. The story of what then took place is one

d which deserves careful attention on the part of those who are inviting me to deal with the present situation.

I,[50] an Athenian and friend of Dion, came as his ally to the court of Dionysios, in order that I might create good will in place of a state of war; in my conflict with the authors of these slanders I was worsted. When Dionysios tried to persuade me by offers of honours and wealth to attach myself to him,[51] and with a view to giving a decent colour to Dion's expulsion to be a witness and friend on his side, he failed completely in his attempt.

e Later on, when Dion returned from exile, he took with him from Athens two brothers,[52] who had been his friends, not from community in philosophic study, but with the ordinary companionship common among most friends, which they form as the result of relations of hospitality and the intercourse which occurs when one man initiates the other in the mysteries.[53] It was from this kind of intercourse and from services connected with his return that these two helpers in his restoration became his companions.

334 a Having come to Sicily, when they perceived that Dion had been misrepresented to the Sicilian Greeks, whom he had liberated, as one that plotted to become monarch, they not only betrayed their companion and friend, but shared personally in the guilt of his murder, standing by his murderers as supporters with weapons in their hands. The guilt and impiety of their conduct I neither excuse[54] nor do I dwell upon it. For many others make

it their business to harp upon it, and will make it their business 334 b
in the future. But I do take exception to the statement that,
because they were Athenians,[55] they have brought shame upon
this city. For I say that he too is an Athenian who refused to
betray this same Dion, when he had the offer of riches and many
other honours. For his was no common or vulgar friendship,
but rested on community in liberal education, and this is the
one thing in which a wise man will put his trust, far more than
in ties of personal and bodily kinship. So the two murderers of
Dion were not of sufficient importance to be causes of disgrace c
to this city, as though they had been men of any note.

All this has been said with a view to counselling the friends
and family of Dion. And in addition to this I give for the third
time to you the same advice and counsel which I have given
twice before to others[56]—not to enslave Sicily nor any other
State to despots—this is my counsel—but to put it under the
rule of laws—for the other course is better[57] neither for the
enslavers nor for the enslaved, for themselves, their children's d
children and descendants; the attempt is in every way fraught
with disaster. It is only small and mean natures that are bent
upon seizing such gains for themselves, natures that know
nothing of goodness and justice, divine as well as human, in this
life and in the next.

These are the lessons which I tried to teach, first to Dion,
secondly to Dionysios, and now for the third time to you. Do
you obey me, thinking of Zeus the Preserver, the patron of third
ventures, and looking at the lot of Dionysios and Dion, of
whom the one who disobeyed me is living in dishonour, while he e
who obeyed me has died honourably. For the one thing which is
wholly right and noble is to strive for that which is most
honourable for a man's self and for his country, and to face the
consequences whatever they may be. For none of us can escape
death,[58] nor, if a man could do so, would it, as the vulgar
suppose, make him happy. For nothing evil or good, which is
worth mentioning at all, belongs to things soul-less; but good or 335 a
evil will be the portion of every soul, either while attached to
the body or when separated from it.

And we should in very truth always believe those ancient and sacred teachings,[59] which declare that the soul is immortal, that it has judges, and suffers the greatest penalties when it has been separated from the body. Therefore also we should consider it a lesser evil to suffer great wrongs and outrages than to do them. The covetous man,[60] impoverished as he is in the soul, turns a deaf ear to this teaching; or if he hears it, he laughs it to scorn with fancied superiority, and shamelessly snatches for himself from every source whatever his bestial fancy supposes will provide for him the means of eating or drinking or glutting himself with that slavish and gross pleasure which is falsely called after the goddess of love. He is blind and cannot see in those acts of plunder which are accompanied by impiety what heinous guilt is attached to each wrongful deed, and that the offender must drag with him the burden of this impiety while he moves about on earth, and when he has travelled beneath the earth on a journey which has every circumstance of shame and misery.

It was by urging these and other like truths that I convinced Dion, and it is I who have the best right to be angered with his murderers in much the same way as I have with Dionysios. For both they and he have done the greatest injury to me, and I might almost say to all mankind, they by slaying the man that was willing to act righteously, and he by refusing to act righteously during the whole of his rule,[61] when he held supreme power, in which rule if philosophy and power had really met together, it would have sent forth a light to all men, Greeks and barbarians, establishing fully for all the true belief that there can be no happiness either for the community or for the individual man, unless he passes his life under the rule of righteousness with the guidance of wisdom,[62] either possessing these virtues in himself, or living under the rule of godly men and having received a right training and education in morals. These were the aims which Dionysios injured, and for me everything else is a trifling injury compared with this.

The murderer of Dion has, without knowing it, done the same as Dionysios. For as regards Dion I know right well, so far as it is possible for a man to say anything positively about

335 b

c

d

e

other men, that,[63] if he had got the supreme power, he would
never have turned his mind to any other form of rule, but that,   336a
dealing first with Syracuse, his own native land, when he had
made an end of her slavery, clothed her in bright apparel, and
given her the garb of freedom, he would then by every means in
his power have ordered aright the lives of his fellow-citizens by
suitable and excellent laws; and the thing next in order, which he
would have set his heart to accomplish, was to found again all
the States of Sicily and make them free from the barbarians,
driving out some and subduing others, an easier task for him
than it was for Hiero. If these things had been accomplished by   b
a man who was just and brave and temperate and a philosopher,
the same belief with regard to virtue would have been established
among the majority which, if Dionysios had been won over,
would have been established, I might almost say, among all
mankind and would have given them salvation.[64] But now some
higher power or avenging fiend has fallen upon them, inspiring
them with lawlessness, godlessness and acts of recklessness
issuing from ignorance, the seed from which all evils for all
mankind take root and grow and will in future bear the bitterest
harvest for those who brought them into being. This ignorance[65]
it was which in that second venture wrecked and ruined everything.

And now, for good luck's sake, let us on this third venture   c
abstain from words of ill-omen. But nevertheless I advise you
his friends to imitate in Dion his love for his country and his
temperate habits of daily life, and to try with better auspices to
carry out his wishes—what these were, you have heard from me
in plain words. And whoever among you cannot live the simple
Dorian life according to the customs of your forefathers, but   d
follows the manner of life of Dion's murderers and of the Sicilians, do not invite this man to join you, or expect him to do any
loyal or salutary act; but invite all others to the work of re-
settling all the States of Sicily and establishing equality under
the laws, summoning them from Sicily itself and from the whole
Peloponnese—and have no fear even of Athens; for there,[66]
also, are men who excel all mankind in their devotion to virtue

and in hatred of the reckless acts of those who shed the blood of friends.

But if, after all, this is work for a future time,[67] whereas immediate action is called for by the disorders of all sorts and kinds which arise every day from your state of civil strife, every man to whom Providence has given even a moderate share of right intelligence ought to know that in times of civil strife there is no respite from trouble till the victors make an end of feeding their grudge by combats and banishments and executions, and of wreaking their vengeance on their enemies. They should master themselves and, enacting impartial laws, framed not to gratify themselves more than the conquered party, should compel men to obey these by two restraining forces,[68] respect and fear; fear, because they are the masters and can display superior force; respect, because they rise superior to pleasures and are willing and able to be servants to the laws. There is no other way save this for terminating the troubles of a city that is in a state of civil strife; but a constant continuance of internal disorders, struggles, hatred and mutual distrust is the common lot of cities which are in that plight.[69]

Therefore those who have for the time being gained the upper hand, when they desire to secure their position, must by their own act and choice select from all Hellas men whom they have ascertained to be the best for the purpose. These must in the first place be men of mature years,[70] who have children and wives at home, and, as far as possible, a long line of ancestors of good repute, and all must be possessed of sufficient property. For a city of ten thousand householders their number should be fifty;[71] that is enough. These they must induce to come from their own homes by entreaties and the promise of the highest honours; and having induced them to come they must entreat and command them to draw up laws after binding themselves by oath to show no partiality either to conquerors or to conquered, but to give equal and common rights to the whole State.

When laws have been enacted, what everything then hinges on is this. If the conquerors show more obedience to the laws than the conquered, the whole State will be full of security and happiness, and there will be an escape from all your troubles. But if they do not, then do not summon me or any other helper to aid you against those who do not obey the counsel I now give you. For this course is akin to that which Dion and I attempted to carry out with our hearts set on the welfare of Syracuse. It is indeed a second best[72] course. The first and best was that scheme of welfare to all mankind which we attempted to carry out with the co-operation of Dionysios; but some chance, mightier than men, brought it to nothing. Do you now, with good fortune attending you and with Heaven's help, try to bring your efforts to a happier issue.

337 e

Let this be the end of my advice and injunction and of the narrative of my first visit to Dionysios. Whoever wishes may next hear of my second journey and voyage, and learn that it was a reasonable and suitable proceeding. My first period of residence in Sicily was occupied in the way which I related before giving my advice to the relatives and friends of Dion. After those events I persuaded Dionysios by such arguments as I could to let me go; and we made an agreement as to what should be done when peace was made; for at that time there was a state of war in Sicily.[73] Dionysios said that, when he had put the affairs of his empire in a position of greater safety for himself, he would send for Dion and me again;[74] and he desired that Dion should regard what had befallen him not as an exile, but as a change of residence. I agreed to come again on these conditions.

338 a

b

When peace had been made, he began sending for me; he requested that Dion should wait for another year, but begged that I should by all means come. Dion now kept urging and entreating me to go. For persistent rumours came from Sicily that Dionysios was now once more possessed by an extraordinary desire for philosophy. For this reason Dion pressed me urgently not to decline his invitation. But though I was well aware that as regards philosophy such symptoms were not uncommon in young men, still it seemed to me safer at that time to part company altogether with Dion and Dionysios; and I offended both of them by replying that I was an old man, and

c

that the steps now being taken were quite at variance with the previous agreement.

After this, it seems, Archytes[75] came to the court of Dionysios.

338 d Before my departure I had brought him and his Tarentine circle into friendly relations with Dionysios. There were some others in Syracuse who had received some instruction from Dion, and others had learnt from these,[76] getting their heads full of erroneous teaching on philosophical questions. These, it seems, were attempting to hold discussions with Dionysios on questions connected with such subjects,[77] in the idea that he had been fully instructed in my views. Now he is not at all devoid of natural gifts for learning,[78] and he has a great craving for honour and glory. What was said probably pleased him, and he felt some

e shame when it became clear that he had not taken advantage of my teaching during my visit. For these reasons he conceived a desire for more definite instruction, and his love of glory was an additional incentive to him. The real reasons why he had learnt nothing during my previous visit have just been set forth in the preceding narrative.[79] Accordingly, now that I was safe at home and had refused his second invitation, as I just now related, Dionysios seems to have felt all manner of anxiety lest certain

339 a people should suppose that I was unwilling to visit him again because I had formed a poor opinion of his natural gifts and character, and because, knowing as I did his manner of life, I disapproved of it.

It is right for me to speak the truth, and make no complaint if anyone, after hearing the facts, forms a poor opinion of my philosophy, and thinks that the tyrant was in the right. Dionysios now invited me for the third time, sending a trireme to ensure me comfort on the voyage; he sent also Archedemos[80]—one of those

b who had spent some time with Archytes, and of whom he supposed that I had a higher opinion than of any of the Sicilian Greeks—and, with him, other men of repute in Sicily. These all brought the same report, that Dionysios had made remarkable progress in philosophy. He also sent a very long letter, knowing as he did my relations with Dion and Dion's eagerness also that I should take ship and go to Syracuse. The letter was

framed in its opening sentences to meet all these conditions, and
the tenor of it was as follows: "Dionysios to Plato", here
followed the customary greeting and immediately after it he
said, "If in compliance with our request you come now, in the
first place Dion's affairs will be dealt with in whatever way you
yourself desire; I know that you will desire what is reasonable,
and I shall consent to it. But if not, none of Dion's affairs will
have results[81] in accordance with your wishes, with regard either
to Dion himself or to other matters." This he said in these
words; the rest it would be tedious and inopportune to quote.
Other letters arrived from Archytes and the Tarentines, praising
the philosophical studies of Dionysios and saying that, if I did
not now come, I should cause a complete rupture in their
friendship with Dionysios, which had been brought about by me
and was of no small importance to their political interests.

When this invitation came to me at that time in such terms,
and those who had come from Sicily and Italy were trying to
drag me thither, while my friends at Athens were literally
pushing me out with their urgent entreaties, it was the same old
tale—that I must not betray Dion and my Tarentine friends and
supporters. Also I myself had a lurking feeling that there was
nothing surprising in the fact that a young man, quick to learn,
hearing talk of the great truths of philosophy, should feel a
craving for the higher life. I thought therefore that I must put
the matter definitely to the test to see whether his desire was
genuine or the reverse, and on no account leave such an im-
pulse unaided nor make myself responsible for such a deep and
real disgrace,[82] if the reports brought by anyone were really
true. So blindfolding myself with this reflection, I set out, with
many fears and with no very favourable anticipations, as was
natural enough. However, I went, and my action on this
occasion at any rate was really a case of "the third to the
Preserver,"[83] for I had the good fortune to return safely; and for
this I must, next to the God, thank Dionysios, because, though
many wished to make an end of me, he prevented them and paid
some proper respect to my situation.

On my arrival, I thought that first I must put to the test the

339 c

d

e

340 a

b

question whether Dionysios had really been kindled[84] with the fire of philosophy, or whether all the reports which had come to Athens were empty rumours. Now there is a way of putting such things to the test which is not to be despised and is well suited to monarchs, especially to those who have got their heads full of erroneous teaching, which immediately on my arrival I found to be very much the case with Dionysios. One should show such men what philosophy[85] is in all its extent, what the

340 c range of studies is by which it is approached, and how much labour it involves. For the man who has heard this,[86] if he has the true philosophic spirit and that godlike temperament which makes him akin to philosophy and worthy of it, thinks that he has been told of a marvellous road lying before him, that he must forthwith press on with all his strength, and that life is not worth living if he does anything else. After this he uses to the full his own powers and those of his guide in the path, and relaxes not his efforts, till he has either reached the end of the whole course of study or gained such power that he is not

d incapable of directing his steps without the aid of a guide. This is the spirit and these are the thoughts by which such a man guides his life, carrying out his work, whatever his occupation may be, but throughout it all ever cleaving to philosophy, and to such rules of diet[87] in his daily life as will give him inward sobriety and therewith quickness in learning, a good memory, and reasoning power; the kind of life which is opposed to this he consistently hates. Those who have not the true philosophic temper, but a mere surface colouring of opinions penetrating, like sunburn, only skin deep, when they see how great the range of studies

e is, how much labour is involved in it, and how necessary to the pursuit it is to have an orderly regulation of the daily life, come to the conclusion that the thing is difficult and impossible for

341 a them, and are actually incapable of carrying out the course of study; while some of them persuade themselves that they have sufficiently studied the whole matter and have no need of any further effort. This is the sure test and is the safest one to apply to those who live in luxury and are incapable of continuous effort; it ensures that such a man shall not throw the blame upon

his teacher but on himself, because he cannot bring to the pursuit all the qualities necessary to it. Thus it came about that I said to Dionysios what I did say on that occasion.[88]

I did not, however, give a complete exposition, nor did Dionysios ask for one. For he professed to know many, and 341 b those the most important, points, and to have a sufficient hold of them through instruction given by others. I hear also that he has since written about what he heard from me, composing what professes to be his own handbook, very different, so he says, from the doctrines which he heard from me;[89] but of its contents I know nothing. I know indeed that others have written on the same subjects; but who they are,[90] is more than they know themselves. Thus much, at least, I can say about all writers, past or future, who say they know the things to which I c devote myself, whether by hearing the teaching of me or of others, or by their own discoveries—that according to my view it is not possible for them to have any real skill in the matter. There neither is nor ever will be a treatise of mine on the subject.[91] For it does not admit of exposition like other branches of knowledge; but after much converse about the matter itself and a life lived together, suddenly[92] a light, as it were, is kindled in one soul by a flame that leaps to it from another, and there- d after sustains itself. Yet this much I know[93]—that if the things were written or put into words, it would be done best by me, and that, if they were written badly, I should be the person most pained. Again, if they had appeared to me to admit adequately of writing and exposition, what task in life could I have performed nobler than this, to write what is of great service to mankind and to bring the nature of things[94] into the light for all e to see? But I do not think it a good thing for men that there should be a disquisition, as it is called, on this topic—except for some few, who are able with a little teaching to find it out for themselves. As for the rest, it would fill some of them quite illogically with a mistaken feeling of contempt, and others with lofty and vain-glorious expectations, as though they had learnt something high and mighty.

On this point I intend to speak a little more at length; for 342 a perhaps, when I have done so, things will be clearer with regard to my present subject. There is an argument[95] which holds good against the man who ventures to put anything whatever into writing on questions of this nature; it has often before been stated by me, and it seems suitable to the present occasion.

For everything that exists there are three instruments by which the knowledge of it is necessarily imparted; fourth, there is the knowledge itself, and, as fifth, we must[96] count the thing itself which is known and truly exists. The first is the name, the second the definition, the third the image, and the fourth the knowledge.[97] If you wish to learn what I mean, take these in the case of one instance, and so understand them in the case of all. A circle is a thing spoken of, and its name is that very word which we have just uttered. The second thing belonging to it is its definition, made up of names and verbal forms.[98] For that which has the name "round", "annular", or "circle", might be defined as that which has the distance from its circumference to its centre everywhere equal. Third[99] comes that which is drawn and rubbed out again, or turned on a lathe and broken up—none of which things can happen to the circle itself—to which the other things mentioned have reference; for it is something of a different order from them. Fourth[100] comes knowledge, intelligence and right opinion about these things. Under this one head we must group everything which has its existence, not in words nor in bodily shapes, but in souls—from which it is clear that it is something different from the nature of the circle itself and from the three things mentioned before. Of these things intelligence comes closest in kinship and likeness to the fifth, and the others are farther distant.

The same applies to straight as well as to circular form, to colours, to the good, the beautiful, the just, to all bodies whether manufactured or coming into being in the course of nature, to fire, water, and all such things, to every living being, to character in souls, and to all things done and suffered. For in the case of all these no one, if he has not somehow or other got hold of the four things first mentioned, can ever be completely a partaker of knowledge of the fifth. Further,[101] on account of the weakness

of language, these (i.e. the four) attempt to show what each thing is like, not less than what each thing is. For this reason no man   343 a
of intelligence will venture to express his philosophical views in language,[102] especially not in language that is unchangeable, which is true of that which is set down in written characters.

Again you must learn the point which comes next. Every circle, of those which are by the act of man drawn or even turned on a lathe, is full of that which is opposite to the fifth thing. For everywhere it has contact with the straight.[103] But the circle itself, we say, has nothing in it, either smaller or greater, of that which is its opposite. We say also that the name is not a thing of permanence for any of them,[104] and that nothing prevents the   b
things now called round from being called straight, and the straight things round; so for those who make changes and call things by opposite names, nothing will be less permanent (than a name). Again with regard to the definition, if it is made up of names and verbal forms, the same remark holds that there is no sufficiently durable permanence in it. And there is no end to the instances of the ambiguity from which each of the four suffers; but the greatest of them is that which we mentioned a little earlier, that, whereas there are two things,[105] that which has real being, and that which is only a quality, when the soul is   c
seeking to know, not the quality, but the essence, each of the four, presenting to the soul by word and in act that which it is not seeking (i.e. the quality), a thing open to refutation by the senses, being merely the thing presented to the soul in each particular case whether by statement or the act of showing, fills, one may say, every man with puzzlement and perplexity.

Now in subjects in which, by reason of our defective education, we have not been accustomed even to search for the truth, but are satisfied with whatever images are presented to us, we are not held up to ridicule by one another, the questioned by questioners, who can pull to pieces and criticise the four things.   d
But[106] in subjects where we try to compel a man to give a clear answer about the fifth, any one of those who are capable of overthrowing an antagonist gets the better of us, and makes the man, who gives an exposition in speech or writing or in replies

to questions, appear to most of his hearers to know nothing of the things on which he is attempting to write or speak; for they are sometimes not aware that it is not the mind of the writer or speaker which is proved to be at fault,[107] but the defective nature of each of the four instruments. The process however of dealing
343 e with all of these,[108] as the mind moves up and down to each in turn, does after much effort give birth in a well-constituted mind to knowledge of that which is well constituted. But if a man is ill-constituted by nature (as the state of the soul is naturally in the majority both in its capacity for learning and in what is called moral character)—or it may have become so by deteriora-
344 a tion—not even Lynkeus could endow such men with the power of sight.

In[109] one word, the man who has no natural kinship with this matter cannot be made akin to it by quickness of learning or memory; for it cannot be engendered at all in natures which are foreign to it. Therefore if men are not by nature and kinship allied to justice and all other things that are honourable, though they may be good at learning and remembering other knowledge of various kinds—or if they have the kinship but are slow learners and have no memory—none of all these will ever learn
b to the full the truth about virtue and vice. For both must be learnt together; and together also must be learnt, by complete and long continued study, as I said at the beginning, the true and the false[110] about all that has real being. After much effort, as names, definitions, sights, and other data of sense, are brought into contact and friction one with another, in the course of scrutiny and kindly testing by men who proceed by question and answer without ill will, with a sudden flash[111] there shines forth understanding about every problem, and an intelligence whose
c efforts reach the furthest limits of human powers. Therefore every man of worth, when dealing with matters of worth, will be far from exposing them to ill feeling and misunderstanding among men by committing them to writing. In one word, then, it may be known from this that, if one sees written treatises[112] composed by anyone, either the laws of a lawgiver, or in any other form whatever, these are not for that man the things of

most worth, if he is a man of worth, but that his treasures are
laid up in the fairest spot that he possesses.[113] But if these things
were worked at by him as things of real worth, and committed   344 d
to writing, then surely, not gods, but men "have themselves
bereft him of his wits".[114]

Anyone who has followed this discourse and digression[115]
will know well that, if Dionysios or anyone else, great or small,
has written a treatise on the highest matters and the first
principles of things, he has, so I say, neither heard nor learnt any
sound teaching about the subject of his treatise; otherwise he
would have had the same reverence for it, which I have, and
would have shrunk from putting it forth into a world of discord
and uncomeliness.[116] For he wrote it, not as an aid to memory—   e
since there is no risk of forgetting it, if a man's soul has once laid
hold of it; for it is expressed in the shortest of statements[117]—
but if he wrote it at all, it was from a mean craving for honour,
either putting it forth as his own invention, or to figure as a man
possessed of culture, of which he was not worthy, if his heart was
set on the credit of possessing it. If[118] then Dionysios gained   345 a
this culture from the one lesson which he had from me, we may
perhaps grant him the possession of it, though how he acquired
it—God wot,[119] as the Theban says; for I gave him the teaching,
which I have described, on that one occasion and never again.

The next point which requires to be made clear to anyone who
wishes to discover how things really happened, is the reason why
it came about that I did not continue my teaching in a second
and third lesson and yet oftener. Does Dionysios, after a single
lesson, believe himself to know the matter, and has he an   b
adequate knowledge of it, either as having discovered it for himself or learnt it before from others, or does he believe my
teaching to be worthless, or, thirdly, to be beyond his range and
too great for him, and himself to be really unable to live as one
who gives his mind to wisdom and virtue? For if he thinks it
worthless, he will have to contend with many who say the
opposite, and who would be held in far higher repute as judges
than Dionysios. If, on the other hand, he thinks he has discovered or learnt the things and that they are worth having as

part of a liberal education, how could he, unless he is an extra-
345 c ordinary person, have so recklessly dishonoured the master[120]
who has led the way in these subjects? How he dishonoured him,
I will now state.

Up to this time[121] he had allowed Dion to remain in possession
of his property and to receive the income from it. But not long
after the foregoing events, as if he had entirely forgotten his
letter to that effect, he no longer allowed Dion's trustees to send
him remittances to the Peloponnese, on the pretence that the
owner of the property was not Dion but Dion's son, his own
d   nephew, of whom he himself was legally the trustee. These were
the actual facts which occurred up to the point which we have
reached. They had opened my eyes as to the value of Dionysios'
desire for philosophy, and I had every right to complain,
whether I wished to do so or not. Now by this time it was
summer and the season for sea voyages; therefore I decided that
I must not be vexed with Dionysios rather than with myself
e   and those who had forced me to come for the third time into the
strait of Skylla,

> *that once again I might*
> *To fell Charybdis measure back my course,*[122]

but must tell Dionysios that it was impossible for me to remain
after this outrage had been put upon Dion. He tried to soothe
me and begged me to remain, not thinking it desirable for himself[123] that I should arrive post haste in person as the bearer of
such tidings. When his entreaties produced no effect, he
346 a promised that he himself would provide me with transport.
For my intention was to embark on one of the trading ships[124]
and sail away, being indignant and thinking it my duty to face
all dangers, in case I was prevented from going—since plainly
and obviously I was doing no wrong, but was the party wronged.

Seeing me not at all inclined to stay, he devised the following
scheme to make me stay during that sailing season. On the next
day he came to me and made a plausible proposal: "Let us put
b   an end", he said, "to these constant quarrels between you and
me about Dion and his affairs. For your sake I will do this for

Dion. I require him to take his own property and reside in the Peloponnese,[125] not as an exile, but on the understanding that it is open for him to migrate here, when this step has the joint approval of himself, me, and you his friends; and this shall be open to him on the understanding that he does not plot against me. You and your friends and Dion's friends here must be sureties for him in this, and he must give you security. Let the funds which he receives be deposited in the Peloponnese and at 346 c
Athens, with persons approved by you, and let Dion enjoy the income from them but have no power to take them out of deposit without the approval of you and your friends. For I have no great confidence in him, that, if he has this property at his disposal, he will act justly towards me, for it will be no small amount; but I have more confidence in you and your friends. See if this satisfies you; and on these conditions remain for the present year, and at the next season [126] you shall depart taking the   d
property with you. I am quite sure that Dion will be grateful to you, if you accomplish so much on his behalf."

When I heard this proposal I was vexed, but after reflection said I would let him know my view of it on the following day. We agreed to that effect for the moment, and afterwards when I was by myself I pondered the matter in much distress. The first reflection that came up, leading the way in my self-communing, was this: "Come, suppose that Dionysios intends to do none of   e
the things which he has mentioned, but that, after my departure, he writes a plausible letter to Dion, and orders several of his creatures to write to the same effect, telling him of the proposal which he has now made to me, making out that he was willing to do what he proposed, but that I refused and completely neg-   347 a
lected Dion's interests. Further, suppose that he is not willing to allow my departure, and without giving personal orders to any of the merchants, makes it clear, as he easily can, to all that he does not wish me to sail, will anyone consent to take me as a passenger,[127] when I leave the house of Dionysios?"

For in addition to my other troubles, I was lodging at that time in the garden which surrounds his house, from which even the gate-keeper would have refused to let me go, unless an order had been sent to him from Dionysios. "Suppose however that I wait for the year, I shall be able to write word of these things to Dion, stating the position in which I am,[128] and the steps which I am trying to take. And if Dionysios does any of the 347 b things which he says, I shall have accomplished something that is not altogether to be sneered at; for Dion's property is, at a fair estimate, perhaps not less than a hundred talents. If however the prospect which I see looming in the future takes the course which may reasonably be expected, I know not what I shall do with myself. Still it is perhaps necessary to go on working for a year, and to attempt to prove by actual fact the machinations of Dionysios."

Having come to this decision, on the following day I said to c Dionysios, "I have decided to remain. But", I continued, "I must ask that you will not regard me as empowered to act for Dion, but will along with me write a letter to him, stating what has now been decided, and enquire whether this course satisfies him. If it does not, and if he has other wishes and demands, he must write particulars of them as soon as possible, and you must not as yet take any hasty step with regard to his interests."

This was what was said and this was the agreement which was made, almost in these words. Well, after this the trading-ships took their departure, and it was no longer possible for me to take d mine, when Dionysios, if you please, addressed me with the remark that half the property must be regarded as belonging to Dion and half to his son. Therefore, he said, he would sell it, and when it was sold would give half to me to take away, and would leave half on the spot for the son. This course, he said, was the most just. This proposal was a blow to me, and I thought it absurd to argue any longer with him; however, I said that we must wait for Dion's letter, and then once more write to tell him e of this new proposal. His next step was the brilliant[129] one of selling the whole of Dion's property, using his own discretion with regard to the manner and terms of the sale and the selection of the purchasers. He spoke not a word to me about the matter from beginning to end, and I followed his example and never talked to him again about Dion's affairs; for I did not think that

I could do any good by doing so. This is the history so far of my efforts to come to the rescue of philosophy and of my friends.

After this Dionysios and I went on with our daily life, I with my eyes turned abroad like a bird yearning to fly from its perch, and he always devising some new way of scaring me back and of keeping a tight hold on Dion's property. However, we gave out to all Sicily that we were friends. Dionysios, now deserting the policy of his father, attempted to lower the pay of the older members of his body guard.[130] The soldiers were furious, and, assembling in great numbers, declared that they would not submit. He attempted to use force to them, shutting the gates of the akropolis; but they charged straight for the walls, yelling out an unintelligible and ferocious war cry. Dionysios took fright and conceded all their demands and more to the peltasts then assembled.

A rumour[131] soon spread that Herakleides had been the cause of all the trouble. Hearing this, Herakleides kept out of the way. Dionysios was trying to get hold of him, and being unable to do so, sent for Theodotes to come to him in his garden. It happened that I was walking in the garden at the same time. I neither know[132] nor did I hear the rest of what passed between them, but what Theodotes said to Dionysios in my presence I know and remember. "Plato", he said, "I am trying to convince our friend Dionysios that, if I am able to bring Herakleides before us to defend himself on the charges which have been made against him, and if he decides that Herakleides must no longer live in Sicily, he should be allowed (this is my point) to take his son and wife and sail to the Peloponnese and reside there, taking no action there against Dionysios and enjoying the income of his property. I have already sent for him and will send for him again; and if he comes in obedience either to my former message or to this one—well and good. But I beg and entreat Dionysios that, if anyone finds Herakleides either in the country or here, no harm shall come to him, but that he may retire from the country till Dionysios comes to some other decision. Do you agree to this?" he added, addressing Dionysios. "I agree", he replied,

348 a

b

c

d

e

"that even if he is found at your house, no harm shall be done to him beyond what has now been said."

On the following day Eurybios and Theodotes came to me in the evening, both greatly disturbed. Theodotes said, "Plato, you were present yesterday during the promises made by Dionysios to me and to you about Herakleides?" "Certainly," I replied. "Well," he continued, "at this moment peltasts are scouring the country seeking to arrest Herakleides; and he must be somewhere in this neighbourhood. For Heaven's sake come with us to Dionysios." So we went and stood in the presence of Dionysios; and those two stood shedding silent tears, while I said: "These men are afraid that you may take strong measures with regard to Herakleides contrary to what was agreed yesterday. For it seems that he has returned and has been seen somewhere about here." On hearing this he blazed up and turned all colours, as a man would in a rage. Theodotes, falling before him in tears, took his hand and entreated him to do nothing of the sort. But I broke in and tried to encourage him, saying: "Be of good cheer, Theodotes; Dionysios will not have the heart to take any fresh step contrary to his promises of yesterday." Fixing his eye on me, and assuming his most autocratic air, he said, "To you I promised nothing small or great." "By the gods," I said,[133] "you did promise that forbearance for which our friend here now appeals." With these words I turned away and went out. After this he continued the hunt for Herakleides, and Theodotes, sending messages, urged Herakleides to take flight. Dionysios sent out Teisias and some peltasts with orders to pursue him. But Herakleides, as it was said, was just in time, by a small fraction of a day, in making his escape into Carthaginian territory.

After[134] this Dionysios thought that his long cherished scheme not to restore Dion's property would give him a plausible excuse for hostility towards me; and first of all he sent me out of the akropolis, finding a pretext that the women were obliged to hold a sacrificial service for ten days[135] in the garden in which I had my lodging. He therefore ordered me to stay outside in the house of Archedemos during this period. While I was there, Theodotes sent for me and made a great outpouring of indignation at these occurrences, throwing the blame on Dionysios. Hearing that I had been to see Theodotes he regarded this as another excuse, sister to the previous one, for quarrelling with me. Sending a messenger he enquired if I had really been conferring with Theodotes on his invitation. "Certainly", I replied. "Well", continued the messenger, "he ordered me to tell you that you are not acting at all well in preferring always Dion and Dion's friends to him." And he did not send for me to return to his house,[136] as though it were now clear that Theodotes and Herakleides were my friends, and he my enemy. He also thought that I had no kind feelings towards him because the property of Dion was now entirely done for.

349e

After this I resided outside the akropolis among the mercenaries. Various people then came to me, among them those of the ships' crews who came from Athens,[137] my own fellow citizens, and reported that I was evil spoken of among the peltasts, and that some of them were threatening to make an end of me, if they could get hold of me. Accordingly I devised the following plan for my safety.

350a

I sent to Archytes and my other friends in Taras, telling them the plight I was in. Finding some excuse for an embassy from their city, they sent a thirty-oared galley with Lamiskos, one of themselves,[138] who came and entreated Dionysios about me, saying that I wanted to go, and that he should on no account stand in my way. He consented and allowed me to go, giving me money for the journey. But for Dion's property I made no further request, nor was any of it restored.

b

I made my way to the Peloponnese to Olympia, where I found Dion a spectator at the Games, and told him what had occurred. Calling Zeus to be his witness, he at once urged me with my relatives and friends to make preparations for taking vengeance on Dionysios—our ground for action being the breach of faith to a guest—so he put it and regarded it, while his own was his unjust expulsion and banishment. Hearing this, I told him that he might call my friends to his aid, if they wished to go; "But for myself," I continued, "you and others in a way forced me to

c

be the sharer of Dionysios' table and hearth and his associate in the acts of religion. He probably believed the current slanders, that I was plotting with you against him and his despotic rule;

350 d yet feelings of scruple prevailed with him, and he spared my life. Again, I am hardly of the age for being comrade in arms to anyone; also I stand as a neutral between you, if ever you desire friendship and wish to benefit one another; so long as you aim at injuring one another, call others to your aid." This I said, because I was disgusted with my misguided journeyings to Sicily and my ill-fortune there. But they disobeyed me and would not listen to my attempts at reconciliation,[139] and so brought on their own heads all the evils which have since taken

e place. For if Dionysios had restored to Dion his property or been reconciled with him on any terms, none of these things would have happened, so far as human foresight can foretell. Dion would have easily been kept in check by my wishes and influence. But now, rushing upon one another, they have caused universal disaster.

351 a   Dion's[140] aspiration however was the same that I should say my own or that of any other right-minded man ought to be. With regard to his own power, his friends and his country the ideal of such a man would be to win the greatest power and honour by rendering the greatest services.[141] And this end is not attained if a man gets riches for himself, his supporters and his country, by forming plots and getting together conspirators, being all the while a poor creature,[142] not master of himself, overcome by the

b cowardice which fears to fight against pleasures; nor is it attained if he goes on to kill the men of substance, whom he speaks of as the enemy, and to plunder their possessions,[143] and invites his confederates and supporters to do the same, with the object that no one shall say that it is *his* fault, if he complains of being poor.[144] The same is true if anyone renders services of this kind to the State and receives honours from her for distributing by decrees the property of the few among the many—or if, being in charge of the affairs of a great State which rules over

c many small ones, he unjustly appropriates to his own State the possessions of the small ones. For neither a Dion nor any other man will, with his eyes open, make his way by steps like these to a power which will be fraught with destruction to himself and his descendants for all time; but he will advance towards constitutional government and the framing of the justest and best laws, reaching these ends without executions and murders even on the smallest scale.[145]

This course Dion actually followed, thinking it preferable to suffer iniquitous deeds rather than to do them;[146] but, while taking precautions against them, he nevertheless, when he had reached the climax of victory over his enemies, took a false step $\quad$ 351 d and fell, a catastrophe not at all surprising. For[147] a man of piety, temperance and wisdom, when dealing with the impious, would not be entirely blind to the character of such men; but it would perhaps not be surprising if he suffered the catastrophe that might befall a good ship's captain, who would not be entirely unaware of the approach of a storm, but might be unaware of its extraordinary and startling violence, and might therefore be overwhelmed by its force. The same thing caused Dion's downfall. For he was not unaware that his assailants were thoroughly bad men, but he was unaware how high a pitch of infatuation and of general wickedness and greed they had reached. This was the $\quad$ e cause of his downfall, which has involved Sicily in countless sorrows.

As[148] to the steps which should be taken after the events which $\quad$ 352 a I have now related, my advice has been given pretty fully and may be regarded as finished; and if you ask my reasons for recounting the story of my second journey to Sicily, it seemed to me essential that an account of it must be given[149] because of the strange and paradoxical character of the incidents. If in this present account of them they appear to anyone more intelligible, and seem to anyone to show sufficient grounds in view of the circumstances, the present statement is adequate and not too lengthy.

LETTER VIII

352 b Plato *to* the relatives and friends of Dion. Welfare.

Welfare[1]—Yes, and I will try, so far as my powers go, to describe to you what are the views most essential for you to hold in order to secure true welfare. And I hope to give advice

c which is profitable not to you alone, but to you in the first instance, and in the second place to all those at Syracuse, and thirdly to your enemies and opponents, unless any of them has done an act of monstrous impiety.[2] For such acts are incurable, and no one can wash out their stain. Consider what I have now to say.

Since the overthrow of the tyranny you have had throughout all Sicily every sort of conflict about that one issue, one side wishing to recover sovereign power, the others to put the finishing stroke to their escape from the tyranny. Now to the

d generality of men in such circumstances the right advice seems to be that one should recommend what will bring about as much harm as possible to their enemies and as much good as possible to their friends. But it is by no means easy for a man, who does much harm to others, to avoid suffering much harm himself.[3] You have not far to go in order to see clearly lessons of this sort in the events which have taken this course on the spot in Sicily— acts of aggression from one party and of retaliation from the

e other. You have only to tell the stories of these things to others, and you will always be capable teachers. Of lessons like this there is, I suppose, no lack. But those steps which will either be to the advantage of all, both foes and friends, or do the least harm to both sides—these are things which it is not easy to see, nor, having seen, to bring to pass. Such advice as this, and the exposition of it in words, seems something of the nature of a

353 a prayer.[4] Well, a prayer let it be by all means; for it is right to make the Gods the starting-point of all our speech and thoughts: and may it be brought to pass, giving to us, as it does, counsel to this effect:

You and your enemies, ever since the strife between you began, have been ruled over almost 5 continuously by one family, which your fathers set in authority as a counsel of utter despair at the time when the Greek States of Sicily were in imminent danger of being destroyed by the Carthaginians and completely absorbed among the barbarians. For they then chose Dionysios, as a young and warlike man, to direct those acts of war which were suited to his character, and Hipparinos, an older man, to be his adviser, in order to secure the safety of Sicily, entitling them monarchs with absolute power,6 as their phrase is. Now, whatever view anyone wishes to adopt about the cause of the safety which was then secured, whether it is attributed to the dispensation of providence and the act of God, or the personal qualities of those in power, or to both causes combined with the efforts of the citizens —let everyone hold his own opinion about this. In any case the fact remains that safety was secured by this step to the men of that generation.

353 b

Seeing then what sort of men they proved themselves, it is right, I suppose, that all should be grateful to those to whom they owe their safety. And if during the time which ensued the royal house made improper use of the gift which the State put in their hands, for this they have paid the penalty in part, and let them now pay what is still outstanding. What penalties therefore would be indubitably right in view of their present position? If you were able to secure your escape from them easily and without great dangers and efforts, or if they were able readily to re-establish their rule, it would not be possible to give the advice which I am now going to formulate. But, as it is, you must both of you reflect and remind yourselves, how often you have each of you cherished a hope which has again and again made you believe7 at the moment that you only needed some very trifling thing to enable you to carry out all that you desired; and yet the result has been that that very trifling thing has always been 8 the cause of great and unending troubles; and you never get to the end of the chapter, but a new beginning always starts out of what seemed to be an end of the old; and, as the wheel goes round, both the tyrannical and the popular party will run the risk of being

c

d

e

utterly destroyed by it; and if the probable result happens, which God forbid, the Greek language will become as good as obsolete throughout all Sicily, which will pass under the power and rule of Carthaginians or Oscan[9] tribes. These are the symptoms for which all the Greeks must, with all the zeal they may, find a cure.[10]

354a If then anyone has anything that is more right and good than what I am about to propose, let him bring it forward, and he will have the best right to be called a Phil-Hellene. What my views under the present circumstances are, I shall attempt to show with all outspokenness, and shall make a just and impartial proposal.

Speaking, in a manner, as arbitrator between two parties, ex-monarch and ex-subject, and treating each as a single person, I give my old advice.[11] Now once more my word of counsel to every absolute monarch would be to fly from that name and

b thing, and change his position, if that be possible, into a limited monarchy. And it is possible, as that wise and good man Lykourgos proved in fact, who, seeing that his kinsmen[12] in Argos and Messene had advanced from the position of constitutional to that of absolute monarchs, and had thus each of them brought to ruin themselves and their respective States, and fearing for his own State and also for his own family, prescribed as a medicine the office of Senator, and the salutary check of the Ephorate on the royal power,[13] so that it has been preserved for

c all these generations without loss of prestige, since law was made the true sovereign power over men, instead of making men masters of the laws.

So this is now my word of exhortation to all—to the aspirants for tyranny, that they should turn their backs and fly at the top of their speed[14] from that ideal of happiness which attracts foolish men of insatiable appetite, and try to change the constitution to a limited monarchy, and be subject to laws befitting constitutional kings, retaining the highest personal honours as a free

d gift from their subjects and from the laws. To those on the other hand who pursue principles of freedom, and fly from the yoke of subjection as an evil thing, my counsel would be that they should have a care lest, in their insatiable craving for unseasonable liberty, they fall one day into the malady of their forefathers, which the men of that time suffered through carrying to excess their opposition to authority, being victims of a passion for liberty which knew no bounds. For the Sicilian Greeks of those days before the rule of Dionysios and Hipparinos lived what they supposed to be a happy life—a life of self-indulgence in which they ruled over their rulers; and they actually stoned[15] to death, without any legal trial, the ten generals who preceded Dionysios, with the object, if you please, that they might be subject to no master, even if his power rested on justice or on law, and might enjoy complete and absolute freedom. It was from this cause that tyrannies became their lot.[16] For subjection and freedom, if either of them is carried to excess, are all-evil; but each of them within proper bounds is all-good. Subjection within proper bounds is the service of God—that which exceeds proper bounds is subjection to men. God, for men of discretion, means law[17]—but pleasure is the God of fools.

354e

355a

Since this is the fundamental nature of things, I call on the friends of Dion to declare to all the Syracusans my advice, which is the joint counsel of Dion and myself. As his spokesman I will set forth what he would now have said to you, if he were alive and able to speak. "Well," someone will say, "what message does Dion's advice unfold to us about the present position of affairs?" It is as follows:

"Men of Syracuse, your first and foremost duty is to put yourselves under laws which show unmistakeably that their effect will not be likely to turn your minds with desire towards money-making and wealth, but which, since there are three[18] things to be considered, soul, body, and possessions, give the highest honour to excellence of soul, the second to excellence of body as lying beneath that of the soul, and put third and last the honour due to possessions, as subject both to soul and body. The ordinance which gives effect to this will be a law rightly enacted for you, making those who follow it truly happy.[19] But that way of talking which calls the rich happy is miserable in itself, being indeed the foolish talk of women and children, and it makes miserable those who believe it.

b

c

"You have only to taste and see the effect of my advice about

laws, and the truth of what I am now telling you will be known to
you by actual experience, which seems to be the surest test in all
355 d cases. Next, after receiving laws of this character,[20] since Sicily
is beset with danger and you are neither in a position of full
mastery nor, on the other hand, are decisively under the
mastery of others, it will perhaps be fair and expedient for both
parties among you to take a middle course[21]—I mean, for you
who are trying to escape the severity of any form of supreme
power, and for those who are eager to get the supreme power into
their own hands again. Now the ancestors of these latter on that
occasion saved the Greeks from the barbarians—the greatest of
all services—and one which renders it possible now to discuss
forms of constitution. For had they been overwhelmed then,
there could have been no discussion nor hope of any kind any-
e where. Now, therefore, let the one side enjoy freedom under
monarchical rule, and the others supreme power in the form of a
responsible monarchy, with the laws holding absolute authority
not only over the other citizens but also over the kings themselves, if they attempt anything unconstitutional.

"On the basis of all this do you, with all sincerity and soundness of purpose and with the Gods helping you, set up as king—
in the first place, my own son,[22] as a reward for two services, that
356 a rendered by me, and that rendered by my father; for he at that
time freed the city from barbarians, and I have now twice freed
it from tyrants, as you yourselves have witnessed. As your
second king appoint my father's namesake, the son of Dionysios
(i.e. of Dionysios the elder) in gratitude for the help which he
has now rendered you and his pious temperament; for, though
the son of an autocrat, he is voluntarily setting his country free,[23]
and thus gaining for himself and his family everlasting honour in
place of a shortlived and wrongful despotism. The third person[24]
whom you must invite to be king of Syracuse, a willing sovereign
b of a willing State, is the man who is now in chief command of the
forces of your enemies, Dionysios, the son of Dionysios, if he will
consent voluntarily to change to the status of constitutional monarch, fearing the despot's doom and pitying his own country,
with her temples robbed of their worship and graves[25] neglected,

lest he may, to gratify his ambition, involve everything in utter destruction, with the barbarians exulting over his fall.

"Your three kings, whether you give them the powers of the Spartan kings,[26] or something less by compact, you must appoint in something like the following way, which has already been described to you,[27] but which nevertheless you must once more listen to. If the family of Dionysios and Hipparinos are willing to put an end to the present disorders with a view to the safety of Sicily, receiving honours for themselves and their descendants for the future as well as for the present, you must on this understanding invite, as was said before, commissioners, approved of by both parties, either men on the spot, or from elsewhere, or both, and in such numbers as the parties shall agree to, and these must have full powers to draw up the terms of the settlement. These commissioners, on their arrival, must first draw up laws and a constitution, in which it is fitting that the kings shall have control of religion, and such other matters as may suitably be assigned to those who have been public benefactors. But the executive power in war and peace must be put in the hands of thirty-five nomophylakes[28] acting jointly with the assembly of the people and the Senate. They must establish law-courts for the different classes of cases, but the thirty-five must be judges in all cases where the penalty is death or banishment; and with them must be associated judges selected every year from the magistrates of the preceding year,[29] one from each magistracy who seems to be the best and most just. These must act as judges in the ensuing year in all cases where the penalty is death, imprisonment, or deportation. A king must not be permitted to be a judge in cases of this kind, being like a priest, who must be pure from all contact with bloodshed, imprisonment and exile.

"This is the constitution which, while I lived, I thought ought to be established for you, and I still think so; and at the time, when with your aid I had got the better of our enemies, I should, if powers of evil working by the hands of friends[30] had not prevented me, have established it; and afterwards, if events had answered the purpose, I should have resettled the rest of Sicily, taking from the barbarians, excepting those who fought on our

356c

d

e

357a

b

side in defence of liberty against the tyranny, the portion which is in their hands, and re-establishing the former inhabitants of the Greek territories in their ancient and ancestral abodes. And now my advice to all is that you should jointly adopt these same aims and take action upon them, that you should invite all to aid in these actions, and treat as a common enemy anyone who refuses.

"These are not impossibilities. For when a policy has already been adopted by two minds, and presents itself as obviously the best course for reasoning men to adopt,[31] surely the man who

357 c pronounces it an impossibility is ill-advised. The two minds that I mean are those of Hipparinos the son of Dionysios and my own son. For now that these two have come to an agreement,[32] I assume their views are shared by the rest of the Syracusans who care for their country. But do you, after offering worship and prayer to all the Gods and to all the powers which it is fitting to worship with the Gods, persuade and exhort both friends and adversaries, gently and in every way you can, and cease not, until

d you have worked out in the light of the day and brought to a prosperous completion those things which I have told you as heaven-sent visions vouchsafed to the waking eye."[33]

LETTER IX

Plato *to* Archytas the Tarentine. Welfare.

e Archippos and Philonides with their party have arrived, bringing the letter which you gave them and reporting the news of you. Their mission to the city they have accomplished without difficulty—for it was not an altogether laborious matter. In the news of you which they have given to me they state that you are a little troubled because you cannot free yourself from the want of leisure[1] caused by your public duties. It is of course obvious to anyone that the pleasantest thing in life is to devote oneself to

358 a one's own pursuits, especially if a man choose such pursuits as you have chosen.[2] But you must also bear in mind that each of

us is not born for himself alone, but our country has its share in our birth, our parents have their share, and so have the rest of our friends; the course of events too in which our life is involved makes many claims upon us. When our country's voice calls us to public duties, it is surely strange conduct to turn a deaf ear. For we cannot do so without leaving[3] the ground clear to inferior characters, who approach public affairs from motives which are not the highest. Enough of this.

358b

Echekrates is already an object of care to me, and shall continue to be so in the future for your sake, and for that of his father, Phrynion, as well as for the qualities of the young man himself.

LETTER X

Plato *to* Aristodoros. Welfare.

I hear that you are, and have consistently been, one of the most devoted supporters of Dion, showing the wisest disposition in matters appertaining to philosophy. For constancy, good faith, soundness of mind[1]—these are the things which I call true philosophy. Other forms of wisdom and cleverness, which have other objects, I think I should call by their right name, if I described them as accomplishments.[2]

c

Farewell, and keep the same disposition which you now have.

LETTER XI

Plato *to* Laodamas. Welfare.

I wrote to you before that, with a view to all the objects which you mention, far the best course is for you to come to Athens yourself. But since you say that this is impossible, the next best course, as you urged in your letter, was that, if it were possible, I or Sokrates[1] should go to you. Now Sokrates is in a state of poor health[2] caused by stranguria, and for me to go and fail in the objects for which you invite me would not be creditable.[3]

d

e

But I have no great hope of the possibility of accomplishing those objects—my reasons for this would require another long letter giving full details; besides, at my time of life I have not the bodily strength requisite for travelling and facing the sort of dangers which meet one by land and sea; and at the present time all the routes are full of dangers.[4]

359 a   I can, however, give to you and the colonists a piece of advice which, in Hesiod's words,[5] may seem trivial when I have uttered it, but was not easy to think of. For if they suppose[6] it possible for a constitution to be well established by the passing of laws, however good they may be, without the existence of any authority which looks after the manner of life of free citizens and of slaves, making it temperate and manly, they are mistaken.

b   Now this authority might be created, if there are men worthy of holding such power. But if you need someone to educate them, then, as I think, you neither have your future educator, nor those who will be taught by him, and you can only pray to the Gods for the future.[7] For it was in much the same way that States got their constitutions in former days and afterwards were well administered,[8] as a result of conjunctions of important events occurring in war or in other affairs, when at such crises there has arisen a man of fine character with great power in his hands. It

c   is necessary and essential that there must first be a desire for such ideals; you must, however, believe them to be the kind of thing which I am telling you, and must not be under any illusions, supposing them to be easy of accomplishment. Good luck to you.

LETTER XII

Plato *to* Archytas the Tarentine. Welfare.

d   I was delighted beyond measure to receive the notes which have arrived from you, and am completely lost in wonder[1] at their author. The man seems to me to be worthy of those old forefathers of his: for these are spoken of in the story as the Ter

Thousand,² and are said to have belonged to those driven out of Troy in the time of Laomedon, good men, as the tradition shows.

My notes, about which you wrote to me, are not yet completed; but, such as they are, I send them to you. With regard to their 359 e safe-keeping³ we are both agreed; so there is no need for admonitions.

LETTER XIII

Plato *to* Dionysios, Monarch of Syracuse. Welfare.   360 a

Let me begin my letter to you with something that will serve as a token that it comes from me. Once when you were giving a banquet to the young men from Lokroi and when you were seated at a distance from me, you rose up, came over to me, and in an affectionate way said something which was happily expressed, as it seemed to me and to my neighbour, a man of the   b better sort, who thereupon¹ said; "Truly, Dionysios, you are much benefited in wisdom by Plato." "And in many other things too", you replied, "for immediately after sending for him, I felt myself benefited by the mere fact that I had sent for him." Keep this spirit in order that the benefits we get from one another may go on always increasing.

With a view to promoting this object now I am sending you   c some bits of Pythagorean² work and some specimens of division, and with them, as it was then agreed between us, a man of whom you and Archytes, if Archytes³ has by this time come to you, might be able to make some use. His name is Helikon. He belongs by birth to Kyzikos,⁴ and is a pupil of Eudoxos and well up in all the teaching of Eudoxos. He has also had lessons from one of the pupils of Isokrates, and from Polyxenos,⁵ one of Bryson's school. What is a rare thing in a man of such antecedents, he is not an unpleasing man to converse with, and looks not at all a bad sort, but would seem rather to be a cheery⁶ and   d simple-hearted person. I say this with fear and trembling, because I am speaking of one of the genus "homo", an animal not altogether to be despised,⁷ but still a changeable creature, with the exception of very few individuals in a few spheres of action. About him also I had my doubts, and therefore observed him for myself when I was conversing with him, and made enquiries from his fellow-citizens; but none had anything unfavourable to report of him. Observe him for yourself, however, and be on your guard. Above all, if you have any spare time[8]

360 e whatever, learn from him and carry on your other philosophical studies. If you have no time, get someone else taught by him, that you may learn when you have leisure, and may become a better man and make a name for yourself;[9] there will then be no cessation in the benefits which you receive from me. Enough of this.

361 a With regard to the things which you asked me to send you— I had the Apollo made, and Leptines is bringing it to you. It is the work of an excellent young sculptor called Leochares.[10] Another work in his atelier was very charming as it seemed to me. I therefore bought it, wishing to give it to your wife, because she cared for me in health and sickness in a way worthy of you and me. Please give it to her, unless you disapprove. I also send twelve jars of sweet wine for your children,

b and two of honey. I arrived after the season for storing figs.[11] Myrtle-berries had been stored, but had gone bad. But we will manage better another time. Leptines will give you all information about our plants.

The money to meet these expenses, both for the foregoing items and for certain dues to the State, I got from Leptines, telling him what seemed to me to put my own conduct in a proper light, besides being true—that the money which I had spent on the Leukadian ship, about sixteen minae, was my own.[12]

c I therefore took this sum from him and used it for my own purposes and for these things which I send to you.

Next let me tell you how things stand for you in the matter of money, both your own money at Athens and mine. As I said to you before, I shall make use of your money in the same way as I do that of my other friends. I use as little as possible, the minimum that seems to be necessary or just or creditable to me and to the men upon whom I am drawing. Now a need of this kind has arisen

for me at the present time. There are four daughters of those 361 d
nieces of mine who died on the occasion when I did not put on a
garland, though you urged me to do so :¹³ one of them has now
reached a marriageable age, one is eight years old, another a little
over three, and another not quite a year; it is for me and my friends
to find marriage portions for them, if I am alive when the time
comes; if not, they must take their chance. I am not called on to
find portions for those whose fathers become richer than I; but,
as it is, I am in easier circumstances than they, and it was I who
found portions for their mothers with the aid of Dion and other   e
friends. The first of these is about to marry Speusippos, being
his sister's daughter. For her I require thirty minae and no
more;¹⁴ this is a decent dowry with us. Also, if my mother dies,
I shall require ten minae and no more for her monument.¹⁵
With regard to expenses this is about all that is necessary for me
at the present time. But if any other outlay, public or private,
falls upon me because of my visit to you, I must do as I said to
you at the time, namely, use every effort to make the outlay as
small as possible, but the cost, where it is unavoidable, must fall   362 a
upon you.

The next point which I have to tell you concerns the expenditure of your money here at Athens. In the first place, if I
have to incur any public expenditure for furnishing (on your
behalf)¹⁶ a chorus or anything of that sort, there is not, as we
fancied there would be, any agent of yours who will give it. In
the next place, if there is any matter which is of great importance
to you personally, and prompt payment will advance your
interests, but delay till some representative of yours arrives will
be prejudicial to you, such an occurrence not only causes
difficulties but brings you discredit. Now I have put this to the   b
test myself by sending Erastos to your correspondent Andromedes the Aeginetan,¹⁷ from whom you used to tell me to obtain
funds, if ever I needed them; for I wished, in accordance with
your instructions,¹⁸ to send other more substantial things. He
sent back a reasonable and natural answer, that he had formerly
incurred expenditure for your father and had had great difficulty
in recovering the money, and that now he would give a small

sum and no more. Under these circumstances I took the money from Leptines, and I must praise Leptines for this—not that he gave the money, but that he gave it readily, and in all other

362 c matters he was evidently doing for you, both in speech and action, whatever a friend can do. For it is right for me to report to you conduct of this kind and the reverse,[19] and to give you my impressions of the way in which different individuals are acting towards you.

With regard to money matters I shall speak plainly to you; for this is right, and at the same time I shall be speaking with some experience of the people you have about you. Those who make reports to you from time to time with regard to any expenditure which they think it suitable to propose, are reluctant to report

d the facts for fear of incurring your ill-will. You must accustom and compel them to speak about these and other matters. For you ought to know all details, as far as you can, and judge for yourself, and not shirk knowledge. For of all things this will be the most serviceable to your position as ruler; and I know that your verdict is, and will be, that accuracy in incurring and repaying expenditure is a good thing generally and tends to augment your resources. Therefore do not let those who profess to care for your interests bring you into discredit with the world. For it is neither good nor creditable to your reputation

e that you should be considered difficult to deal with.

In the next place I will speak about Dion.[20] With regard to other points I cannot yet speak till letters arrive from you, as you promised. With regard, however, to that special point, which you forbade me to mention, I have not mentioned it nor talked about it; but I tried to see whether he would take it well or ill, if such a step were carried out, and it seemed to me that he would be not a little aggrieved. In other respects Dion's speech and action with reference to you seems to me to show good feeling.

363 a To my friend Kratinos,[21] brother of Timotheos, let us make a present of a hoplite's cuirass, one of the padded ones used by infantry, and to the daughters of Kebes three under-tunics of the seven-cubit size, not the costly ones of Amorgos fabric, but of Sicilian linen. The name of Kebes is familiar to you; for he is

represented in the Sokratic dialogues as speaking to Sokrates along with Simmias in the discussion about the soul,[22] and is a friend and well-wisher to us all.

With regard to the pass-word[23] which indicates the letters 363b which I am writing urgently and the reverse, I fancy you remember, but nevertheless you must understand and attend to it. For there are many who press me to write to whom I cannot give a simple refusal. The urgent letter has "God" in the superscription, and the less serious one "Gods".

The[24] ambassadors begged me to write to you, and naturally so,—for they are loud in their praises of you and me in all directions—especially Philagros, who at that time was suffering from a bad hand. Philaides also, who had arrived from a   c mission to the King of Persia, spoke about you. If it did not require a long letter, I should have written what he said. As it is, you must make enquiries from Leptines.

If you send the cuirass or any other of the things which I mention, entrust them to any one whom you select, or else give them to Terillos.[25] He is one of those who are constantly making the journey, a friend of mine and a man of sound views both in philosophy and in other matters. He is connected by marriage with Teison, who was one of the Board of Works when I left you.

Farewell.—Devote yourself to philosophy and encourage the rest of your contemporaries to do the same. Give my greetings   d to your tennis-club.[26] Instruct them all and particularly Aristokritos that if any message or letter arrives from me for you, they must see that you know of it as soon as possible, and re-mind you to attend to its contents. When you receive this, do not forget about the repayment of the money due to Leptines, but pay it without loss of time, in order that other people, when they see how he is treated, may be more anxious to do us good service.

Iatrokles, who was set free by me (you know when) along with   e Myronides, is sailing now with those whom I am sending. Take him into your service in some paid capacity, and make any use of him that you wish;—for he is devoted to you. Keep this letter or a memorandum about it, and be the same good friend you always were.

NOTES

ABBREVIATIONS

Bt. = J. Burnet. *Phil.* = *Greek Philosophy from Thales to Plato.* Rit. = C. Ritter. *N.U.* = *Neue Untersuchungen.* Tayl. = A. E. Taylor. Hack. = R. Hackforth. Raed. = H. Raeder. Ad. = R. Adam. Andr. = W. Andreae. Sou. = J. Souilhé. Wtz. = U. von Wilamowitz-Moellendorff. How. = E. Howald. Kar. = H. T. Karsten.

For titles of the works referred to see the list which follows the preface.

EPISTLE I

Introductory Remarks

This letter must remain an unsolved problem. The style is not that of Plato, and the writer's relations with the tyrant whom he addresses bear no resemblance to those of Plato with Dionysios II. The early editors did not improve matters by altering the name in the heading from Plato to Dion. For even if we allow, what is most unlikely, that Dion would have written to Dionysios in Attic Greek, a Syracusan would not have spoken of Syracuse as "your city". The poetical quotations suggest the idea of a school exercise. It is not the ordinary type of fictitious letter, and Bt. (*Phil.* p. 205) regards it as a genuine fourth-century letter, "which has got into its present place by mistake". His idea perhaps was that a former pupil of the Academy had been attached to the service of some tyrant, and, having returned to Athens after a rupture with him, wrote this angry letter, and placed a copy of it among Academy papers.

The atmosphere of the letter suggests the affairs of Syracuse and, if it was addressed to Dionysios II, the plural pronouns in the earlier part of it (ὑμῖν, ὑμῶν) may be regarded as referring to his father as well as himself. The abrupt change to the singular σύ is then accounted for. But it is not easy to assign the letter to any known person in connection with Sicilian affairs. Immisch (*Philologus*, vol. LXXVIII) suggests that it may be an expansion by Timaios of a genuine letter from the Spartan Dexippos to Dionysios I, which may, he imagines, have been preserved in the history of Philistos. But it is not likely that anyone, editing a collection of letters which professed to be by Plato, would have transferred to it one which appeared under another name in a well-known work. The letter was known to the author of the 24th Sokratic Epistle, who regards it as a letter from Plato, and it has probably been in its present place from a date prior to Aristophanes of Byzantium. The stilted style and poetical quotations are suggestive of a rhetorical exercise, composed perhaps by a writer who assumes the character of Dion, but deals rather freely with his historical circumstances.

1. "Welfare." Εὖ πράττειν covers the two meanings—"May your actions and your fortune be good". Plato adopted this greeting instead of the usual χαίρειν for reasons which he gives at the beginning of the 3rd letter. Any member of his School may have followed his practice. The formula seems to be confined to the Platonic Epistles and to imitations of them. See Ep. III n. 1.

2. 309 b 2. αὐτοκράτωρ, a common word in connection with Syracusan affairs. Στρατηγὸς αὐτοκράτωρ was a title assumed by Gelon, Dionysios I and II, Dion and Agathokles, and was applicable to anyone holding an appointment which set him above the Ekklesia; cf. 353 b 3.

3. 309 b 7. τρόπον ἀπανθ. The words which follow (σὺ δὲ κ.τ.λ.) belong to a passage in iambic verse. A line of the same passage may have ended with ἀπάνθρωπον τρόπον. For ἀπάνθρωπον we have to choose between the meanings "inhuman" and "remote from humanity". Plutarch (Dion, 7) uses the word in the former sense, and may have given it that sense here. The other meaning is supported by Aesch. P.V. 20, and was given to the word by the author of Sokr. Ep. 24. If we had the piece of poetry in full, we might find the words ἀπάνθρωπος τρόπος used to describe a character of the type of Timon. We should then have an explanation of the curious myth that Plato himself, on his return from Syracuse, adopted for a time the habits of Timon.

4. 309 c 6. ὥστε with an imperative clause is in character with the poetical style of the letter; cf. Soph. El. 1172, θνητὸς δ' Ὀρέστης· ὥστε μὴ λίαν στένε.

5. 309 d 5. διότι for ὅτι (that) is usually regarded as a sign of late Attic Greek; but it is used by Isokrates (Plataicus, 23; Antid. 133) and may have been common in the colloquial and epistolary language of the fourth century.

6. 310 a 1. φίλων ἔρημος κ.τ.λ. An iambic senarius, probably from some lost play. The words τοῖς νοῦν ἔχουσιν κ.τ.λ. in the following sentence are also a senarius; but the metre may be only a result of the high-flown style.

7. 310 a 4. οὐ χρυσὸς κ.τ.λ. These verses are only known as quoted here. The lyric poem from which they are taken may have been one resembling that which Horace had in mind when he wrote:

Non ebur neque aureum
Mea renidet in domo lacunar (Od. II. 18).

How. points out that there is a prosaic touch in δοκιμαζόμενα and αὐτάρκεις. He thinks that the lyric belongs to the fourth century, and may have been composed by the writer of the letter. I have translated Bt.'s text; but the second line evidently calls for correction, and Immisch's restoration seems probable; οὐκ ἀδάμας οὐδ' ἀργύρου κλεινὰ πρὸς ἄνθρωπον δοκιμαζομένα στράπτει πρόσοψις, "Nor does adamant nor the glorious sight of silver flash forth when put to the test in comparison with a man"; i.e. A good man and true is worth more than steel or silver. This gets rid of the unnecessary "couches", and removes difficulties of concord which are hardly possible even in lyric poetry. Immisch's further suggestion of βρίθοντ' (=βρίθοντι) for βρίθοντες is unnecessary and spoils the metre; γύαι is, of course, from the masc. γύης.

8. 310 b 1. τοσ. ἡμ. διημ. can hardly mean, as Post and Bury render, "how great a loss you have suffered in me". It must be, "that you have gone so far astray from me", i.e. failed so completely to understand me.

EPISTLE II

Introductory Remarks.

Dionysios has sent Archedemos, a Syracusan philosopher, much esteemed by Plato, to Athens conveying

(1) A request that Plato will restrain his associates from speech and action adverse to Dionysios.

(2) An enquiry what the future relations between Plato and the monarch are to be.

(3) A model connected with his mathematical or astronomical studies.

(4) A question as to Plato's fundamental position in philosophy.

(5) Some messages about personal matters.

This letter purports to be the reply which Plato sent back by the hand of Archedemos. The first point is dealt with briefly in the first fifteen lines, and the personal matters in the last nineteen lines. The rest of the letter is devoted to the philosophical relations between Plato and Dionysios. There is nothing about politics, and no reference to Dion's property, which figures so largely in the 7th and 3rd letters. The writer's object is to impress two points on the mind of Dionysios: (1) that if he intends to make a serious study of philosophy, he must begin by feeling and showing a proper respect for his teacher; (2) that in philosophy he must not expect to jump at once to the solution of ultimate questions, and that enlightenment is only likely to come after a prolonged period of study.

Two questions call for discussion: (1) Is the letter genuine? (2) If so, was it written during the interval between Plato's two visits to the younger Dionysios or after his last visit?

(1) On the question of genuineness the most important evidence is that of the letter itself. It is certainly not a letter which might have been written by anyone. Its contents are remarkable, and while some critics feel that it contains things which Plato could not possibly have written, others are convinced that there are portions of it which no mind but that of Plato is likely to have produced. These opposite impressions have been caused by the cryptic passage in 312 e and the two following pages. To me this passage seems to afford the strongest evidence of the genuineness of the letter. If Plato was not the author of it, who was, and where are his other writings? For the writer was

certainly a master of thought and language; he was not working up
material which is to be found in Plato's Dialogues, and only a very
small part of the thought occurs in the 7th Epistle. It seems waste of
time to argue with those who condemn all mystery-making as un-
Platonic. Surely the Dialogues afford sufficient evidence that Plato was
fond of combining a jest with the things that are most earnest, and that,
like Goethe, he never lost his liking for a little piece of mystification.
One of the earliest charges brought against him by adverse Greek
critics was that he had "much of the hierophant about him" (Demetrius Phalereus, ap. Dion. Hal. *Ep. ad Pomp.* § 760).

On the other side it is urged that the list of monarchs associated with
philosophers and poets in the earlier part of the letter is long and
tedious, and that the request that Dionysios will take the initiative in
honouring Plato is unworthy of the character of the philosopher. It
must be remembered, with regard to the first of these points, that the
writer's object is not to create a work of art, but to produce certain
effects on the mind of Dionysios—a man still young and not without
good points in his character, in spite of tendencies to self-indulgence
and conceit, gifted with intelligence and anxious to shine in philosophy,
at the same time the absolute ruler of what was then the greatest power
in the Greek world. A careful study of the central part of the letter will
show that it is not ill adapted to produce the effect desired by the writer.

As regards the second point we have to face the fact that Plato's
outspoken request for marks of honour, which gives a shock to the
modern reader, is not out of character. He has to make it clear that the
absolute monarch, who wishes to learn philosophy, must give the place
of honour to his teacher, and he would not have regarded it as an act
of undue assumption, when the *bhikku* Nigrodha took his seat on the
throne of the emperor Asoka (*Mahavaṃsa*, v, 65). By the Greek of
Plato's day the pursuit of honour was regarded as an essential feature in
the ideal character. Plato himself had a strong feeling of its importance
and makes no secret about it (cf. *Laws*, 727 a, 921 e, Ep. IV *ad init.*).
The Stoic depreciation of δοξάριον belongs to a later age. (See note on
312 b 8.)

The style of the letter resembles that of the 7th, which the writer has
been accused of imitating. It differs in the fact that there is no effort
to avoid illegitimate hiatus. But this is intelligible, if Ep. II was written
by Plato at an earlier date, when he had not formed the habit of avoiding hiatus, but difficult to account for if it was the work of a later writer
imitating Ep. VII. Rit.'s attempt to prove by stylometric tests that the
2nd, 6th and 13th letters form a group with characteristics of their own
breaks down completely. The three letters undoubtedly agree in their
use of certain words and particles. But if the argument is to be worth
anything, these must be proved to be confined to this group. Many of
them certainly are not, but occur in other letters which Rit. himself
accepts as genuine. Some, as ταῦτα μὲν ταύτῃ, are common in the later
Dialogues.

The writer's attitude with regard to philosophy and its teaching harmonises with what we learn of Plato in his later life from his Dialogues, from the statements made about him by Aristotle, and from those which he makes about himself in the 7th Epistle. In particular this is true of his refusal to give a written answer to the question, What is the nature of his First Principle in philosophy? His answer is confined to a few remarks in enigmatical language, which admit of more than one explanation (see note on 312 e 1). But Dionysios is told to state all his difficulties to Archedemos, and we must assume that Archedemos has received instructions from Plato as to a course of study to be carried out by Dionysios under his directions. If, after completing this, Dionysios still has difficulties, Archedemos may be sent to Plato again with a statement of them. After some few periods of instruction carried out in this way Dionysios will find that he is gaining an entirely new light on the questions which are troubling him.

Raed., who accepts the letter as genuine, holds that the whole passage about the proposed visits of Archedemos is ironical, and that Plato is simply jeering at the question of Dionysios. The word θεοφιλεστέραν (313 e) shows that such a view is out of the question. In Ep. VII we are told that Archedemos was a pupil of Archytas, and that Plato thought more highly of him than of anyone else in Sicily (339 a), and was for some time living in his house. He may have been quite serious in proposing that the personal teaching, so essential in philosophy, might be given to the monarch by such a man. The visits of Archedemos to Athens, to refer doubtful points to Plato, are a not unnatural concession to the self-importance of Dionysios. Plato may have smiled, as he made that part of the suggestion, and yet have been in earnest in his desire to encourage study on the part of Dionysios.

A small indication of genuineness worth notice is the hint at contending philosophical views in the lines 312 a 3–7. The inner meaning here has been missed by some editors, but must have been at once apparent to Dionysios (see notes 12 and 13). No forger would have indicated the point in so delicate a manner.

(2) The question of the date of the letter is connected with that of its genuineness. The fact that its supporters cannot agree as to its date has been made a ground for suspicion. It professes to have been written not long after a celebration of the Olympic Games at which both Plato and Dion were present. Are the Games referred to those of 364 B.C. or those of 360 B.C.? In other words, are we to suppose that the letter belongs to the interval between Plato's last two visits to Syracuse or to the period after his final return to Athens? The two historians who accept the letter as genuine, Grote and E. Meyer (whose opinion is entitled to great weight), prefer 360 B.C., when both Plato and Dion are known to have been present. Recent commentators, Raeder, Apelt, Andreae and Post, prefer 364 B.C. It is in fact possible to make out a plausible case against either date. Let us first suppose the Games of Ep. II to be those of 360 B.C. The objectors urge that in that case Plato

is giving Dionysios an untrue account of what occurred. But this by no means follows. Plato is answering the charge that his associates had spoken evil of Dionysios. He replies that he had heard nothing of the sort, and that the monarch's informants must have had better ears than his. There is nothing here that is necessarily inconsistent with the account of the happenings at Olympia in 360 B.C. given in Ep. VII 350 b–d. Dion had then, no doubt, spoken against Dionysios; but he is expressly excluded by the terms of the question with which Plato is dealing in Ep. II. We have no information as to anything said by Plato's other friends, and it is not impossible that he was able truthfully to contradict the report which had found its way to Dionysios.

Plato may, of course, have attended the Games of 364 B.C.; and the fact that his visit on that occasion is not mentioned would be no obstacle to our assigning the letter to that date if its other contents harmonised with it. But on the question of date, as on the question of genuineness, the philosophical contents of the letter are the most important part of the evidence. In the 2nd letter we are told (313 a, b) of an interview between Plato and Dionysios "in the garden under the laurels", in which deep philosophical questions were discussed; and Dionysios professed to have already arrived at his own solution of certain problems. Can such an interview have taken place during the earlier of Plato's two visits to Dionysios?

In the 7th letter the philosophical relations between Plato and Dionysios are fully dealt with. Speaking of the latter part of his first visit to the tyrant, Plato states that Dionysios refused to receive any instruction in philosophy from him (330 a, b). Again, when speaking of the state of Dionysios' knowledge during the interval between his two visits (338 d, e), he said that Dionysios had received no instruction from him during his first visit. One of the main objects of Plato's last visit was to give to the monarch instruction in philosophy, if he was in earnest in desiring it; and in the 7th Epistle (340 b–341 b) we have an account of his procedure. Again, in 345 a, Plato states definitely that he gave Dionysios one lesson (μία συνουσία), and one only, and no other on any subsequent occasion. If, therefore, we regard the 2nd and 7th letters as both genuine, it follows that the discussion in the 2nd letter must be the same as the συνουσία described in the 7th, and we have no choice except to date the 2nd letter after the Games of 360 B.C.*

---

* I have not thought it necessary to discuss Mr Post's later attempt (Cl. Rev. vol. XLI, p. 58) to show that the interview under the laurels of Ep. II, 313 a, may, without inconsistency with the statements in the 7th Epistle, be regarded as having taken place during Plato's first visit to the younger Dionysios, on the ground that what passed in it was only information and exhortation, not instruction. I can only ask the reader to refer again to Plato's thrice repeated statement (330 a, b, 338 d, e, 345 a) about the intercourse between himself and Dionysios during his first visit to the monarch, and to decide for himself whether Plato could have used such language if the philosophical discussion described in Ep. II, 313 a, b, had taken place during that visit.

Is 360 B.C. an improbable date for the letter on other grounds? Rit. (*N.U.* p. 372) states that, if the contents oblige us to assign it to this date, it must necessarily be a forgery. He does not give his reasons; but apparently he means that the breach between Plato and Dionysios at this date was so complete as to render further correspondence between them impossible. This is a deduction from his own purely arbitrary theory that Plato's only motive for making his last journey to Sicily was to look after the interests of Dion. But a fair reading of the 7th Epistle shows that Plato was quite as much influenced by the desire not to miss a chance, if there was one, of the conversion of Dionysios to the philosophic life. It is also clear from what he said to Dion at Olympia (350 c, d) that he cherished no animosity against Dionysios personally. He was not a vindictive man, and he regarded philosophy as much the most important concern for any man, whoever he might be. He recognised that Dionysios had good natural ability (338 d 6), and it is not unreasonable to suppose that, if he saw any possibility of helping him, even at the eleventh hour, to a sounder study of the necessary groundwork of philosophical thought, he would try to take advantage of it. If we suppose that the mission of Archedemos took place at some date not long after the Olympic Games of 360 B.C., it may well have put Plato's mind once more into the state so vividly described in Ep. VII, 339 e—unwillingness to take the risk of missing any opportunity of saving a soul.

At the same time we need not imagine that the mission arose from any desire for salvation on the part of Dionysios. We may assume that his informants, on their arrival from Olympia, told him that Dion had been talking big about reprisals. It was worth his while to take steps to embarrass Dion, and Plato might suitably be requested to use his influence with his own friends. There had been no outward breach of friendly relations between them: Plato owed and acknowledged a debt of gratitude to the monarch, and had openly refused to assist the action threatened by Dion. Dionysios may well have pressed him to go farther and prevent his own associates from joining in any aggressions. Plato could not be expected to restrain Dion from taking action with the aid of his Peloponnesian friends, but he might prevent him from getting supporters from Athens.

Read in this light, the early part of the 2nd Epistle applies very well to the position in the latter part of 360 B.C., before Dion had actually begun to enlist mercenaries—better, in fact, than to the state of affairs in 364 B.C.

There is one minor point in the 2nd Epistle which harmonises better with the later than with the earlier date. The request of Speusippos (314 e) that Dionysios would lend him the services of his court physician Philistion is not likely to have been made before Speusippos had visited Syracuse.*

* Some portions of the above, which deal with the date of the letter, are reprinted from a paper by me in the *Classical Review* for December, 1926.

1. 310 c 5. μέγας. In *Laws*, 732 a, we have μέγας for a "a man of high ideals". Here it more probably has the sense of "powerful", as in tragedy; cf. Eur. *Med.* 549; *Tro.* 669. I have made λόγῳ refer to Plato's teaching; but it may be a reference to his intention of being neutral, announced in 350 d.

2. 310 c 7. For Polyxenos see Bt., *Phil.* p. 254, and Tayl., *Var. Soc.* pp. 87–8. Ep. XIII 360 c shows that he was a pupil of the Megarian Bryson, and had himself been one of the teachers of Helikon. From the mention of him below, 314 c, it appears that he went to Sicily with an introduction from Plato. He made a considerable name as a representative of the Megarian School of Philosophy, and as inventor of the celebrated τρίτος ἄνθρωπος argument used by opponents of the doctrine of εἴδη. Plato's use of this argument in the *Parmenides* and elsewhere shows that he himself considered it valid against that doctrine, when held in a certain form. It seems safe to infer that Polyxenos became a prominent figure at the court of Dionysios and inspired some of his criticisms of Plato. A similar position is implied by the mention of him in the Sokr. Epp. 35 and 36. Such a person would be likely to visit the Olympic Games, if he had an opportunity of joining a party from the court of Dionysios.

3. 310 d 7. Hack., following Ad., finds this inconsistent with the questions of Dionysios mentioned in 312 b and 313 c. But there is no inconsistency: it is characteristic of Plato's procedure in his later works to begin by preparing the ground in this way, and later to introduce the monarch's definite questions.

4. 310 e 5. πέφυκε κ.τ.λ. The writer has been charged with borrowing from Ep. VII, 335 d. But there is nothing in common between the two passages except the words δύναμις μεγάλη and φρόνησις. The point of the passage in Ep. VII, as in the passages parallel to it in *Rep.* 473 d and *Laws*, 711 c, is that there is no hope of political salvation except by a coalition between these two forces, and that the chances of such a coalition are remote. Here the point is that the two have a natural tendency to combine, and this is illustrated from history and poetry. The opposite view is stated by A. Zimmern, *Learning and Leadership*, p. 66. "The relationship between the philosopher and the statesman is the oldest problem of civilisation. Knowledge and power, thought and action, intellectual insight and practical mastery, have confronted one another in all ages. Each is indispensable to the other in the scheme of human life; yet each, in its self-sufficiency and in the natural reluctance of opposite natures to collaborate, would make as little use of the other as possible." Plato's desire to encourage a young ruler may have made him more sanguine.

5. 310 e 8. ἕν τε...ποιήσεσιν. This is said to be put together from scraps taken from various sources, *Laws*, 957 c, *Rep.* 366 e, and *Soph.* 232 c. A reference to these passages will show on what trivial grounds the charge of copying is sometimes made.

6. 311 a 1 ff. Xenophon's *Hieron*, which had probably appeared at this date, is a dialogue between Hieron and Simonides. For the intercourse between Solon and Croesus see Herod. I, 29 ff. The writer may have originally stopped after Σόλωνα in 311 a 6; Hercher brackets the other words; but they may have been added by the writer himself as an afterthought; cf. Herod. III, 36, where Croesus appears as the adviser of Cyrus and Cambyses. Pindar refers to the virtue and wisdom of Croesus, *Pyth.* I, 184, οὐ φθίνει Κροίσου φιλόφρων ἀρετά. As Apelt points out, Croesus has a double relation, that of ruler in his intercourse with Solon, and of counsellor with Cyrus. The passage, as it stands, looks like the rough draft of a letter.

7. 311 b 1. Polyidos was a soothsayer at the court of Minos, who restored to life Glaukos, the son of Minos. The story is unfamiliar to modern readers, because the tragedies of Sophokles and Euripides, which dealt with it, have been lost. Nestor, Odysseus and Palamedes are a triplet of sages attached to Agamemnon.

8. 311 b 3. This addition of Prometheus and Zeus is characteristic of Plato, but hardly likely to have occurred to a forger.

9. 311 d 2. A thoroughly Platonic idea; cf. *Soph.* 246 d 7. The whole of this passage is well conceived for a letter to a young man. 311 d 3, where strict grammar requires τούς for τοῖς, is suggestive of the first draft of a letter; the writer began with the intention of connecting τοῖς with ἑξείη, and altered the plan of his sentence, as he wrote.

10. 311 d 6. σὺν θεῷ εἰπεῖν. This phrase was a favourite one with Plato in his later years; cf. *Laws*, 858 b; *Theaet.* 151 b; *Ep.* IV, 320 b, c. It is an indication that the pieties of speech received attention in the Academy. My rendering is borrowed from Jowett.

11. 311 d 8–312 a 2. The train of thought here is: "If you and I maintain a high standard of conduct and also devote ourselves to philosophy, we shall be securing the honour of philosophy and our own salvation. For all higher intellectual study brings us into contact with that which is most truly divine in the universe. My own motive for visiting Syracuse was to secure the honour of philosophy." Godliness (εὐσέβεια) is here identified with the intellectual life, as in *Tim.* 47 b; *Laws* 967 d; *Epin.* 989, 990; cf. Farnell, *Greek Cults*, IV, p. 243: "the exalted conception of the philosophers, that the pursuit of intellectual truth was a divine function and an act of worship". For Plato, to aim at the honour of philosophy is the same thing as to aim at the glory of God. His attitude is the same as that presupposed in Dion's appeal to him in Ep. VII, 328 e, urging him to come to the rescue of philosophy which is now held in dishonour by mankind at large. There is no suggestion that the πλῆθος are to become philosophers, and no inconsistency with *Rep.* 494 a, where the impossibility of such a thing is insisted on. The point here is that philosophy will come into her proper rights, if she has the support of a powerful ruler.

12. 312 a 2. εὐαγῆ. Cf. Soph. *O.T.* 921: ὅπως λύσιν τιν' ἡμῖν εὐαγῆ πόρῃς. In what follows some editors have misunderstood the reason given by Plato for his failure. Plato sometimes uses πρᾶγμα with a

philosophical signification, for which see note on Ep. VII, 340 b 8.
Here it is "my position", or "my views". So ἄλλα ἐσπούδακας refers
to other views in philosophy, not to other occupations or business.
For the philosophical controversies which are probably referred to see Intr.
pp. 26, 27.

13. 312 b 8. For this claim for marks of honour see Intr. Rem.
This passage may have suggested the charge of φιλοτιμία made against
Plato by Dionysios of Halicarnassos (*Ep. ad Pomp.* 756). The stories
preserved by Diog. Laert. show that he was commonly charged with
τῦφος in the gossip of the philosophical schools, a charge which may
have had its origin in the well-known σεμνότης of his bearing. He took
himself and his own occupations seriously, and he probably had, as was
said of his English translator, an adequate sense of his own importance.
There is nothing unsuitable in his recognition of a desire to be well
reputed as a proper motive for action on the part of Dionysios. A
sovereign has to consider how his conduct will be regarded by the
public; and it is not wise on the part of a philosopher to ignore this
necessity. The other teachers referred to are, no doubt, those
mentioned at 314 c, Polyxenos, Lykophron and the others, where
the "others" include probably Aischines of Sphettos and Aristippos
of Kyrene. The influence of Aristippos was most important. See
Intr. (*l.c.*)

14. 312 d 2. σφαιρίον; probably a model illustrating either the
geometry of the sphere or the movements of the planets, brought by
Archedemos. Cicero (*Rep.* I, 14. 21) describes two models, made by
Archimedes and brought to Rome by Marcellus. They showed the
movements of the sun, moon and five planets, in accordance with the
theory of homocentric spheres formulated by Eudoxos. The orrery
of Dionysios may have been a less successful attempt to illustrate the
same theory: his skill in making toys and models is alluded to by
Plutarch. Archedemos, no doubt, was to take back the model and point
out its defects. The abrupt style here, so suitable to a letter accompanied
by the model, is too clever a touch for a Greek forger.

Andr. explains σφαιρίον as the spherical atom which Demokritos
supposed to be the material of the soul (*Philologus*, LXXVIII, pp. 78–9).
This would only be possible if Archedemos had been the bearer of a
written letter, in which the word had been used by Dionysios. In any
case it seems improbable that the theory would be alluded to by the
singular noun σφαιρίον.

15. 312 d 7. τῆς τοῦ πρώτου φύσεως. Here Andr. (*l.c.*) gives the
right clue by explaining τὸ πρῶτον as the soul, and referring to the
arguments in *Laws*, x, for the priority of soul to body.

16. 312 d 8. ἵν' ἄν τι κ.τ.λ. Plato has worked into his sentence
fragments of a passage in a lost tragedy. For the use of πτυχαῖς cf.
Soph. *O.T.* 1026, ἐν Κιθαιρῶνος πτυχαῖς, and Eur. *Hel.* 44, ἐν πτυχαῖσιν
αἰθέρος. It is not possible to say whether the word δέλτος is a part of
the quotation; but in any case the word belongs to the poetic colouring,

and does not justify an inference that the letter was written on wax tablets; *v. inf.* note on 314 c 6.

17. 312 e 1. βασιλέα. The chance that his letter might go astray gave Plato an excuse for parrying the question of Dionysios. The riddle with which this is done is, if a forgery, a most clever imitation of Plato's manner, and none the worse because critics differ as to its meaning. Even for βασιλέα, which looks easy, we have to choose between three solutions, each of which, in the absence of the others, seems possible:

(1) The "Idea of the Good", which in *Rep.* 509 d is said βασιλεύειν νοητοῦ γένους τε καὶ τόπου.

(2) The Creator of the *Timaeus* (cf. *Tim.* 28 c 3, 37 c 7, 41 a 7).

(3) Νοῦς, as in *Phileb.* 28 c 7.

Apelt cuts the knot by making the "Idea of the Good" convertible with "die Gottheit". This identification has the support of E. Zeller, J. Adams, and others. But how can anyone, who accepts as trustworthy Aristotle's description of Plato's lecture on the "Idea of the Good", believe that the philosopher would have accepted this simplification of his views? Further reasons against it are given by Bt., *Phil.* p. 336. The first of the three solutions derives some support from Plutarch, who (*Dion*, 14) makes the court party at Syracuse complain that Dionysios is being made to sacrifice his strong position as tyrant in order to pursue τὸ σιωπώμενον ἀγαθόν. A mystic ἀγαθόν was recognised even by the general public as a special feature of Plato's teaching. The comic dramatist Amphis makes one of his characters say:

> τὸ δ' ἀγαθὸν ὅ τί ποτ' ἐστὶν οὗ σὺ τυγχάνειν
> μέλλεις διὰ ταύτην, ἧττον οἶδα τοῦτ' ἐγώ,
> ὦ δέσποτ', ἢ τὸ Πλάτωνος ἀγαθόν.

If we make βασιλεύς the "Idea of the Good", we are almost bound to explain δεύτερον and δεύτερα as the sun and the world of phenomena. But τρίτον and τρίτα remain a problem. On the whole Andr. (*l.c.* p. 80) again seems right in taking βασιλεύς as the Creator, and in comparing *Laws*, 904 a, where the Creator is spoken of as βασιλεύς, and *Tim.* 30 a 7, which explains αἴτιον ἁπάντων τῶν καλῶν. For the two pairs of doublets, δεύτερον and δεύτερα, τρίτον and τρίτα, we are left to our imagination. But Andr.'s suggestion that the first doublet represents the World-Soul and the stars, and the second the human soul and the world of sense, seems the least improbable of the solutions offered. It is most like Plato to put the human soul and the world of sense in the lowest place, and, if this is done, the order of creation in the *Timaeus* is best preserved here by giving the second place to the World-Soul and heavenly bodies. It is true that these, as perceived by sight, form a part of the world of sense. But for Plato they are on a higher level, because their movements are regulated by νοῦς.

These cryptic sentences became one of the commonplaces of the Schools of Alexandria, and were interpreted by the Christians as an anticipation of their doctrine of the Trinity; cf. Clem. Alex. *Strom.*

v, 598 D (Paris Edn); *ib. Adm. ad Gent.* 45 C; Athenag. *Leg. pro Christ.* 26 A.

18. 312 e 5, ποῖ' ἄττα. 313 a 3, ποῖόν τι. The confusion between τὸ ποῖόν τι and τὸ ὄν or τὸ τί is referred to in the philosophical digression in Ep. VII (see 342 e 3, and note on 343 b 8) as one of the main causes of difficulty to a learner. Plato is there thinking of the earlier stages in the attainment of knowledge, more especially mathematical knowledge. Here he is thinking of the danger of raising the question ποῖόν τι when dealing with the ultimate truths of metaphysics. The Stoics were trying to answer this question when they identified God with a material πνεῦμα running through the universe. The Epicurean atoms were another attempt to answer the same question. Both these systems were attempts to provide the ordinary man with a philosophy which could be expressed in a few simple dogmas. It is possible, as I have suggested (Intr. pp. 26, 27), that Dionysios had learnt from Aristippos and others some form of materialism, which provided an easy answer to the question ποῖόν τι. The translation assumes a stop after τοιοῦτον, 313 a 2.

19. 313 a 7. "In the garden under the laurels." Rit. (*N.U.* p. 361) regards the details as characteristic of a forger, and parallel to St John's Gospel, i, 46, "When thou wast under the fig-tree, I saw thee". But even if we regard both passages as fictions, they are not parallel. For in the Gospel the speaker's acquaintance with the detail is part of a miraculous incident and an evidence of his supernatural powers. In the letter there is no miraculous incident, and the detail is mentioned to identify a particular occasion. It may be a forger's device to give *vraisemblance* to the letter; but there is nothing in the facts, style or language which makes it suspicious. "The garden" is mentioned as the scene of interviews with Dionysios in Ep. III 319 a and Ep. VII 348 c, and Plato's own lodging was in it.

20. 313 b 4. For the change from infin. to virtual or. obl. in opt. cf. 328 c 3, and Intr. Sect. pp. 93, 94.

21. 313 b 7. For κατέδησας cf. *Meno*, 98 a, where we are taught that right opinion must be tied up and made fast before it can become knowledge. For ἄττει in the sense of unstable movement cf. *Theaet.* 144 a, ἄττοντες φέρονται ὥσπερ τὰ ἀνερμάτιστα πλοῖα. ἄττει σοι is Bt.'s highly probable conj. The two best MSS have ἀλλαττισοι and ἀλλ' αἴττι σοι. From these the early editors extracted ἀλλ' ἄττεις, which gives something like the right sense. But the original must have had letters corresponding to σοί.

22. 313 d 7. ἐμπορεύομαι here and in e 4 suggests the journeys of a trader; cf. λόγοισιν Ἑρμόδωρος ἐμπορεύεται, a proverbial saying, which arose from the fact that Hermodoros, a pupil of Plato, sold his works in Sicily.

23. 314 a 3. ἄκουσμα does not occur in any genuine Platonic dialogue, but Diog. Laert. III, 39 quotes a saying of Plato, ἀεὶ εἶναι ἥδιστον ἀκουσμάτων τὴν ἀλήθειαν.

24. 314 a 7–b 7. This is a remarkable passage, and typical of a mind with a strong bent towards mysticism: it is most unlikely to have been written by a forger, or by anyone who was not in earnest. I know no parallel to it in the Dialogues, and there is nothing quite like it in the 7th Epistle. The sudden vision, which a man sometimes has, of another world, more real than that with which he has been in contact in his previous life, is an experience which philosophy shares with religion, and which may change for him the whole aspect of things. Compare W. James, *The Varieties of Religious Experience*, p. 382: "The simplest rudiment of mystical experience would seem to be that deepened sense of a maxim or formula, which occasionally sweeps over one. 'I've heard that said all my life,' we exclaim, 'but never realised its meaning till now.' 'When a fellow-monk', said Luther, 'one day repeated the words of the Creed "I believe in the forgiveness of sins", I saw the scripture in an entirely new light; and straightway I felt as if I were born anew. It was as if I had found the door of Paradise thrown wide open'". James also refers to the remarkable passage in which Newman describes how his whole view of church history was altered by hearing a friend repeat the words "securus judicat orbis terrarum" (*Apologia*, p. 117, 1891 edn). "Who can account", says Newman, "for the impressions which are made on him? For a mere sentence, the words of St Augustine, struck me with a power which I had never felt from any words before."

25. 314 c 1. In Ep. VII, 341 c, there is a similar statement, οὔκουν ἐμόν γε περὶ αὐτῶν ἔστιν σύγγραμμα οὐδὲ μήποτε γένηται, and the usual charge of copying has been made. Hack. and Ad., who find fault with the "forger" for overlooking the limitation introduced by περὶ αὐτῶν, have overlooked περὶ τούτων in the first clause of the sentence here. There is no reason why Plato, writing his 7th Epistle for general circulation in 354 B.C., should not have reproduced the substance of something which he said in a private letter in 360 B.C., and which may well have been a remark which he was fond of repeating in conversation and lectures. The words τὰ δὲ νῦν λεγόμενα κ.τ.λ. only mean that the Dialogues must be regarded not as the teaching of Plato himself, but as an idealised picture of the conversations of Sokrates. The omission of the reference to Sokrates in 353 B.C., when he must have published some, at least, of the non-Sokratic Dialogues, is intelligible enough; but the remark about him in Ep. II is "both possible and natural in Plato's own mouth when the *Philebus*, *Timaeus*, and *Laws*, and possibly the great dialectical Dialogues were unwritten. It is much more unlikely that a forger, with the whole series of Plato's works before him, should have thought of making such a remark" (Tayl., note on p. 124 of *Mind*, N.S. no. 69). The sentence is quoted in Sokr. Ep. 15.

26. 314 c 6. There is no need to suppose an inconsistency between this direction to burn the letter and the mention of wax tablets in 312 d. If, as seems clear, that passage is a familiar quotation, it is not necessary to suppose that the letter actually sent was written on wax tablets. Nor is there anything improbable in the supposition that, after giving such a direction, Plato preserved his own draft of the letter, which has in due course been the source of our text. Ad. (*l.c.* p. 20) contends that, as the instruction to burn the letter implies that it was written on papyrus, it must be a late work by a forger resident in Alexandria. But papyrus was in use as a material for letters among Greeks in Plato's time. See Gardthauser, *Griech. Palaeographie*, Leipzig, 1911, p. 162 (quoted by Andr.).

27. 314 c 7. ταῦτα μὲν ταύτῃ; cf. 318 d 1, e 4, 360 e 3; *Laws*, 676 a 1, and Plutarch, *Demosth.* 4.

28. *Ib.* For Polyxenos see above, note 2. I have assumed that Bt. is right in following the best MSS and cutting out οὐ before πέμψαιμι, which the earlier editors retained. The passage gives a better continuous sense, if we suppose Dionysios to have expressed surprise that such a person as Polyxenos had received a recommendation from Plato. The next sentence is in the hasty style of a letter-writer; the first καί is " also ", and the depreciatory remark is meant to apply to Polyxenos as well as to Lykophron and the rest. Rit., in his otherwise useful note on Polyxenos (*N.U.* pp. 393–4), assumes that the text is οὐ πέμψαιμι. But with that reading it is impossible to account for the presence of Polyxenos at the court of Dionysios, which is implied in 310 c. Lykophron cannot be identified with any certainty; he may be the sophist of that name mentioned by Aristotle, *Pol.* 3, 9.

29. 314 e 1. Philistion, one of the most eminent of the Italian physicians of the day, was born at Lokroi in southern Italy, a city under the rule of Dionysios. At this date he was evidently court physician to Dionysios, and it is probable that a visit to Athens would have been acceptable to him. The mention of Speusippos, who accompanied Plato on his last visit to Syracuse, and this request of his, are both natural, if the present letter was writter after that visit. We know from other sources that Speusippos suffered from very poor health (Diog. Laert. iv, 1; Sokr. Ep. xxxv). If Philistion went to Athens, he may, as M.Wellmann has suggested, have been the Sicilian physician whom Epikrates introduces in his caricature of a nature-study lesson at the Academy; cf. Athenaeus, ii, 59 d; Kock, *Frag. Com. Att.* Epikrates Fr. 11.

30. 314 e 4. τὸν ἐκ τῶν λατομιῶν. Nothing is known of this person nor of the others who are mentioned in the following sentences. The stone quarries are the underground quarries used as prisons.

EPISTLE III.

Introductory Remarks.

In this letter we have moved on about four years from the date of Ep. II. All possibility of friendly relations between Plato and Dionysios has been removed by Dion's expedition (357 B.C.). Plato is no longer a neutral, as he wished to be after his return from Sicily, and is doing

what he can, from a distance, to support his friend's venture. He refers
to such efforts in the opening sentences of Ep. IV. Written in the form of
a personal letter to Dionysios, we have here a political pamphlet,
intended to meet charges circulated by him in Syracuse (see Intr.
p. 38). It tells its own story, and the only question to be discussed is
whether it is genuine.

Here again, it is important to remember the writer's object. We are
not dealing with a work of art, intended for the world at large and for
posterity, but with something written to serve a temporary purpose, and
addressed to a limited audience. The writer shows an accurate knowledge of the state of affairs at the moment. The charges are just those
which Dionysios is most likely to have made; they rested on a sufficient
basis of fact to make them plausible, and it was important for Dion to
meet them. But the writer not only knows the facts. He has also, if he
was not Plato himself, been singularly successful in throwing the letter
into a form which Plato, and no one else, would have been likely to
adopt. The charges made by Dionysios were that his original intention
to re-establish the ruined cities of Sicily and to convert the tyranny
into a constitutional monarchy had been thwarted by Plato and Dion.
But Plato, with the fondness for digressions so characteristic of his
later manner, is reminded by these new charges of the earlier slanders
spread by Philistos and others at the time of his own visits to Syracuse,
that he had been the chief adviser of Dionysios, and was responsible for
his oppressive government. The earlier charges must be dealt with
before he answers the later ones, and they are met by an autobio-
graphical sketch of the relations between himself and the monarch.

The charges which Dionysios is now circulating are next dealt with
(318 e 6); and their dishonesty is shown by a dramatic account of one of
his latest interviews with Dionysios, in which the monarch had taunted
him with preventing the re-establishment of the ruined cities of Sicily.
On that occasion he had wrung from ⸺ ⸺onysios an acknowledgment
that his advice had been, not that the scheme should be abandoned, but
only that it should be deferred till he had received some education.

The contents of the letter are as unlike the ordinary pamphleteer or
rhetorician as its arrangement. There is no personal abuse of Dionysios,
whose character such a writer would certainly have assailed; but
incidentally the letter shows him up as a shifty, pleasure-seeking man,
who would have been most unlikely to initiate any generous policy
towards the Syracusans or the homeless citizens of the ruined cities.
At a first reading one is surprised to find Plato, of all people, writing an
angry letter. But it was natural that, in writing a public pamphlet, he
should throw force into his language and give expression to some of the
indignation which he felt. No ordinary rhetorician could have risen to
the elevated style of 315 c 1–5 and 317 c 8–d 4, to the vigour of 318 d
4–e 5, to the quiet and convincing force of the narrative in 316 c 3–e 4,
or to the dramatic power of the scene described in 319 a 2–c 6. As a
pamphlet for circulation in Syracuse the letter is not likely to have been

of much use; but it is not at all ill-adapted for the purpose of clearing the character of Plato himself in the opinion of readers of the more intelligent sort. The honourable nature of his own intentions would carry with it as a corollary the vindication of those of Dion.

As in its contents and arrangement, so also in its style Ep. III resembles Ep. VII. We do not get in it the long and unwieldy sentences which occur sometimes in the longer work; they would be out of place in a pamphlet of this nature. But in other respects the two closely correspond; there are the same avoidance of hiatus and attention to the clausula, the same inversions of order and the same tendency to say the thing which the reader does not expect (see note on 316 c 6 and 318 e 6). Those who regard Ep. III as an exercise produced in a rhetorical school, or as written in order to form with others a historical novel, shut their eyes to the difficulty of maintaining such an unusual style throughout a composition of such length. A forger would have betrayed himself again and again.

Most critics have, like Rit., come round to the view that, if the 7th and 8th letters are accepted as genuine, the 3rd must be accepted also. Wtz., however, who has recanted his earlier condemnation of the 7th and 8th letters, still clings to his disbelief in the 3rd, which (*Pl.* I, 645) he dismisses summarily (along with the 2nd and 4th) as a forgery constructed with material drawn from the 7th and the 8th, and often transferred bodily. He is followed by How. and Sou., the latter of whom gives (pp. lxxxii–lxxxvi) in detail a number of arguments against the matter and style of the Epistle, which he regards as a product of the rhetorical schools. The following are his more important points.

(1) Ep. III is an open letter, intended for the public. Is it likely that within the short period of a few months Plato wrote two such letters, the 3rd and the 7th? The answer is that the letters are separated by two years at least, that during the interval the expulsion of Dionysios and the murder of Dion had entirely changed the political position, and that, while the 3rd letter was written to assist Dion at Syracuse, the 7th is Plato's Apologia to the Greek world at large and to posterity.

(2) The opening is in the style of a school exercise, being an imitation of *Charm.* 164 d, which passed into a commonplace of the schools, and reappears in Sokr. Ep. 36. A careful reading of the passage of the *Charmides* in its context will show that the two passages have nothing really in common except that both contain the word χαίρειν, and both mention the Delphic Oracle. The quotation in Sokr. Ep. 36 only proves that when that Epistle was written the 3rd Platonic Epistle was a well-known classic.

(3) The author has borrowed from the *Apology* the idea that the defence is against two groups of accusers, one earlier, and one later. It is true that the language in 316 b shows a reminiscence of *Apology*, 18 b. But this is not the only place in which Plato in his later writings has reproduced thoughts and language from earlier works. The *Laws* abound in such passages (see the remarkable list in Jowett's *Plato*, v,

p. 20); and there are not a few in Ep. VII (see note on 330 c 9). In such passages Plato is merely carrying out his own motto, δὶς τὸ καλὸν ῥηθὲν οὐδὲν βλάπτει (*Laws*, 754 c), and καλὸν δὲ τό γε ὀρθὸν καὶ δὶς καὶ τρίς (*ib.* 956 e).

(4) Material from Ep. VII is served up again, but used with regard to different circumstances. The instances given are 316 a of this letter compared with 341 b of the 7th, and 318 b of this letter compared with 348 a of the 7th. I can only refer the reader to the passages; in both cases the resemblances are very trifling, and give no real support to the idea of a transfer of material.

(5) Finally the dramatic scene described in Ep. III 319 a ff., which occurred twenty days before Plato's final departure, is analysed in order to show that it is a reconstruction of the earlier scene described in Ep. VII, 349 a ff., with judicious variation of names, dates and circumstances. Sou. distinguishes correctly between these two interviews, and does not conceal the fact that the author of Ep. III mentions briefly the earlier interview in its proper place. This fact in itself renders his suggestion most unlikely; nor is it at all likely that a forger could have produced a piece of fiction so striking and dramatic as the account of the later interview. The scene tallies so exactly with the characters of the two actors that it is difficult to account for it except on the supposition that it is either a relation of actual facts or the work of a master of the art of dramatic fiction.

It is, however, true that there is some disagreement on two points between what is said in the two letters about the Herakleides incident (see Intr. pp. 28, 29). In the 7th letter Herakleides runs away to save his life; in the 3rd he is said to have been driven out by Dionysios. But it is not unnatural that in a polemical pamphlet the tyrant should be charged with having driven out a man who had fled to escape his anger. Again the remark of Dionysios, which in the 7th letter is conveyed to Plato by a messenger, is reported in the 3rd (318 c 5) as having been made in the course of the interview which both letters mention. But is it impossible that the same remark was both made at the interview and later sent to Plato as a message? In any case it is easy to make too much of such discrepancies. In describing the events of their own lives men often wander far from the facts without any intention to deceive. Scenes, incidents and conversations, which have been much brooded over by the chief actors in them, assume a new complexion and are liable to be reproduced in a form which renders them hard to recognise. It is more likely that after an interval of two or three years Plato told the story differently than that a forger, with the 7th letter before him, altered the facts.

Ad. (p. 21), who uses these incidents to prove the 3rd Epistle a forgery, tries to strengthen his case by tampering with the evidence, suppressing the mention of this remark in 318 c 5, and taking advantage of the fact that in 319 a 5 a different remark, which has a slight resemblance to it, is mentioned in connection with the later interview.

With the remark thus transferred he has no difficulty in showing that the forger of Ep. III has gone widely astray in his facts and dates. This is a typical specimen of his unfair criticisms, which are only worth mentioning because, like those of Kar., they still form a part of the artillery of references with which the Epistles are attacked. This charge, the misdating of the remark of Dionysios, is brought up again by How. (p. 190), and Ad. is referred to as having *proved* it. It is worth noting that the same forger, whom Ad. regards as a muddle-headed person betraying himself by his own blunders, appears to Sou. a highly ingenious author of romance, who has deliberately varied the facts in order to give *vraisemblance* to his fiction. The French critic has at least the discernment to take some account of the merits of the letter.

1. 315 a 6. This and the following sentences are suitable in an open letter. Plato, who had had previous correspondence with Dionysios, would not have required, in a private letter, to justify his ordinary formula of greeting. For the formula see Lucian, *de lap. in sal.* ch. 4.

2. 315 b 4. Dionysios may, as Gray suggests, have sent to consult the Oracle after the first successes of Dion in Sicily; or, as Rit. thinks (*N.U.* p. 388), the reference may be to a Pythian festival at which representatives both from Athens and from Dionysios were present. If so, it would be the festival of 358 B.C. There is no reason to doubt that the incident actually happened. The words πόρρω—θεῖον, 315 c 3, should have made critics pause before ascribing the letter to a forger. We have the same sentiment in *Phileb.* 33 b, with the explanation that joy or sorrow is something unseemly for Gods, and in *Epin.* 985 a 6.

3. 315 c 8. πρός τινας τῶν παρὰ σὲ πρεσβευόντων. Compare the opening of the letter of Isokrates to the children of Jason (Ep. 6), a pamphlet published about three years before the date of Plato's 3rd Epistle, ἀπήγγειλέ τίς μοι τῶν πρεσβευσάντων ὡς ὑμᾶς. Any publication of Isokrates must have been studied by Plato, who has evidently borrowed these envoys, to provide a setting for his own pamphlet.

4. 315 d 5. διδάσκοιμι. The optative indicates that λέγειν in 315 c 8 represents an impf. indic.

5. 315 e 3. Philistides is the well-known Philistos, for whom see Intr. The interchange between the patronymic and the simple name was common at Athens. In Aristoph. *Nub.* the same person is called Pheidonides in l. 65 and Pheidon in l. 134. See note of B. B. Rogers on l. 65 and on Ar. *Ran.* 1513.

6. 316 a 3. The laws for which Plato's preambles were used may have been those made for the settlements which Dionysios established at Tauromenion, and at Phoibia on the site of Rhegion. In establishing these places Dionysios was taking the step which he blamed Plato for preventing him from taking. As Tauromenion was refounded in 358 B.C., shortly before Dion's expedition, Plato may well have heard of laws being drawn up for it. In *Laws*, 722 d ff., Plato dwells on the importance of such preambles as a means of educating public opinion. In view of the contemplated refounding of the Greek cities, it was natural that Plato should have drafted preambles for future use. His work on these may have suggested to him the great Dialogue to which his later years were devoted, and in which some of them may have been embodied. For διασκευωρεῖν cf. *Rep.* 540 e 2.

7. 316 c 6. Literally, "Which are most certainly needed by those possessed even of small intelligence". This is one of the passages which puzzled Kar. because the writer says the opposite to what the ordinary reader is expecting. We expect him to say that even a man of *great* intelligence requires age and experience to be an adviser to a sovereign in the position of Dionysios. But Plato approaches his point differently. The words νοῦν καὶ σμικρὸν κεκτημένοις might be dispensed with; and we may suppose that the sentence was first composed in this simple form. Then, wishing to bring in the fact that some modicum of higher intelligence is wanted as a first requisite, he added the clause νοῦν... κεκτημένοις in attachment to μέλλουσι. A rhetorician would have modelled the sentence differently.

8. 316 c 8. ἀπειρίας περὶ σέ. This is not Plato's want of experience of Dionysios, which will be mentioned in the next clause. It is one of his odd circumlocutions with περί, and means "want of experience on your part". See Intr. p. 96.

9 317 a 1. πόλεμος is not metaphorical, as Apelt suggests. In 338 a 4 Plato says definitely that a war was going on *in Sicily* at this time. See note on that passage.

10. 317 a 5. For a fuller account of these events see 337 e ff. It should be noted that in this letter we hear nothing about the philosophical studies of Dionysios, and in the 7th nothing about the scheme suggested by Plato for a union between Dion and Dionysios.

11. 317 c 7. For διαβάλλουσιν see Bt.'s note on *Euthyphro*, 3 b 7.

12. 317 e 4. οἰκειότητα. Plato may have suggested some scheme for uniting the families of Dion and Dionysios by one or more marriages, as Dionysios I had united his own family to that of Hipparinos. ἥν is a loose internal accus. qualifying ἐπείθου; see note on 323 c 1.

13. 318 a 5. In 346 a–d and 347 c–d, the story is told in a slightly different order. The proposal to divide the property into two parts is introduced at a later point, and not when Dionysios was trying to persuade Plato to stay for a year.

14. 318 d 2. κοινωνίας. The gen. belongs to the informal style of a letter: we may take it as depending on the verb of saying implied in ταῦτα μὲν ταύτῃ. See Riddell's *Dig. of Id.* § 26.

15. 318 e 5. λυκοφιλία is not found elsewhere before Marcus Antoninus. But the corresponding adjective and adverb occur in Menander, and the noun may have been in use: so also may ἀκοινωνία, which is ἅπ. λεγ. The reference is to the treaty between the wolves and the sheep (Phaedrus, Appendix, Fab. 21).

16. 318 e 6. The style here seems to be intentionally eccentric. Gray tried to relieve it by proposing συνεχῆ τῷ νυνδὴ γενομένῳ. Rit. also (*N.U.* p. 400) adopts συνεχῆ from Kar. But Bt.'s text, which follows the MSS most closely, is probably right. The order of construction is ὁ λόγος σχεδὸν συνεχὴς τῷ νυνδὴ γενόμενος ἥκει μοι εἰς λόγον περὶ οὖ κ.τ.λ. The hyperbata are characteristic. For the transfer of σχεδόν cf. Ep. VIII, 353 a 3, and for the care in explaining the order of his procedure cf. 330 c 6 with note.

17. 319 a 4. The translation assumes that some word like εἰπεῖν, perhaps, as How. suggests, μέμφεσθαι, can be supplied before ἅ. But there may be corruption of the text. After ἀποδημίας we expect something like εἰπεῖν ἅ νυνδὴ ἔλεγον, ἐμοὶ μεμφόμενον ὡς κ.τ.λ. Bury cuts the knot by inserting εἰπεῖν after λέγεις.

18. 319 b 6, 7. The insult was in the words "received instruction". The parenthesis, διὸ τὸ κ.τ.λ., means that the successes of Dion have given Dionysios a practical lesson; cf. Ep. VII, 333 b 3. What follows is the only allusion in the letters to the course of geometry of which Plutarch gives a highly coloured account (*Dion*, 13). See Intr. p. 22.

19. 319 c 6. Perhaps a verse from a tragedy—μή μοι γένοιτ' ἀντ' εὐρυχωρίας στενός—as suggested in the Bohn trans.

20. 319 e 2. Cf. *Rep.* 529 c, δίκην, ἔφη, ἔχω· ὀρθῶς γάρ μοι ἐπέπληξας. The sense here is, "I deserve to be punished for trusting such a liar".

21. 319 e 3. The reference to a Sicilian poet is appropriate here. For the story see *Phaedr.* 243 a. Stesichoros, like Homer, was said to have been deprived of his eyesight for maligning the character of Helen; but, being a philosopher, he divined the reason, wrote his palinodia to the effect that it was not Helen who went to Troy, but a phantom representing her, and thus recovered his sight.

EPISTLE IV

This letter speaks for itself. We must suppose that Dion has made his expedition to Sicily, and that Plato has heard both of his earlier successes and of the surrender of the citadel by Apollokrates (see Intr. pp. 44, 45). He has also received disquieting reports of collisions between Dion and Herakleides. The main object of the letter is, if possible, to put an end to these, and the point of it lies in the last sentence, in which Dion is urged to be more conciliatory in his treatment of others. Dion's relations with Herakleides have been dealt with in the Intr. Conciliation was not a suitable way of dealing with such a man. Dion ought to have found some effective way of eliminating him at an early stage of the proceedings.

The letter is natural and lifelike in tone, and there is nothing either in the contents or the style which gives any real grounds for suspicion. Those who believe that the 3rd letter is the product of a school of rhetoric have, of course, ascribed the 4th to the same source. But if it is a forgery, it is the work of a very clever forger. Objection has been raised to the difference of attitude between 320 a of this letter, where the writer claims to have been an active supporter of Dion's expedition, and Ep. VII 350 b, where Plato meets Dion's request for support with a refusal. But three years had elapsed and circumstances had altered. When Dion's expedition had actually been launched, it was no longer possible for Plato to intervene as mediator; and, though he did not take part in it, it was natural that he should give to it all the encouragement and support which he could give from Athens.

Plato's complaint of the absence of direct news from Syracuse fits in well with the date assumed above for the letter. The letters of Timonides to Speusippos must have given Plato full information so long as they continued to be sent. But, after the surrender of Apollokrates, Timonides and some others, who accompanied Dion as volunteers, may have returned to their homes. (See Intr. p. 44 note *).

This letter was used by Plutarch, who quotes from its concluding sentence in his Life of Dion, chs. 8 and 52. He quotes it again in his *Moralia* (Adul. ch. 29), adding, "Speusippos also wrote to him not to be elated if his fame stood high among boys and women, but to endeavour to make the Academy famous by his holiness and justice, and by adorning Sicily with the best laws". The letter from Speusippos here mentioned cannot possibly be the 4th Platonic Epistle, and the passage is sufficient disproof of Rit.'s suggestion that Ep. IV was written by him. The view that it was a product of one of the schools of rhetoric is rendered most unlikely by the style and contents.

1. 320 b 2. Plato's *Laws* include provisions for giving marks of honour to successful generals. Honour, he tells us (921 e), is the way in which such men are paid; cf. also 727 a, and Ep. II, 312 b 7.

2. 320 b 3, c 7. For the repeated σὺν θεῷ εἰπεῖν see Ep. II, note 10.

3. 320 c 4. For πλεόν ἢ παίδων Hack. quotes the passage about Isokrates in *Phaedrus*, 279 a. At the end of the sentence How. perhaps improves the text by printing τοὺς...οἶσθα δήπου, and compares Ep. III, 318 a 1, οὓς οἶσθα σύ. Perhaps these words were a slang phrase used by the members of the Academy to describe themselves.

4. 320 d 6. ἀρχαῖον, "out of date"; cf. *Hipp. Mi.* 371 d 4, ἡγούμενος ἀρχαῖον εἶναι τὸν Ὀδυσσέα.

5. 320 e 1. ἀναιρεθέντος. Perhaps a piece of slang: Dionysios has been completely "smashed".

6. 321 a 1 ff. The word θεάτροις shows that there is no reference to races. ἀγωνιστάς covers either actors or competitors in vocal or instrumental competitions, which might be held in a theatre. We are probably meant to think of the actors in a drama. But Plato may have had in his mind the simile of a foot-race introduced by Isokrates at the close of his *Evagoras* (ch. 79, 207 a). The central idea in both passages is similar; but in other respects they have not much in common. In Plato the actors in a play are being applauded by children as well as by their own friends. In Isokrates the competitors in a race are being cheered on by spectators as well as by their friends. Plato has elsewhere borrowed ideas from Isokrates; see notes on Ep. III, 315 c 8, and Ep. VII, 324 d 7. But it should be noted that there is no copying of phraseology; friends are mentioned in both passages, and the words παρακελεύεσθαι and παροξύνειν are common to both; but there is no further parallelism in the language.

7. 321 b 4. The sense is much improved if with Wtz. we read παρά for περί.

8. 321 c 1. αὐθάδεια. See Jebb's note on Theophrastus, *Ch.* 3, The Character of the αὐθάδης. As Jebb points out, such words change their meaning with changes of social usage, and the character described by Theophrastus is not at all that which Plato meant to ascribe to Dion. For Plato the word implied the avoidance of social intercourse, with a suggestion of *hauteur*; cf. *Rep.* 590 a 9, where it is coupled with δυσκολία, or surliness, as a fault to which the man in whom courage is over-developed will be prone. In *Laws*, XII, 950 b, the adj. αὐθάδης is applied to the State which refuses all intercourse with other States.

LETTER V

This letter is a reply to one from Perdikkas, the young king of Macedon (365–360 B.C.), elder brother and predecessor of Philip. Perdikkas has asked Plato to send him an adviser from the Academy, and Plato recommends Euphraios of Oreos. That Euphraios went to the court of Perdikkas and had great influence there appears from the story, told by Karystios the Pergamene and reproduced by Athenaios, that he would not allow anyone to sit at the king's table who was ignorant of geometry and philosophy (Athen. XI, 508 e). Athenaios also (*ib.* 506 e) cites, from a letter of Speusippos quoted by Karystios, a statement that Philip owed his subsequent position to Plato, because it was Euphraios who induced Perdikkas to put him in charge of a district in which he became powerful enough to seize the crown after the death of Perdikkas. Euphraios must have returned to Oreos after the accession of Philip. The end of his career is related in the 3rd Philippic of Demosthenes (chs. 59 ff.). He was active in opposing the paid agents who succeeded in bringing Oreos under the rule of Philip, was thrown into prison, and there committed suicide. The passage mentions the previous residence of Euphraios at Athens, and harmonises with what is said in this letter about his courage.

There is no reason to doubt the genuineness of this letter, and nothing improbable in the relations which it implies between Plato and Perdikkas. It probably belongs to some date not long after the accession of Perdikkas. Plato had been asked, a few years earlier, to make laws for Megalopolis; and other States besides Macedon made use of advisers from the Academy.

Rit. (*N.U.* pp. 397–8) groups the letter with Ep. IV, and thinks, tentatively, that it may have been written by Speusippos. Hack. (p. 74) condemns it on the ground that the passage about the voices of the different forms of government is "a clumsy copying of what is said in the *Republic* (493 a, b)". But the two passages are written from totally different points of view, and there is no trace of copying either of thought or language (see below, note 2).

Wtz. (*Pl.* II, p. 280 n. 3) attacks the letter roughly on three grounds:
(1) The two parts of it have no connection with each other.
(2) It is inconceivable that Plato should have professed to give advice for a democracy better than for any other form of constitution, and that he should have taken a young king into his confidence as to his own relations with the Athenians.
(3) The thought of the concluding sentences is not that of Plato.

To this it may be answered that
(1) The first part of the letter leads the reader on to the second by a quite natural transition.
(2) Plato's critic only urges against him that he professes to be able to advise what is expedient for a democracy, but has not done so. The letter, if genuine, must belong to a date after Plato's first visit to the younger Dionysios, when he must have been assailed by the very criticism which is here dealt with. It was not unnatural that he should refer to it in a contemporary letter to Perdikkas.
(3) The difficulties which Wtz. finds do not arise, if the concluding sentences are taken in the way adopted in this edition.

Wtz. is followed by How. and Sou.; but the latter is more appreciative, and while he regards the letter as a school exercise, a specimen of the epistolary type known as συμβουλευτικόν, he allows that the materials are good, though, of course, borrowed. It is curious that fictitious letters of this date, which reach this high order of excellence, seem to be extant nowhere except in the Platonic Epistles.

Post regards the letter as a "malicious forgery", the work of "a clever opponent of the Academy, who was desirous of fastening on Plato the stigma of favouring monarchy; in particular, of having helped Philip to the throne of Macedon". If this is so, the letter seems singularly ill-adapted to secure its object; for Philip is not mentioned or alluded to. The style is said to be a good imitation of Plato's, but to be without "Plato's characteristic ardour and rhythmic utterance". But are these qualities which we should expect to see in a private and personal letter of introduction? Post's criticism, however, is of value as indicating that the letter is not likely to have been produced by an admirer of Plato during the period shortly after his death, when the Academy was being criticised as the producer of tyrannies. No such difficulty arises, if we regard the letter as written by Plato himself before such criticisms had been heard of. On so short a piece one cannot speak with full confidence, but as addressed to a young and inexperienced monarch, who was not without intelligent aspirations, the letter seems neither unworthy of Plato nor unsuited to the object which it professes.

1. 321 c 5. ἱερὰ συμβουλή, a proverbial phrase; cf. *Theages*, 122 b, λέγεταί γε συμβουλὴ ἱερὸν χρῆμα εἶναι, Xenoph. *An.* v, 6. 4, αὕτη ἡ ἱερὰ συμβουλὴ λεγομένη εἶναι δοκεῖ μοι παρεῖναι.

2. 321 d 5. The voice of each of the three forms of State is simply its public policy and acts. The State is a living organism, and the different types of constitution differ from one another as fundamentally as two animals of different species. The policy, which would be sound for one type, will be disastrous for another. We must not press the animal simile too far; it is dropped after a few lines, and the appropriate policy for a monarchy is spoken of as the λόγος τῆς μοναρχίας. The passage has nothing really in common with *Rep.* 493 a ff., from which Richards and Hack. consider it to be copied. In the *Republic* the populace is a Great Beast, whose moods and the φωναί, by which they are expressed, are studied by the statesmen of the wrong sort, who in their turn try to find the φωναί which will keep the Great Beast in good humour: the successful accomplishment of this humouring process is what passes for statesmanship.

3. 322 a 7. εἰπεῖν, infinitive used as imperative. The next eight lines, Πλάτων...τὰ ἐμὰ συμβουλῆς, I have, following Hack. and H. Jackson, taken as or. recta introduced by ὅτι. The alternative is to make the reported speech end at ποιήσειν, and suppose that in what follows Plato is speaking in his own person, and that the advice is given by the State to him. But it is only by very unnatural straining that we can get any meaning out of this. Wherever we put the inverted commas, we still have the difficulty of the accus. τὴν ἐμὴν συμβουλήν. Stephanus inserted περί; but it is better to suppose that the phrase ταὐτὸν δρᾶσαι governs a second accus. συμβουλήν.

EPISTLE VI.

This letter, like the 2nd, brings us into contact with the religious side of Plato's philosophy; but it belongs to the last years of his life. Two of his former pupils, Erastos and Koriskos, have gone to live in their native city, Skepsis, in the Troad. Erastos is mentioned in the 13th letter (362 b 2). Koriskos is a well-known person; he was a fellow-pupil of Aristotle at the Academy, and maintained a life-long friendship with him. His son, Neleus, was on similar terms with Theophrastos, Aristotle's pupil and successor. Aristotle's library, left by him to Theophrastos, was left by Theophrastos to Neleus, and removed by him from Athens to Skepsis.

The Greek States of Asia Minor were subject to Persia, but during the troubled times of the Satrap Revolt (*c.* 360 B.C.) some of the despots who held power in them had succeeded in making themselves independent. Among these was Euboulos, who held a strip of the coast, a little to the south of the Troad, containing the cities of Atarneus and

Assos. With Euboulos was closely associated Hermeias, a remarkable man, who succeeded him as despot. Before this, Hermeias had visited Athens; and though he does not seem to have made the personal acquaintance of Plato, there was a link between him and Aristotle, who was working with Plato in the Academy. Aristotle's guardian, after his father's death, was Proxenos of Atarneus, and his acquaintance with Hermeias probably began at an early period of his life; the two were certainly connected by an intimate friendship before Plato's death. After that event Aristotle, accompanied by Xenokrates, left Athens, and the two lived for three years at Atarneus with Hermeias, whose adopted daughter Aristotle married. At the end of that period Hermeias was treacherously made prisoner by the Persian satrap and sent up to Artaxerxes, who put him to death (see Diod. xvi, 52. 6, Grote, ch. 90).

The common story about Hermeias represents him as having been a eunuch, and originally the slave of Euboulos, whose position and property he inherited. This rests on the authority of Theopompos (Frs. 210 and 242), who, as a native of Chios, was prejudiced against Atarneus and Hermeias. In *Class. Quart.* Oct. 1926, p. 155, C. M. Mulvany gives reasons for disbelieving the story that Hermeias had been a eunuch and slave. It was probably a mere revival of the story of Hermotimos in Herod. viii, 104–6, the name Hermeias being an abbreviation of Hermotimos. Such discreditable circumstances naturally won their way into history, and having established themselves gave birth to further legends, such as we see in Demetr. περὶ ἑρμ. § 293. If this view is accepted, the relations between Hermeias and Aristotle become more intelligible. It is also quite possible that Pythias, whom Aristotle married, was actually the daughter of Hermeias.

Aristotle put up a monument to Hermeias, and composed in his honour a remarkable ode, which is still extant (Diog. Laert. v, 7; Rose, *Arist. Fr.* 675). The idea of writing this letter may have been suggested to Plato by Aristotle. The absence of any allusion to him in it is a strong evidence of its genuineness. The connection between Aristotle and Hermeias was a matter of such notoriety that a forger could hardly have resisted the temptation to drag in a reference to it. The object of the letter is to promote between Plato's two pupils and Hermeias a friendship based on sympathy in philosophy and religion. The friendship of the three men is alluded to in Theopomp. Fr. 242.

The genuineness of the letter has been attacked, because it describes Plato as not acquainted personally with Hermeias (323 a 1); this conflicts with the statement of Strabo (xiii, 57) that Hermeias, when at Athens, listened to the teaching of Plato and Aristotle. But Strabo wrote more than three centuries after the events, and does not give his authority. The visit of Hermeias to Athens may have occurred during one of Plato's long absences, and Strabo may have been misled by the association between Hermeias and the Platonists.

In all other respects the setting implied by the letter fits exactly the circumstances, as they are known from other sources. The internal evidence is summed up by Wtz. (*Pl.* II, p. 281) in the dictum already quoted, but worth repeating, "Er trägt den Stempel von Platons unnachahmlicher Ältersstyl, und ist ein kostbares Dokument seiner Denkart". Rit. condemned the letter on the ground of style and because the oath enjoined by it is mystery-making. But this little piece of ritual, and the tone, half-jest and half-earnest, in which it is pre-scribed, are both thoroughly characteristic of Plato. Enough has been said in the Introduction about Rit.'s criticisms of the style. The other attacks on the letter do not call for separate mention.

1. 322 d 1. According to Theopompos (Fr. 242) Hermeias contended at the games with costly chariot-teams. The reference here is to horses for a force of cavalry, and the language recalls Ep. VII, 328 d 4. The construction changes as the sentence proceeds, giving one of Plato's simpler anacolutha.

2. 322 d 5. καίπερ γέρων ὤν. L. A. Post (*Class. Rev.* XLIV, p. 116) has rendered comment on this much-disputed phrase unnecessary by pointing out that it is an intentional reminiscence of Soph. *Thyestes,* Fr. 239 (Nauck):

καίπερ γέρων ὤν· ἀλλὰ τῷ γήρᾳ φιλεῖ
χὠ νοῦς ὁμαρτεῖν καὶ τὸ βουλεύειν ἃ δεῖ.

3. 323 b 7. συμφῦσαι, Bt.'s reading, means "cause to grow together". The reading of the first hand in the best MSS is ἐμφῦσαι, and this may be right. It is not impossible to supply φιλότητα καὶ κοινωνίαν as objects to it. "Implant in you, and bind you together once more into, friend-ship" etc. is not a more ungrammatical sentence than many in Plato's later works. συμφῦσαι καὶ συνδῆσαι has been supposed to be modelled on συντῆξαι καὶ συμφῦσαι in *Symp.* 192 e. But there συμφυσῆσαι is the reading of the best MSS, and Bt. is probably right in adopting it. The metaphor is different in the two passages. Here it is that of healing a wound and of tying up again something that has been untied. In the *Symposium* it is that of welding together something that has been cut asunder.

4. 323 c 1. ἥν may be taken as internal accus. with φιλοσοφῶμεν. It has a looseness of construction almost equal to Mrs Gamp's "which": cf. Ep. III, 317 e, ἥν εἰ ἐμοὶ κ.τ.λ.; *Tim.* 59 c 7, ἥν ὅταν τις κ.τ.λ. φιλοσοφεῖν means "to put our philosophy into practice". Philosophy for Plato was a matter of conduct, as well as of intellect. See Ep. x, 358 c 3, where τὸ πιστόν is one of its features.

5. 323 c 3. τὸ ἂν μὴ δρῶμεν. This putting aside of the unfavourable alternative is suggestive of the style of tragedy; cf. Aesch. *Ag.* 499, τὸν ἄντιον δὲ τοῖσδ᾽ ἀποστέργω λόγον.

6. 323 d 1. ἐπομνύντας κ.τ.λ. Three points call for comment.

(*a*) The second ἐπομνύντας, which appears in all the MSS and in the quotation of the passage in Clem. Alex., is unnecessary, and has provoked more than one emendation. Though it can hardly have been inserted intentionally by the writer, it may have been written by him unintentionally in his first draft, and this, preserved among Plato's papers, may be the source of our text.

(b) The coupling of jest and earnest is characteristic of, but not confined to, Plato's later works; cf. *Epin.* 980 a 9, 992 b 3; *Laws*, 688 b 5. It occurs also in *Symp.* 197 e 7, and is one of the resemblances which have led Hack. to describe this letter as produced by a forger working on reminiscences of that Dialogue. The words σπουδῇ μὴ ἀμούσῳ became a familiar quotation; cf. the letter of Timaios the Sophist prefixed to his Vocabulary. The "sister" metaphor is common in the dramatists, and is used by Plato in *Rep.* 404 e, where the best Gymnastic is sister of Music.

(c) The two divinities by whom the oath is to be taken are as problematic as the Trinity of Ep. II, 312 e. The meaning would, no doubt, have been clear to those familiar with the religious teaching of Plato's School. Post's rendering suggests a monotheism which is not in the original. The God described as ἡγεμόνα in d 3 must be the same as the ἡγεμόνος of the next line, and therefore cannot be the same as πατέρα. The mention of two Gods related as Father and Son made the sentence an attractive one to the early Christians, and it is reproduced by Clem. Alex. along with the cryptic passage of Ep. II. The most probable explanation is to be found in the language used about the sun and the Idea of the Good in *Rep.* 506 e, 508 a, 516, 517, where they are respectively ἔκγονος and πατήρ. The sun there is not only the source of light, but manages (ἐπιτροπεύει) everything in the visible world, and is in a fashion the cause (αἴτιος) of what we see there. The title πατήρ is also given to the Creator in the *Timaios*, and it has been supposed that this is the meaning here, the other God being the World-Soul. This is the view of Andr. and of Wtz. (*Pl.* I, p. 707 n. 2). But the language used here is not suitable to the World-Soul, which would hardly be spoken of as ἡγεμὼν καὶ αἴτιος; and the balance of probability seems to be in favour of those who, with the poet Gray, Ast, and Apelt, explain the oath from the passages in the *Republic*.

EPISTLES VII AND VIII.

Introductory Remarks.

These two letters may be considered together. With the rest of the Epistles they remained under a cloud for some time after the attack of Kar., who went so far as to say, of one scene in Ep. VII (348 b ff.), "Profecto neminem fore arbitror quin, hac scena attente perlecta, fateretur eam et rebus et verbis ita comparatam esse ut non Platonem sed potius simium Platonis referat". Rit., speaking of the same scene fifty years later, gives the opinion (*N.U.* p. 408) that "on any unprejudiced reader it cannot fail to produce the impression of the natural outspokenness of a narrative of personal experience".

The critical world could not long remain blind to the fact that the contents of the two letters were sufficient proof of their genuineness, and that in the case of the 7th letter in particular Cicero was not under an illusion when he spoke of it as "praeclara epistula Platonis ad Dionis propinquos" (*Tusc. Disp.* v, 35). Cobet's verdict on the 7th letter, "Platonis ipsius esse hanc epistolam et argumentum et stilus clamant, et neminem alium in Graecia novimus qui de his rebus sic scribere potuisset," could not fail to be adopted by other scholars, as soon as the wave of scepticism had a little subsided. On the internal evidence in its favour enough has been said in the Introduction. The more recent attacks, such as that of Ad. on Ep. VIII, and that of Rit. on the philosophical digression in Ep. VII, have been sufficiently dealt with by other writers and need not be further referred to here.*

If, however, we accept the letters as genuine, two difficulties have to be faced: (1) the extraordinary arrangement of the subject-matter of Ep. VII; (2) the historical puzzle in Ep. VIII caused by the death of Dion's son. The following remarks are, for the most part, taken from a paper in the *Classical Quarterly* (Oct. 1928), in which I attempted to remove these difficulties.

(1)

The 7th Epistle professes to be a reply to a request for help and counsel, addressed to Plato by the friends of Dion at some time not long after his murder. By far the greater part of it is actually Plato's Apologia for himself. He describes and justifies his own career, so far as it brought him into contact with the political affairs of his day, his detachment from the politics of Athens and his intervention in those of Syracuse, his relations with Dionysios the Younger, and the failure of his attempts to influence that monarch for good in politics and philosophy. The justification of Dion is combined with his own; and clearly one of his objects in writing the letter was to raise a worthy memorial to his friend.

The letter, which contains a little over twenty-eight pages of the edition of Stephanus, may be divided roughly into three sections:

(*a*) A section of between six and seven pages, giving an account of the writer's early life, of his visit to Syracuse during the time of Dionysios I, and of the first of his two visits to Dionysios II.

(*b*) A section of about seven pages, which opens with a statement that the writer is now going to give his advice, but of which the greater part consists of a complicated series of digressions, devoted to the justification of his own conduct and that of Dion and to the condemnation of the wickedness of Dion's murderers. The actual advice occupies less than two pages at the end of this section.

(*c*) A section of fourteen pages, of which twelve are occupied with Plato's second visit to Dionysios II and the events which immediately

* Hack., p. 141, Tayl., *Mind*, N. S. LXXXIII, pp. 348–352.

preceded and followed it, no less than five being devoted to their relations as teacher and pupil. Towards the close there is a striking peroration, in which the writer returns to Dion's murder and defends in impassioned terms his friend's character and aims. Two or three formal sentences bring the letter to an end.

This is a plan which might conceivably have been adopted by one of Plato's disciples writing after his death to meet posthumous attacks on his master's intervention in Sicilian affairs. But if we accept the letter as genuine, and believe that it was actually sent to Syracuse in response to an appeal for help and advice from the Dionean party—men with whom Plato had been in intimate relations during his second and third visits to Sicily, and who were well acquainted with the whole story of those visits—the difficulties become overwhelming.* Nor are they removed by supposing that the document was an open letter sent to Sicily for general circulation. Plato did not entirely lose his sense of humour in his old age; and, apart from structural eccentricities, it is hardly likely that the forcible and often-quoted description of the luxury and debauchery of the Sicilian Greeks (326 b, c, d) would have been included in a letter intended primarily for circulation in that region.

If we recognise these facts, and believe that the letter was written, not for Sicily, but for Athens, for the Greek world at large, and for posterity, is it necessary to go on treating the letter from the friends of Dion as actual fact? Is it not clear that the appeal for help and advice mentioned in the first paragraph is merely a literary device, introduced as a picturesque setting for the letter which follows? Plato had a gift for imaginative fiction. No one thinks of taking as actual fact the whole setting of the *Republic* or *Symposium*. It is obvious that in these cases we have the same skilful combination of fact with fiction which we expect in a historical novel. Surely we may credit Plato with the power of providing as good a setting for a letter, and maintaining the illusion by such passages as 326 e 4.

Let us try to put ourselves into the position of Plato at Athens, when the news of Dion's murder reached him. It was conveyed by a letter from Kallippos to the government of Athens describing himself as a tyrannicide (Plut. *Dion*, 58). Kallippos had in fact done what everyone suspected Dion of intending to do.† He had seized the coveted position of tyrant; he was master of the impregnable citadel, and maintained his power by the aid of the mercenaries, with whom he had ingratiated himself by bribery before the murder. The entry to the harbour was commanded by the citadel, and was so narrow that only one ship at a time could leave it; under the tyranny none left it without scrutiny (329 e; Intr. pp. 7, 8). It is most unlikely that any letter from the friends

* For an account of the structural theories framed by Odau and others to remove these difficulties, see *Class. Quart. l.c.*

† For Aristotle's view on Dion and Kallippos see Intr. p. 47, note *.

of Dion was conveyed by the ship that carried the despatch of Kallippos or by any ship that left Syracuse for some time after. Of actual occurrences during the thirteen months rule of Kallippos very little is known. In the course of it (we are not told when) the Dioʌican party were obliged to fly from Syracuse to Leontinoi. From there also communications with Athens must have been difficult. Nor is it likely that the party at that time thought of appealing to Plato for help and advice. They had their own plans for the removal of Kallippos, which were ultimately successful; but they were not plans which Plato was likely to be able to assist in any way.

The letter of Kallippos gave, no doubt, the version of the story which best suited his own purposes; but it would, in the course of time, be supplemented by news from other sources as to the part which he had played in Dion's downfall and the nature of his subsequent rule. There would be much uncertainty about details, but no doubt about the central fact—the complete failure of Dion's schemes, and the final shipwreck of the hopes which enthusiasts had associated with Plato's visits to Sicily. The scraps of literary gossip which have survived are sufficient evidence that adverse critics did not neglect their opportunity; and to anyone reading between the lines of the 7th Epistle it is plain that we have in it the defence of a man who had been the object of unkind attacks. Plato maintains an attitude of dignified aloofness, and does not descend to personal controversy. But the concluding sentences of the letter refer clearly to such attacks; and when (in 330 c) he speaks of those who put the question why he made a second visit to the younger Dionysios, the people whom he means must be at Athens, not at Syracuse.

The position at Athens called for an immediate defence of Plato's intervention in practical politics, of his attitude as a teacher of philosophy, and of his friend Dion. The defence had to be in some literary form; and the dialogue was not suited to such a purpose. Howald suggests that Plato actually wrote a speech. In the middle of the fourth century the writings of Isokrates had made the fictitious speech, published but not delivered, a familiar form for the political pamphlet. But Plato had never been a professional writer of speeches, and it is not likely that he would have entered into competition with Isokrates by adopting this form for his defence. A letter was not open to the same objection. Isokrates had, it is true, thrown three of his pamphlets into this form; but Plato himself had, as we have seen, used it in his 3rd Epistle. It was natural that he should adopt for his defence the form of a similar, but more extensive, letter, enlivened in the same way with dramatic scenes and scraps of dialogue, and provided with a suitable, but purely fictitious, setting; and it was surely a happy thought to make his letter a reply to an appeal from the Dionean party; for it gave him a reason for combining with his own justification that of his friend.

If the letter from the friends of Dion is removed to the region of

fiction to which it belongs, and the 7th Epistle is regarded as a pamphlet
intended for readers at Athens and in the Greek world generally, its
eccentricities of arrangement call for no defence from those who are
familiar with the *Laws*; and it will always be found that, puzzling as the
procedure is, there is some method behind it (see note on 324 b 8).
    Before leaving Ep. VII something must be said about the date of its
publication. Here again we have to depend upon conjecture; but two
things stand out clearly:
    (*a*) The letter must have been written before the end of the rule of
Kallippos. Plato regarded Kallippos as a fiend incarnate, and some
allusion to his downfall would have been inevitable, if it had occurred.
    (*b*) It bears in many places the marks of hurried writing. The
writer's mind is too full of intense feeling for adherence to the conventions of literary prose. Instances of this will be found at 325 c 5–326
b 4, 332 c 6–333 a 5, 335 a 2–c 1, 335 e 3–336 b 8; and most of the
narrative parts of the letter give the impression of having been rapidly
dictated. The whole can hardly have taken more than two or three
months to write. If, therefore, on the evidence stated in my paper
(*Class. Quart. l.c.* pp. 148, 149) we take midsummer 354 B.C. as the
probable date of Dion's murder, and suppose that the letter of Kallippos
reached Athens a few weeks later, the 7th Epistle may well have been
finished and in circulation at the beginning of the following year.

(2)

The 8th Epistle is addressed to the friends of Dion; but the second
sentence states that it is written for the benefit of all parties in Sicily,
and we may assume that it was actually sent to the Dionean party for
circulation. But the letter is the work of a literary artist; it is a careful
composition, intended also for the general public and for posterity. It is
quite independent of the 7th Epistle,* nor does it, like that letter,
profess to be an answer to any previous communication. Before
stating the historical difficulty it will be well to fix its date as nearly
as possible. Those who accept it as genuine have usually dated it
after the expulsion of Kallippos from Syracuse† (Intr. p. 50). There is
nothing in the letter to render such a view necessary, and a good deal
against it. If Kallippos had already been ousted, Plato would surely
have dwelt with emphasis on his defeat; it is most unlikely that he
would have passed over so important a fact without some clear allusion
to it.‡

---

    * For the supposed references to Ep. VII see notes on 354 a 5 and
356 c 1.
    † Raed. (*Rhein. Mus.* vol. LXI, p. 439) leaves it doubtful and calls
attention to the tense of ἐλευθεροῖ.
    ‡ F. Egermann (Diss. on pl. Br. VII and VIII, Vienna, 1928), who
argues strongly in favour of putting the letter after the expulsion of
Kallippos, relies mainly on two points. (1) That the words πᾶσιν τοῖς

What we learn from the letter is that the Dionean party have joined hands with Dion's nephew, Hipparinos, that they have received help from him, that he has shown a pious temperament (ὅσιος τρόπος), that, though the son of a tyrant, he is of his own free will setting the city free (356 a; the present ἐλευθεροῖ shows that the action is still going on). The position is clear, if we suppose: (1) that Kallippos is in possession of the citadel; (2) that Hipparinos has joined the Dioneans; (3) that the Dioneans have not yet had to retire to Leontinoi.

We may now state the historical difficulty. In the latter part of the Epistle Dion is introduced, giving his advice in the form of an address to the Syracusans. He recommends a constitution of the oligarchical type with three titular kings: (1) his own son, whose name is not mentioned, (2) Hipparinos, son of Dionysios I, (3) Dionysios II. Now three other authorities, Plutarch, Nepos and Aelian, state that Dion's son had met his end, either by accident or by suicide, before his father's murder.

It is usually said that there are three conceivable ways of meeting this difficulty: we may say either (a) that the other authorities are wrong and that Dion's son was not dead, or (b) that the news of his death had not reached Plato, or (c) that Plato is referring to Dion's posthumous son, who was born while his mother was shut up in the prison of Kallippos.

The third of these views is rendered impossible by the language used in the letter (see note on 357 b 7), and, if we have decided that the 8th Epistle was written while Kallippos was still holding the citadel, and

------

ἐν Συρακούσαις (352 c 1) prove that Kallippos, the ἀνοσιουργός mentioned two lines later, must have been outside Syracuse. This is pressing the language unduly. The clause πλὴν εἴ τις κ.τ.λ. is merely an afterthought, added to remind the reader that there is one enemy with whom reconciliation is impossible; but it also implies that Kallippos is still a person to be reckoned with. (2) That the altered position of affairs, which the 8th Epistle implies throughout, has been caused by the expulsion of Kallippos. When the 7th Epistle was written, the disorders in Syracuse were so great that it would have been premature to propose reforms (336 d 7, εἰ δ᾽ οὖν ταῦτα μὲν ὕστερα κ.τ.λ.); but now the writer feels that there is sufficient harmony for definite details to be suggested. This is an important point; but it is not necessary to suppose that the improved state of affairs must have been caused by the expulsion of Kallippos. The last sentence of Ep. VIII before the final invocation, if translated with due regard to the tenses, implies that the coalition between the two Hipparinoi had already produced harmony of views among the main body of the citizens (see note on 357 c 2). The case is one in which we have to choose between probabilities; but the probability that Plato had not heard of the expulsion of Kallippos is heightened by the consideration that the news of his expulsion must have been very soon followed, if not accompanied by, tidings that Hipparinos had made himself despot.

Dion's widow was in prison, it becomes doubly impossible. For during the mother's imprisonment no tidings of the posthumous son's birth could have reached Plato at Athens. We have therefore to consider only the first two views. As the historical problem is a nice one, it is worth while to give a full account of the data. Plutarch, the most important authority, who is probably drawing his information from Timaios, relates (*Dion*, 55) that when the conspiracy of Kallippos was being formed, Dion was sitting one evening in the portico of his house. He heard a sound at the other end of the portico, and, looking up, saw a woman of lofty stature, who resembled in dress and feature the Furies of tragedy, and was sweeping the house with a broom. Startled and alarmed, he sent for his friends, told them of the vision, and begged them to stay with him for the night, in case it should reappear. It was not seen again; but a few days later, his son, who was just growing out of boyhood (σχεδὸν ἀντίπαις ὤν), in consequence of some vexation and anger arising from a trifling and childish cause, threw himself from the roof and was killed.

Plutarch adds that Kallippos thereupon spread a rumour that Dion, having lost his own son, was going to adopt Apollokrates, the son of Dionysios, as his successor in the tyranny, and that this helped him to bring his conspiracy to a head.

Nepos probably had some other authority before him. He mentions the suicide parenthetically (*Dion*, 4) and without any precise indication of time, while relating an earlier part of Dion's life. He says that while Dion was in the Peloponnese getting together forces for his expedition, Dionysios, having Dion's family in his power, encouraged the boy in vicious habits so that his character became completely depraved. After the return of Dion, when he was trying to reform his son's character and had placed him under strict guardians, the boy could not endure this new kind of life, and committed suicide by throwing himself down from the roof of the house.

Aelian is certainly following a different authority. He tells the story (*V.H.* III, 4) as a short anecdote with no details of time, grouping it with other instances of the fortitude of parents on the occasion of the death of their children. He says: "Dion, the son of Hipparinos and the associate of Plato, happened to be engaged in public and national affairs, when his son lost his life by falling from the roof into the court of the house. Dion did not allow himself to be affected by this incident, but went on doing that on which he was engaged before". Plutarch tells the story again in his *Consol. ad Apollon.* ch. 33, 119 b, following the same version as Aelian, and making no suggestion of suicide.

These stories do not agree together, and it is easy to criticise each of them individually as suspicious. But they show that the writers had before them more than one independent authority for the fact of the death of Dion's son. That fact is supported by another important piece of testimony, which some of the critics have ignored. Dion's son does not appear on the scene after his father's murder. He was not one of those imprisoned by Kallippos and released at the end of his rule; nor was he with those unfortunates, when they subsequently fled to Hiketas at Leontinoi, and were done to death by him (see Intr. p. 49, note *). If he had been alive during these transactions, his name must have been mentioned.

The only probable supposition is that his death had actually occurred before that of Dion. There may have been, even at the time, some doubt about the circumstances of his death. It may have been, as Aelian's story implies, an accident; and gossip may have converted the accident into a suicide, and then embellished it with details, disparaging to Dionysios, and illustrative of the fortitude of Dion. But it is not sound criticism to dismiss the whole incident as fiction, because Plutarch and others are fond of telling a good story.

Plato, however, certainly wrote under the impression that Dion's son was alive. If there were reason to believe that he had trustworthy evidence before him, the historical difficulty would be serious. So long as people believed that the 7th Epistle was preceded by a letter to Plato from the friends of Dion, the difficulty was serious. If, however, we regard that letter as a literary fiction, the problem is at once simplified. Plutarch's narrative implies that the interval between the death of Dion's son and the crime of Kallippos was a short one. Affairs at Syracuse were in a highly disturbed state; it is at least probable that no communication was sent to Athens during this interval; and after Dion's murder, as we have seen, the correspondence must have been at once stopped by Kallippos. It may have been renewed, somewhat tardily, after the Dionean party had removed to Leontinoi and formed their coalition with Hipparinos and Dionysios, whose ships would probably be the means by which communications would be sent. But need we suppose that the letters of the friends of Dion would, at that time, necessarily refer to the son of Dion, who had been removed from the scene several months before? They would be full of their own attempted operations and other matters which, like the death of Eudemos, belonged to the present. There is no improbability in supposing that the death of Dion's son was left unmentioned, and that Plato wrote the 8th Epistle as well as the 7th in complete ignorance that such an event had taken place. If then we give the 8th Epistle its proper date, and treat as a literary fiction the letter from the friends of Dion mentioned in the 7th Epistle, the historical difficulty is removed.

Two further points bearing on the 7th Epistle may conveniently be dealt with here, viz. (3) the identity of the Hipparinos mentioned at the beginning of the letter, and (4) the relation between the letter and the *Antidosis* of Isokrates.

(3)

The passage in the 7th Epistle (324 a 5) runs as follows: "When I made my first visit to Sicily, being then about forty years old, Dion was of the same age as Hipparinos is now, and the opinion which he then formed was that which he always retained, I mean, the belief that the Syracusans ought to be free and governed by the best laws. So it is no matter for surprise if some God should make Hipparinos adopt the same opinion as Dion about the forms of government".

At the time of Plato's first visit to Sicily Dion was about twenty years old. The Hipparinos referred to must, therefore, have been a person of about twenty when the letter was written. Dion's son, at the time of his death, is said by Plutarch to have been ἀντίπαις, i.e. about eighteen years of age. Now Plato had been on very intimate terms with the family during his second and third visits to Syracuse. He must have known Dion's son well; but he would not have the same precise knowledge of his age which the boy's mother had. Six years had elapsed since his return to Athens, and it is not at all improbable that he figured to himself the youth of eighteen as a young man of twenty, especially if he wished to emphasise a parallel between the young man and his father.

On the other hand there are serious difficulties in the way if we suppose the other Hipparinos, the son of Dionysios the Elder and Aristomachê, to be referred to as a young man of twenty. He too must have been well known to Plato. The circumstances of his birth have been related in the Introduction. If we are to suppose him to have been about twenty years of age in 354 or 353 B.C., he must have been born not less than twenty-four years after his mother's marriage, and she must subsequently have given birth to at least one other child. This is not a physical impossibility; but it is much more likely that the interval of Aristomachê's childlessness was shorter, and that in 354 B.C. her elder son was a man of about thirty. It is therefore simpler to suppose that the Hipparinos here mentioned was Dion's son; and there is nothing in the passage itself which renders this at all unlikely. Language produces different effects on different minds; but surely most readers must feel it more probable that the two persons of whom Plato is here speaking are, not uncle and nephew, but father and son.*

---

* The difficulty arises partly because Plato, speaking through the mouth of Dion in Ep. VIII (355 e 5), makes him mention his son without giving his name, while Plutarch gives two names, (1) Hipparinos on the authority of Timonides, and (2) Aretaios on the authority of Timaios. Plutarch considers Timonides, as an intimate friend of Dion, to be the better witness. It is possible that the young man had both names, the name Aretaios having been added to prevent confusion with his cousin. But we have no right to treat this conjecture as a certainty.

Mr Post has a further note on the points at issue between us in the *Class. Quart.* for April 1930. In this he tries to lower the probable age of Dion's son, relying on Plutarch's description of him as παιδίον at the time of the surrender of the citadel, about a year perhaps before Dion's murder, and on his use of ἀντίπαις (*Pomp.* 76, 5) of another youth, supposed, rather problematically, to be about fifteen. Plutarch had no first-hand knowledge of the age of Dion's son, and it would be a

(4)

L. A. Post (*Thirteen Epistles*, p. 58) rightly emphasises the close connection between the 7th Epistle and the *Antidosis* of Isokrates. Both are apologies in the form of autobiographies; they must have appeared at closely approximate dates, and the connection between Plato and Dion has something in common with that which Isokrates claims to have existed between himself and Timotheos. Some of Post's points are overpressed; it is going too far to say that Isokrates twits Plato with the civil strife and executions which followed from Dion's success.

We may, however, take it as fairly certain that one of the two works inspired the other; and if, as shown above, it is probable on other grounds that the 7th Epistle was in circulation in the early part of 353 B.C., it is most likely that it was the source of inspiration for the *Antidosis*, which appeared in the course of the same year.

Other indications point in the same direction. Isokrates had not the same reasons for an Apologia as Plato. There is nothing in the 7th Epistle which can be construed into an allusion to Isokrates, while unmistakeable references to Plato and his School abound in the speech on the Antidosis. Quite an appreciable part of that work may not unfairly be described as an attempt on the part of Isokrates to justify his own career and activities as against those of Plato.

Both works have a fictitious setting; but their methods of handling the fiction are different, each being characteristic of its author. Plato leaves the reader to find out for himself the little mystification about the letter from the Dionean party; while Isokrates begins by revealing his secret and making sure that his readers are under no mistake about it.

---

mistake to lay too much stress on his language. But the meaning which a Greek would naturally give to ἀντίπαις is clear from Soph. Fr. 139 (Nauck):

οὗτοι γένειον ὧδε χρὴ διηλιφὲς
φοροῦντα κἀντίπαιδα καὶ γένει μέγαν
μητρὸς καλεῖσθαι παῖδα.

Plutarch regarded him as a youth approaching manhood at the time of Dion's death; and Plato, writing a few months later, may very well have spoken of him as being about twenty years of age. The fact that no name is given to the young man in Ep. VIII is explicable, as Wtz. suggests (*Pl.* II, 300), by Plato's desire to avoid confusion with his namesake. As to the probability of a letter being conveyed from Syracuse to Plato, when Kallippos was master of the position, our readers must decide between me and Mr Post; but I must thank him for calling attention to the ill-chosen phrase "purely literary document", which I applied to Ep. VII, when trying to bring out the point that it was not a personal letter.

EPISTLE VII.

1. 324 a 7. Ἱππαρῖνος; the son of Dion; for the difficulty see Intr. Rem. pp. 195, 196.

2. 324 b 3, 4. Notice the religious attitude, and the pleonastic style—both characteristic of Plato's old age.

3. 324 b 8. Νέος ἐγώ κ.τ.λ. Plato has promised to describe the growth of Dion's political views. It is a shock to the reader when, instead of doing so, he plunges abruptly into the story of the growth of his own views. We get back to Dion again in 327 a. For a similar jump aside see 333 d 1, ἦλθον…ἐγώ, with note. This digressional manner is characteristic of the old age of Plato. A good parallel is the transition from the 2nd to the 3rd book of the *Laws*. Plato has been speaking of music and gymnastic in education, and, having dealt with music in the latter part of Bk II, has promised that he will go on next to gymnastic. At the beginning of Bk III we expect him to do so; but, without any apology, he jumps into a digression on the origin of political institutions. After some ten pages he points out (683 a) that this rambling procedure, ἡ πλάνη τοῦ λόγου, has given him a wider outlook. Here he might have said that the account of the formation of his own views made those of Dion intelligible.

4. 324 c 3. εἴς καὶ πεντήκοντα. Further on (325 a 6) the new government receives its usual title, "the Thirty". The name had painful associations, and Plato begins by avoiding it. His narrative here agrees with that of Aristotle (*Ath. Pol.* 35), who, after his account of the appointment of the Thirty, gives among their first acts the creation of these two boards, both of which are evidently new institutions. As to the initial duties of the Eleven, Plato is our best witness; and they, like the Ten in the Peiraeus, may in the first instance have been put in charge of all purely urban matters. These would include the charge of the prison. The wholesale imprisonments and prosecutions carried out by the new government would make their work as a Prisons' Board the most important part of their functions. After the fall of the oligarchy the convenience of having a Prisons' Board was probably recognised, and the Eleven were retained as a permanent part of the constitution.

5. 324 d 1. Plato mentions no names: his "connections" were his uncle Charmides, the brother of his mother Periktione, who was one of the board of Ten in the Peiraeus, and Kritias, the cousin of Charmides, who was leader of the extreme party among the Thirty, and mainly responsible for their policy of wholesale executions. Both of these lost their lives in the final struggles which led to the overthrow of the Thirty.

6. 324 d 4. ἔκ τινος ἀδίκου βίου. Lysias, *cont. Eratosth.* 5, describes the Thirty as professing to aim at a moral reformation, φάσκοντες χρῆναι τῶν ἀδίκων καθαρὰν ποιῆσαι τὴν πόλιν καὶ τοὺς λοιποὺς πολίτας ἐπ' ἀρετὴν καὶ δικαιοσύνην τραπέσθαι. Both he and Plato are probably giving the substance of actual propaganda of the Thirty.

7. 324 d 7. χρυσόν. See Burnet's note on *Phaedo*, 72 b 9, and Cobet

(*Var. Lect.* p. 325), who compares Eur. *Tro.* 436, ὡς χρυσὸς αὐτῷ τἀμὰ καὶ Φρυγῶν κακὰ | δόξει ποτ᾽ εἶναι. Plutarch uses Plato's attractive phrase more than once; cf. *Timol.* XI, 4, χρυσὸν ἀπέδειξαν τὰς ἐν τῇ τυραννίδι συμφοράς. Isokrates in his *Areopagiticus* (152 c) had used similar language: ἐπεὶ καὶ τὴν ἡμετέραν πολιτείαν ᾗ πάντες ἐπιτιμῶσιν, ἣν παραβάλωμεν αὐτὴν μὴ πρὸς τὴν ὑπ᾽ ἐμοῦ ῥηθεῖσαν, ἀλλὰ πρὸς τὴν ὑπὸ τῶν τριάκοντα καταστᾶσαν, οὐδεὶς ὅστις οὐκ ἂν θεοποίητον εἶναι νομίσειεν. The *Areopagiticus* was published in 355 B.C., about two years before Plato wrote this letter; the passage was probably in Plato's mind.

8. 324 e 1. ὃν ἐγὼ κ.τ.λ. An intentional echo of the last sentence of the *Phaedo*, ἀνδρός, ὡς ἡμεῖς φαῖμεν ἄν, τῶν τότε ὧν ἐπειράθημεν ἀρίστου καὶ ἄλλως φρονιμωτάτου καὶ δικαιοτάτου.
When Sokrates and four other citizens were ordered by the Thirty to go to Salamis and arrest Leo, the Salaminian, he walked off home, and the others carried out the arrest. See *Apol.* 32 c. There is a slight anacoluthon in the long sentence 324 d 6–325 a 5. Instead of maintaining the construction of ὁρῶν the writer, after his parenthesis, makes a fresh start at ἃ δὴ πάντα.

9. 325 a 5 ff. Again no names are mentioned. "Those who had returned" were Thrasyboulos and the other exiles, who overthrew the government of the Thirty in 403 B.C.

10. 325 b 6. δυναστεύοντές τινες. This refers to Anytos, one of the most influential of the men engaged in politics after the downfall of the Thirty, and one of the three accusers of Sokrates. For the later legends about Anytos see Intr. pp. 83, 84. Plato evidently knew nothing about them.

11. 325 c 4. The tautology is not attractive, but is typical of the unconventional style affected in Plato's later works. Karsten thought it intolerable and rendered the first participle "unum ex accusatis", and the second as "exules". But in this context τῶν τότε φευγόντων must mean "the exiled party".

12. 325 d 1—326 a 7. οὔτε γὰρ ἄνευ...κατιδεῖν. This long sentence, which is broken up by two parentheses, 325 d 2–5 and 326 a 3–5, states under three heads the difficulties which prevented Plato from taking part in politics—the want of associates, which affected himself personally, the deplorable state of the laws at Athens, and the deterioration of the Greek States generally.

13. 325 d 6. I have followed the other translators in giving an impersonal force to ἐπεδίδου, but can find no parallel; Plato may have simply meant that the laws, written and unwritten, were increasing in bulk. He may have been thinking of the remarkable passage in Isokr. *Areopag.* 147 d, in which the multiplication of laws is spoken of as a sign of deterioration in States. Cf. Tac. *Ann.* III, 27, corruptissima re publica plurimae leges.

14. 326 a 5. λέγειν τε ἠναγκάσθην. Plato here reproduces the substance of two passages in the *Republic*, which must have been familiar to his readers: 473 c, "Until then philosophers are kings, or the kings and princes of this world have the spirit and power of philosophy, and political greatness and wisdom meet in one, and those commoner natures who follow either to the exclusion of the other are compelled to stand aside, cities will never cease from ill—no, nor the human race, as I believe—and then only will our State have a possibility of life and behold the light of day". 499 b, "This was the reason why truth forced us to admit that there is no chance of perfection, either in cities or governments or individuals, until a necessity was laid upon the second small class of philosophers (not the rogues, but those whom we termed useless), that they should take care of the State and obey the call of the State; or until kings themselves or the sons of kings or potentates, were inspired with a true love of philosophy" (Jowett). In his note on the second of these passages J. Adam approves the poet Gray's suggestion that the mention of the "sons of potentates" was added by Plato as a compliment to the younger Dionysios. However this may be, it embodies a thought which he probably owed to his earlier Sicilian experiences. For the form taken by Plato's later views on the subject see Intr. pp. 13, 14.

15. 326 b 6—c 4. ἐλθόντα δὲ...κραθήσεται. This passage is translated by Cicero, *Tusc. Disp.* v, 35, and is quoted by other moralists, as Clement of Alexandria (*Paedagogus*, 150). It was probably included in collections of elegant extracts. The luxury of the Italian and Sicilian Greeks was a shock to the inhabitants of Greece Proper, whose habits were simple and abstemious. Plato (*Rep.* 404 d) speaks with disapproval of Syracusan banquets and the refinements of Sicilian cookery. Athenaios (IV, 166 e) illustrates the self-indulgent habits of the Tarentines by a quotation from Theopompos (Fr. 226), who says that the city had public banquets once a month, and that the life of private citizens was a continuous succession of dissipations. From b 6–d 6 we have another long unwieldy sentence describing Plato's impressions. At εἶναι, d 3, he passes into a virtual or. obl. describing his thoughts, loosely dependent on ἤρεσεν.

16. 326 d 7. The "previous convictions" are those which he has quoted at 326 a 7. Ad. (*Progr.* p. 10) considers that Plato's views were now completed by learning that moral training must precede intellectual. His views on this point were no doubt confirmed by his experiences in these visits. But the view on which he lays stress here is that political instability is the result of moral corruption. For the circumstances of his visit see Intr. Sect. II.

17. 326 e 2. τῶν κρειττόνων. For this use of the word cf. *Soph.* 216 b 4, *Tim.* 77 c 6, *Laws* 718 a 5, *Epin.* 991 d 5. Plato's visit led to consequences so far-reaching that it was natural to see in it the working of a higher power. Whether the consequences to Syracuse were to be good or bad, would depend, Plato implies, on the action taken with regard to his advice. The rejection of this by Dionysios II had led to disasters, and similar disasters would follow, if it was now rejected by the friends of Dion.

18. 327 b 5, 6. περί is used loosely to describe various relations: in b 5 "in accordance with", in b 6 "in the case of". See Intr. p. 96.

19. 327 c 3–6. Cf. *infr.* 328 c 2, πείσας γὰρ ἕνα μόνον κ.τ.λ. Plato was thinking perhaps of his own words (*Rep.* 502 b 4), that his ideal could be realised, if a single competent man could be found who had a city ready to obey him. For the periphrastic tense συμβῆναι γενόμενον cf. Intr. p. 96.

20. 327 c 7. With ἐκ παντὸς τρόπου here and again in d 8, and in 338 b 4, cf. the letter on p. 131 of Deissmann's *Licht vom Osten*, ἀπόστειλον ἡμῖν ἐκ παντὸς τρόπου τὸν αὐλητὴν Πέτωον.

21. 327 d 5, 6. Here, as throughout, the moral reformation of the community was the thing uppermost in Plato's mind.

22. 327 e 5. καταλέγων δὲ. In place of a verb for this subject a fresh sentence is started at 328 b 1. Richards would remove the anacoluthon by reading δή for δέ. This is unnecessary.

23. 328 a 3. ἀδελφιδοῦς. The two sons of Dion's sister, Aristomachê, were probably approaching manhood in 368 B.C. Their mother was married to Dionysios I in 398 B.C., but remained childless for some years, it is not known how many. Dion may have had other nephews of whom nothing is known.

24. 328 b 4. For the changeableness of the young cf. *Laws*, 929 c 5.

25. 328 b 8. For the superfluous δεῖν see Intr. p. 96.

26. 328 c 6. παντάπασι λόγος κ.τ.λ. The Greek is very emphatic, "wholly and solely words, if I may say so". In Eur. *H.F.* the Chorus of old men call themselves ἔπεα μόνον and the aged Amphitryon describes himself as οὐδὲν ὄντα πλὴν γλώσσης ψόφον (*H.F.* 111 and 229). This reference to the opinion of his conduct, which some had formed, is important as showing that there had been real detraction of Plato on account of his Sicilian journeys. Absurd charges with regard to them are common in the later literature. The change of construction at κινδυνεύσειν to virtual or. obl. is due to the same studied negligence which we have in other passages; cf. note on 331 a 2, 3.

27. 328 d 4. It is natural that Plato, the writer of Dialogues, should pass into direct speech; cf. 346 a 7, e 1, 348 c 5, 349 a, b, and Dion's speech, 355 ͣ

28. 328 d 4. οὐχ ὁπλιτῶν; cf. 322 d 1. What follows is an important testimony to Plato's personal influence over his pupils.

29. 328 e 3. φιλοσοφία; cf. *Tim.* 47 b 1, φιλοσοφίας γένος, οὗ μεῖζον ἀγαθὸν οὔτ' ἦλθεν οὔτε ἥξει ποτὲ τῷ θνητῷ γένει δωρηθὲν ἐκ θεῶν.

30. 329 b 4. Διὸς ξενίου, i.e. from guilt as regards duty to friends; τῆς φιλοσόφου μοίρας is merely a periphrasis for τῆς φιλοσοφίας; cf. *Phileb.* 60 b, where ἡ τοῦ ἀγαθοῦ μοῖρα=τὸ ἀγαθόν.

31. 329 b 7. ἐλθὼν δέ κ.τ.λ. Cf. Plutarch, *Dion*, 14. Plato summarises the events of which Plutarch gives fuller details, taken probably from Timaios. See Intr. Sect. II.

32. 329 d 3. τὸν ἐμέ. Cf. *Theaet.* 166 a 5, γέλωτα δὴ τὸν ἐμὲ ἐν τοῖς λόγοις ἀπέδειξεν. Campbell remarks that the use of the article has a humorously pathetic effect; cf. also *Phileb.* 20 b 1.

33. 329 e 2. For the entrance to the harbour see pp. 23, 24.

34. 330 a 4. Codling and Short here suggest themselves as a parallel.

35. 330 b 7. On this passage Grote (*Hist.* ch. 84) remarks: "This is a strange account; but it reads like a real picture of a vain and weak prince, admiring the philosopher, coquetting with him, and anxious to captivate his approbation, so far as it could be done without submitting to the genuine Platonic discipline". For παραποδισθείη (330 b 3) see *Laws*, 652 b 1, with England's note.

36. 330 c 6. Plato is evidently referring to contemporary critics who had asked this question. In the next line the ἔργα are his advice to his correspondents, and the πάρεργα the narrative of his proceedings. Plato begins to be on doubtful ground here, and this may account for the cumbrous and laboured style of the following pages. For a parallel to his careful explanation of the order of his treatment of the subject see the opening of Bk ix of Wordsworth's *Prelude*.

37. 330 c 9. What follows is partly built up with materials from *Rep.* iv, 425 e–426 d: such repetitions are a common feature in an old man's writings. With Plato's attitude towards the disorganised State compare the saying of Confucius: "A sage will not enter a tottering State nor dwell in a disorganised one. When right principles of government prevail, he shows himself; but when they are prostrated, he remains concealed" (*Confucianism and Taoism*, by A. O. Douglas). With his attitude towards slaves in 331 b compare *Laws*, 777 b–778 a. The spirit there is the same as here; but in the *Laws* the attitude is sterner. We are there told not to advise but to order a slave. In both passages force must be applied in cases of disobedience, and in both the treatment of a slave is sharply marked off from that of a free man.

38. 331 a 2, 3. There are three difficulties here: (1) The plural ὑπηρετοῦντας after the singular συμβούλῳ. (2) The optative κελεύοιεν where we expect a participle κελεύουσιν to balance προαγορεύουσιν. (3) The singular γίγνοιτο where we expect γίγνοιντο with subject supplied from βουλήσεσιν.

(1) For the change from singular to plural, as due to studied negligence of style, cf. *Epin.* 982 c 5–d 7, 990 c 3, 4; with notes in my edition.

(2) The more difficult κελεύοιεν cannot have arisen from the easier reading κελεύουσιν, which appears as a correction in one MS. κελεύοιεν is a throw-back to the clause εἰ μὲν συμβουλεύοιτο. It is tacked on as a sort of parenthetical afterthought—"Suppose they should bid them". An εἰ has to be supplied for it from εἰ συμβουλεύοιτο. Egermann proposes to make the sentence grammatical by inserting εἰ after συμβουλεύειν and striking out δέ after ταῖς. But without δέ the sentence is very lame; and it is not impossible for an agile mind to repeat the εἰ from εἰ συμβουλεύοιτο. For a similar omission of εἰ cf. *Rep.* 337 e 6, ἀπειρημένον αὐτῷ εἴη, where it is not possible, with J. Adam, to eject εἴη;

but an εἰ can be supplied from the implied condition in the preceding participles εἰδώς and φάσκων. In both passages the change of construction is meant to suggest the informality of conversation. (3) γίγνοιτο must be taken as impersonal; cf. 325 e 4, ἄμεινον ἂν γίγνοιτο. Here, as often, Plato has made a slight change in his phrasing, so as to give the reader something which he does not expect.

39. 331 b 4. ἀφοσιωσάμενος. The metaphor is that of doing a thing as a mere matter of ceremonial. See *Laws*, 752 d 4.

40. 331 c 1. Another quotation—from *Crito*, 51 c 2. It introduces here a passage full of strong feeling. Milton has something of Plato's spirit in *Par. Reg.* IV, 143:

> *What wise and valiant man would seek to free*
> *These thus degenerate, to themselves enslaved?*

41. 331 d 2. βίαν κ.τ.λ. For the accumulated genitives cf. 324 b 5, ὁ τρόπος τῆς γενέσεως αὐτῆς. A few pages farther on Plato allows the threat of force (337 a). Again, in *Polit.* 296 d, he maintains that the true statesman will take the course required by scientific government, κἂν πείσας, κἂν μὴ πείσας. But in both these cases the force is to be used by persons who hold the supreme power. Plato here condemns the use of force to effect a revolution. Cicero (*ad Fam.* I, 9. 18) quotes with approval Plato's condemnation of force; but he is probably referring to the *Crito*. For the prayers which are to accompany the abstinence from action cf. Ep. XI, 359 b 3, and the note on εὐχή, 352 e 5.

42. 332 a 5. This numerical computation of the inferiority of Dionysios to Darius is quite in Plato's manner. Compare the calculation of the numerical values of the happiness of the different types of men, *Rep.* 587 d. In what follows the Mede must be the Pseudo-Smerdis in the version of the story given by Herodotus (III, 70 ff.). The facts are told by Darius on his Behistun inscription, and agree on the whole with the narrative of Herodotus. The pretender was a Magian priest from Media, by name Gaumata, who professed to be Bardiya (i.e. Smerdis), the younger son of Cyrus. Cambyses, before his departure for Egypt, had had Bardiya murdered, and kept his death a secret. This gave the pretender his opportunity. Plato must have had a wrong version of the story; he refers to it again in *Laws*, 695 b, and again calls the pretender a eunuch, and uses the number seven where we should expect six, as here in 332 b 2.

43. 332 b 8. ἐμβεβλημένας. Thucydides uses this word, both in active (c. dat.) and in passive, of ships ramming others and being rammed. The "seventy years" describes roughly the period 478–404 B.C.

44. 332 c 3. The wholesale transfer to Syracuse of the population of city States was one of the points in the policy of Dionysios which gave a most severe shock to Greek feelings. His friendlessness, like his literary ambition, finds a parallel in Frederick the Great, of whom it has been said: "He lived and died friendless, because he did not understand that friendship meant giving as well as taking, and he was content, for the most part, to be surrounded by sycophants, whom he was free to insult either in speech or in the practical jokes of a rare brutality" (article by C. Whibley, *Blackwood*, Feb. 1917, p. 288). **45.** 332 c 6—333 a 2. ἃ δὴ...ὄντως. Plato here describes and justifies the treatment which he and Dion attempted to apply to the neglected mind of Dionysios. The key to the passage is in the words ἔμφρονά τε καὶ σώφρονα (331 e 2). Plato wished to do two ἱ·ings for Dionysios before allowing him to embark on political activity: (1) to waken his intelligence; (2) to give him self-control. He had not received the παιδεία and συνουσίαι which others receive; συνουσίαι are lessons from teachers, "conférences" (cf. *Protag.* 335 b 3). To make him ἔμφρων this missing education must be supplied by a definite course of teaching. The procedure is the same as that described in *Laws*, 711 e 7: ὡσαύτως δὲ καὶ συμπάσης δυνάμεως ὁ αὐτὸς πέρι λόγος, ὡς ὅταν εἰς ταὐτὸν τῷ φρονεῖν τε καὶ σωφρονεῖν ἡ μεγίστη δύναμις ἐν ἀνθρώπῳ συμπέσῃ, τότε πολιτείας τῆς ἀρίστης καὶ νόμων τῶν τοιούτων φύεται γένεσις, ἄλλως δὲ οὐ μή ποτε γένηται. The verb φρονεῖν there covers the same ground as our adjective ἔμφρονα. Commentators have gone wrong through failing to see the significance of this word. We have σώφρων τε καὶ ἔμφρων again, 351 d 2, to describe the character of Dion.

I have followed Bt. in supposing a lacuna after πρῶτον. How. proposes to fill this up by repeating words from 331 d 7 ζῆν μὲν τὸ καθ' ἡμέραν κ.τ.λ. Post also inserts in brackets "(regulate his daily life)". This only gives us σώφρονα and leaves out ἔμφρονα. The missing words should describe the provision of παιδεία and συνουσίαι. These would include the much criticised course of geometry. For Plato's reticence about this see Intr. p. 22. The lacuna after πρῶτον can hardly be accidental. Nor can we, with How., suppose that Plato was merely saving himself the trouble of writing something over again; for the passage in 331 d 7 does not admit of verbatim reproduction here. The simplest explanation is to suppose that the ultimate source of our text was a copy filed in the Academy, and that Plato struck out the missing words with a view to a revision which was never carried out. The traditional text ἐπὶ ταῦτα, which Egermann wishes to retain, can be made to give the right meaning, but it has no MS authority, and it is not easy to see how such a corruption as ἔπειτα ταύτῃ could have arisen.

46. 333 a 5. φόρον. Gelon, after his victory at Himera (480 B.C.), made the Carthaginians pay an indemnity of 2000 talents. Dionysios, after his defeat at Kronion (379 B.C.), made a peace, by which he restored to them his conquests west of the Halykos and paid an indemnity of 1000 talents. Holm (*Gesch. Sic.* II, p. 142) suggests that if, as is probable, this sum was paid in instalments, we have an explanation of the statement that Dionysios paid tribute to the barbarians. For the impersonal ἕτοιμον εἶναι cf. *Rep.* 567 a 10 with J. Adam's note.

47. 333 b 2. I have translated Bt.'s text, but Hermann may be right in striking out τά after πράγματα. The "short time" will then be

that taken in telling the story. The interval between Dion's expulsion
and his return was about ten years, which seems too long for ἐν ὀλίγῳ
χρόνῳ. It should be noticed that Plato insists on the point that the
expedition proceeded from Athens as much as from Corinth and the
Peloponnese. **48.** 333 b 4. δίς. Cf. 356 a 1. The first deliverance was from
Dionysios the Younger, the second from Nypsios the Neapolitan.
49. 333 b 7. ὁ δὲ τοῖς κ.τ.λ. A violent anacoluthon of the nominativus pendens type. The writer begins as if a verb like ἐπείθετο were
going to follow, but substitutes for it the words ταῦτα τότε ἐνίκησεν,
where ταῦτα is the charge of aiming at the tyranny, which was brought
against Dion. **50.** 333 d 1–d 7. ἦλθον...διήμαρτεν. This mention of Plato's last
visit to Syracuse is quite outside the story, which is dealing with the
events which followed Dion's victory. It is a parenthesis, intended to
show the contrast between Plato's conduct and that of Dion's murderers.
For the digressional style see note on 324 b 8. The stress which Plato
lays on his own freedom from political corruption, and on the importance of this as removing any possible stain from the good name of
Athens, will give a shock to those who forget that there is often a strong
vein of egoism in characters otherwise very noble. **51.** 333 d 5. γενέσθαι describes the single act of joining Dionysios,
γίγνεσθαι the permanent state resulting from it. **52.** 333 e 1. For Plato's reticence about names cf. 324 d 1. Plutarch
(*Dion*, 54) gives the name of Kallippos, but, though he uses this passage
for the origin of his friendship with Dion, he does not mention his
brother. Nepos (*Dion*, 9) speaks of two brothers, giving their names as
Callicrates and Philostratus. It is not clear what his authority was; but
it is possible that Kallippos, after seizing the supreme power, may have
changed his name to the more high-sounding Kallikrates. For fuller
details about the murder see Intr. p. 48. **53.** 333 e 4. μυεῖν and ἐποπτεύειν are complementary: "to initiate
and to be initiated". It is inferred that Kallippos initiated Dion into
the Eleusinian Mysteries. **54.** 334 a 6. For παρίεμαι cf. *Apol.* 17 c 7. Richards's προσίεμαι
(*Platonica*, p. 264) is uncalled for. His other conjectures, ἐξαρνοῦμαι for
ἐξαιροῦμαι in b 2, and αἰτίω for ἀξίω in b 7, are useful as showing how
Plato has avoided the phraseology which the reader expects. The
rendering which I have given for ἀξίω puts some strain on the word,
but is not impossible. **55.** 334 b 1–c 2. The strong feeling for Athens is characteristic of
Plato's later writings; *v. infr.* on 336 d 5. **56.** 334 c 5, 6, and d 7. The advice is that referred to in 354 a 5 as
his παλαιὰ συμβουλή, to make an end of the tyranny. For the occasions
on which it was given see 334 d 5. The third time is the auspicious
time. The Athenians connected it with the third libation to Zeus Soter;
cf. 340 a 3.

206 NOTES

57. 334 c 8. The language here becomes impressive, and poetical words and phrases appear, e.g. οὐκ ἄμεινον (cf. Heraclit. Fr. 104) and ὀλέθριος.

58. 334 e 3. Lit. "None of us is undying". In 335 a we are told that the soul (ψυχή) is undying or immortal. There is no inconsistency. A man is not only soul, but soul in combination with a body (ψυχὴ καὶ σῶμα παγέν, *Phaedr*. 246 c). The Stoic view that man is only the reasoning soul (λογικὴ ψυχή) and not the body at all, was not Platonic. Simplicius (Pref. to *Comm. on Epict. Ench.*) states this doctrine, quoting the proof of it in the *First Alkibiades*. But that is one of many indications that that Dialogue was not the work of Plato. For the view that good and evil things belong specially to the soul see *Laws*, 896 c, d, a passage which harmonises with what is said here.

59. 335 a 3. The παλαιοὶ καὶ ἱεροὶ λόγοι, like the παλαιὸς λόγος of *Phaedo*, 70 e, refer to Orphic doctrines: see Bt.'s *Phaedo*, Intr. p. xviii. For the Orphic teaching see L. R. Farnell, *Greek Hero Cults*, ch. xiv, and for fuller details Miss J. Harrison's *Prolegomena to Greek Religion*; and for a classified collection of all important passages in Plato which refer to Orphism see P. Frutiger, *Les Mythes de Platon*, Paris, 1930, pp. 254–260. Farnell, with reference to Plato's indebtedness to Orphic teaching, says (p. 380), "his debt seems to have been great, his gratitude small". This is hardly just to Plato. It is true that he often borrows the imagery of Orphism, as here in the reference to the soul's πορεία; but there are usually words, like παλαιοὶ καὶ ἱεροὶ λόγοι here, which acknowledge the debt. He is, however, careful to distinguish his own view, that the soul's purification is accomplished by the philosophic life, from those which prescribed ritual cleansings. For the πορεία ὑπὸ γῆς cf. *Phaedr*. 256 d 6 and *Rep*. 615 a 2; and for a full statement of what is briefly indicated in this passage see *Laws*, x, 903 b–905 c, where Plato's eschatology is given in its most mature form.

60. 335 a 7–c 1. ὤν...πανταχῇ. For the doctrine that it is better to suffer wrongs than to inflict them cf. *Gorgias*, 523, where, as here, the reason for it is found in a future judgment. The statement of it here bears the marks of strong conviction, and the irregularities of the language arise from the writer's struggles to give full expression to deep feelings. In a 7 ὤν refers back to the λόγοις of a 3; and it would be better, as Richards suggests, to substitute a colon for the comma after δρᾶσαι. At ὤν begins a description of the tyrant in language parallel to that of *Rep*. ix. φιλοχρήματος must be translated "covetous", but, for the reason given in *Rep*. 580 e, it covers the whole range of desire. πένης τὴν ψυχήν recalls *Rep*. 579 a, ὁ τῷ ὄντι τύραννος πλείστων ἐνδεέστατος, ἐάν τις ὅλην τὴν ψυχὴν ἐπίστηται θεάσασθαι; cf. Wordsw. *Prel*. ix, 35,

That voluptuous life
Unfeeling, where the man who is of soul
The meanest thrives the most.

In b 2 ὡς οἴεται must be connected closely with καταγελῶν; cf. Ep. iii, 319 b 6. The ridicule is only fancied, because such beliefs are not really ridiculous, though to many people they seem so. The translation follows the Clar. Press text, in which Hermann's emendation τοὐμπίμπλασθαι is adopted. τοῦ μὴ πίμπλασθαι, the reading of the MSS, is certainly corrupt. The emendation is supported by the rhythm of the sentence and rendered almost imperative by the closely parallel passage about the man absorbed in the pursuit of wealth in *Laws*, 831 d, e, μηδὲν δυσχεραίνοντα, ἐὰν μόνον ἔχῃ δύναμιν κάθαπερ θηρίῳ τοῦ φαγεῖν παντοδαπὰ καὶ πιεῖν ὡσαύτως καὶ ἀφροδισίων πᾶσαν πάντως παρασχεῖν πλησμονήν. An old man uses his material more than once, and in his letter Plato was probably reproducing in an expanded form what he had written not long before in the *Laws*, adding a characteristic protest against using the name of a goddess to describe anything so gross as the sexual act.

After οὐχ ὁρῶν we have a hyperbaton, and the construction is οὐχ ὁρῶν κακὸν ἡλίκον ἀεὶ (ἔστιν) μετ' ἀδικήματος ἑκάστου (ἐν τούτοις) τῶν ἁρπαγμάτων οἷς συνέπεται ἀνοσιουργία, ἣν ἀναγκαῖον τῷ ἀδικήσαντι συνεφέλκειν κ.τ.λ. ἀνοσιουργία recalls the temple robberies of Dionysios I, and the sacrilegious oath of Kallippos in the sanctuary of the Korê, described by Plutarch, *Dion*, 56. In Ep. VIII ἀνοσιουργός is used again of Kallippos. συνεφέλκειν suggests a vision of something like the "burden" of Bunyan's pilgrim. νοστήσαντι is poetical; *v. supr.* note 57. Post's proposals for reconstructing the text seem to add to its difficulty.

61. 335 d 1. See note on 326 a 5, and Intr. pp. 13, 14, with the passage there quoted from *Laws* 709 e. The reformation which might have been accomplished by Dionysios, as young tyrant, was something more extensive and deep-rooted than that which Dion might have carried out, if he had survived.

62. 335 d 6, 7. Cf. *Rep.* 590 d, where Plato describes the foundations on which his theory of government rests; the two passages agree closely, but the *Republic* adds that the principles of wisdom and justice in the minds of the best men are divine.

63. 335 e 5. The superfluous ὡς following ὅτι is in accordance with Attic idiom and was not felt to be an anacoluthon; cf. *Rep.* 470 d with J. Adam's note, and *Hipp. Ma.* 281 c. But after ὡς there is an anacoluthon, harsh even for Plato's later style: the infinitive which ought to follow ἐπὶ τό never comes, and there is an ungrammatical change of construction to the finite verbs ἐκόσμησεν and προὐθυμεῖτο. At τούτων the construction changes again to accus. and infin. dependent on a verb supplied from οἶδα in 335 e 4. The whole passage suggests rapid composition: see Intr. Rem. φαιδρύνας is poetical, but is used in *Laws*, 718 b, τὸν αὐτοῦ βίον φαιδρυνάμενον κατὰ νόμον κοσμεῖν δεῖ, a passage which may have been running in Plato's head when this was written; σχήματι shows that the metaphor here is that of the bright apparel of the free woman as contrasted with the sordid dress of slavery or mourning. Hieron in a 8 may be a mistake on Plato's part for Gelon.

64. 336 b 4. ἀπέσωσεν has the same emphatic meaning as in *Laws*,

208 NOTES

692 c, another passage which may have been in Plato's mind here. There is no difficulty in supplying an object to the verb, like πάντα in that passage, and no need for the emendations of Hercher and Apelt. The verb is used again without an object in *Phileb.* 26 c 1.

65. 336 b 8. There is no need to amend αὕτη. The sentence, like the anacoluthon dealt with in note 49, starts with a nominativus pendens, and in place of the verb required by δαίμων and ἀλιτήριος the main sentence is resumed at αὕτη with a change of construction. The avenging fiend is the spirit which inspired Dion's murderers, who are mentioned again below, d 7; cf. 357 a 4, ξενικαὶ ἐρίνυες. ἀλιτήριος does not occur elsewhere in Plato, but it is used freely by the orators; cf. Antiphon, *Tetral. A.* ὅ τε γὰρ ἀποθανών, στερόμενος ὧν ὁ θεὸς ἔδωκεν αὐτῷ, εἰκότως θεοῦ τιμωρίαν ὑπολείπει τὴν τῶν ἀλιτηρίων δυσμένειαν. The provisions laid down in *Laws*, 865 d, to prevent the visits of the ghost of a victim of homicide show that Plato was inclined to treat such beliefs seriously. He may even be suggesting here that Dion's murderers were inspired by an ἀλιτήριος exacting vengeance for Herakleides. With the plurals τόλμαις and τόλμας in b 6 and d 7 cf. φθόνων in 344 b 6 and *Laws*, 869 a, μανίαις ὀργῆς, with Jowett's remarks, Intr. to *Laws*, p. 16. Similar plurals are not uncommon in poetry, especially in lyric passages of elevated style; cf. Aesch. *Ag.* 1576, μανίας μελάθρων ἀλληλοφόνους ἀφελούσῃ.

66. 336 d 5. *v. sup.* note 55, and compare the remark of the Spartan Megillos, *Laws*, 642 c: "The common saying is quite true, that a good Athenian is more than ordinarily good, for he is the only man who is freely and genuinely good by the inspiration of nature, and is not manufactured by the law".

67. 336 d 8. At first sight one is inclined to give to ὕστερα the idiomatic sense of "too late". But the context shows that Plato did not regard it as too late for taking action of the kind just described; action cannot, however, be taken, till, by means of moderation on the part of the victorious side, the civil strife has been brought out of the acute stage. What follows will seem a commonplace to those whose acquaintance with revolutionary struggles is derived from books. But Plato, who had been through them, knew how rare it is for the victorious party to show the moderation which he recommends. The spirit of his recommendation here is like that of *Laws*, 628 a–d.

68. 337 a 4. διτταῖς ἀνάγκαις κ.τ.λ. Cf. *Rep.* 465 a 10, ἱκανὼ γὰρ τὼ φύλακε τὼ κωλύοντε, δέος τε καὶ αἰδώς.

69. 337 b 3. φιλεῖ. Schema Pindaricum, not infrequent in Plato; cf. *Euthyd.* 302 c, ἔστι γὰρ ἔμοιγε καὶ βωμοὶ καὶ ἱερὰ οἰκεῖα, and *Rep.* 363 a, 463 a, *Symp.* 188 b; the verb is usually ἔστι or γίγνεται; here γίγνεσθαι φιλεῖ is equivalent to γίγνεται. In *Tim.* 45 a a plural subject occurs with προσέφυ.

70. 337 b 6. The qualifications resemble those required from the Director of Education in *Laws*, 765 d.

71. 337 c 1. ἀριθμὸν κ.τ.λ. It is not easy to see any point in this parenthesis. The number of male citizens at Syracuse was far in excess of 10,000. The body with which we have to do is not a permanent part of the new constitution, but a temporary committee appointed to draw up laws. It corresponds to the πρέσβεις of Ep. VIII, 356 c 6, whose numbers are left to be settled, not to the thirty-five νομοφύλακες of 356 d 4, 5. The number of such a committee would not be fixed in any special proportion to the population, and fifty seems much too large. In *Laws*, 702 c 5, a similar committee appointed to frame laws for the colony of Knossos consists of ten members only. The new laws introduced at Syracuse by Timoleon were framed by two commissioners from Corinth. The words may be a marginal suggestion of some not very clear-headed person, who felt the need of a definite proposal here, and who remembered the phrase μυρίανδρος πόλις. If the sentence is retained, the grammatical difficulty can be removed, as Egermann has suggested (*l.c.* p. 43), by treating the words ἱκανοὶ τοιοῦτοι as a parenthesis, independent of the construction of χρή; but to make sense τοιοῦτοι must be changed to τοσοῦτοι.

72. 337 d 6. δευτέρα μήν. For the first scheme see above, 335 d 1 and note 61; by the second scheme he means the reforms at which Dion was aiming at the very end of his career, when he sent for commissioners from Corinth, who were to design a new constitution of an aristocratic type; see Plut. *Dion*, 53. When Plato speaks of himself as acting jointly with Dion in this, he probably means that he had been active in advising the scheme.

73. 338 a 4. πόλεμος ἐν Σικελίᾳ. Plato cannot have been making a mistake about the facts here, nor is he likely to have described in these words the Lucanian war to which the passage is supposed by E. Meyer to refer. The hostilities with Carthage, which were in progress at the beginning of the reign of Dionysios, may have been still going on. But our materials for the history of Sicily during these years are very meagre, and we can only conjecture what the war here mentioned was.

74. 338 a 5. The full stop after ἀμφότεροι in the Clar. Press text should be altered to a colon, or to a comma with a dash. The words εἰρήνης δὲ γενομένης do not describe something previous to συνωμολογήσαμεν in order of time; but belong to μεταπέμψεσθαι in a 6. The hyperbaton is unaffected by the break of construction after ἀμφότεροι. This is a good instance of the studied negligence of Plato's later style. The point is important for the history. Odau (*Diss.* p. 8) has misunderstood the passage.

75. 338 c 6. Tayl. has pointed out that in the text of the Epistles the Attic form Ἀρχύτης is used (see below, 339 b), and not the Doric Ἀρχύτας which appears in the headings of Epistles IX and XII, and that this is one of the minor indications of genuineness. For the relations between Plato and Archytas see Intr. p. 16. In what follows I have assumed, in spite of the note of Richards (*Plat.* p. 281), that παράκουσμα here (and in 340 b 6) means "erroneous teaching". διακηκοότες is a *vox technica* for the relation of pupils to a philosopher. The detailed account, which follows, of the philosophical side of Plato's motives for his last journey to Sicily is important. If we had only the 3rd letter we might suppose, as Rit. has done, that Plato's only motive for the journey was to try to secure justice for Dion. The 7th letter shows that his desire to satisfy his conscience as a teacher of philosophy was quite as strong a motive with him (see note 82). When he looked back at the events from some distance of time, he seems to have regarded this as the most important of the reasons for his visit.

76. 338 d 2. τούτων, sc. διακηκοότες. This seems to be the only possible way of taking τούτων, and it is so taken by Andr., How. and Sou. Apelt makes it gen. after ἄλλοι, "different from these", i.e. different from the Pythagoreans, who are described in the preceding words, and translates on the supposition that it is only the second group who are filled with erroneous views. Post's translation implies the same construction. As I have shown above (Intr. pp. 26, 27), there most probably was a second group, consisting of hedonistic followers of Aristippos, and Plato was probably thinking mainly of them as the people who were stuffed full of erroneous views. But that group would draw its members from those who had picked up a little philosophy either from talks with Dion, or from those who had learnt from him. Dion was not a teacher of philosophy, and ἄττα shows that Plato is speaking in a depreciatory way of the scraps of knowledge picked up from him: ἔμμεστοι qualifies those who had heard him personally as well as the others. Bt.'s punctuation shows that he took this view of the passage.

77. 338 d 4, 5. τῶν περὶ τὰ τοιαῦτα. Is τῶν mas .. or neut.? Apelt makes it masc. and gen. after οἵ, "Diese letzteren unter den dortigen Philosophiebeflissenen". According to his view of the previous sentence, those engaged in philosophy, οἱ περὶ τὰ τοιαῦτα, have been divided into two groups, the Pythagoreans, and a second group different from them, τούτων τινὲς ἄλλοι, and the relative clause refers only to this second group—Andr.'s translation implies the same view of τῶν περὶ τὰ τοιαῦτα, though he does not follow Apelt in the previous sentence. The other translators make τῶν neuter, as I have done: the gen., as Sou. points out, is partitive and presents no difficulty. If τῶν is masc., we have a sentence which is forced and unnatural even for the informal style of Ep. VII.

78. 338 d 6. This is important. The fact that the young monarch had a real gift for philosophy helps to make Plato's attitude in the 2nd and 13th Epistles intelligible. What is said about the natural gifts of Dionysios at 314 d 4 is not a meaningless compliment. Hack. (p. 120) notes this as a sentence very unlikely to have been written by a forger.

79. 338 e 4. ἐν τοῖς ἄνω...λόγοις. Cf. 330 a, b.

80. 339 a 7. For Archedemos see Intr. Rem. to Ep. II.

81. 339 c 6. ἕξει is middle. There is no need to suppose with Richards (*Plat.* p. 267) that the text is corrupt. Strict grammar would require γιγνόμενον to agree with οὐδέν; the plural is due to the intervening τἆλλα.

82. 339 e 7. This is important as evidence of Plato's mental attitude; *v. sup.* note 75. The real disgrace would have been to have missed an opportunity of saving a soul.

83. 340 a 3. τὸ τρίτον τῷ σωτῆρι. *V. sup.* note 56.

84. 340 b 2. ἐξημμένος. For the metaphor cf. 341 c 7 (οἷον ἀπὸ πυρός κ.τ.λ.), 344 b 7 (ἐξέλαμψε φρόνησις), and *Rep.* 498 b 1, where ἐξάπτονται describes the kindling of the fire of philosophy.

85. 340 b 8. Lit. "What the thing (τὸ πρᾶγμα) as a whole is". So again in the next sentence, what the learner is akin to and worthy of is τὸ πρᾶγμα. "The reiterated τὸ πρᾶγμα seems to mean something like 'the grand concern'" (Tayl.). The phrase was perhaps part of the current slang of the Academy. Andr. compares *Phaedr.* 232 e; *Phaedo*, 61 c 9; *Theaet.* 168 b. Apelt (note 67) suggests that the test applied by Plato to Dionysios was not confined to a single interview, but took the form of a short course of introductory lessons in philosophy. This is in direct conflict with what Plato says here and at 345 a. The contents of the following pages have been fully discussed and the greater part of them (341 a–345 c) translated by Tayl. ("Analysis of ΈΠΙΣΤΗΜΗ in Plato's Seventh Epistle", *Mind*, N.S. No. 83). My translation, though made independently, owes much to corrections made after consulting his version, and I have with permission reproduced some of his notes. I have also derived help from Andr., "Die Philosophische Probleme in den Platonischen Briefen", *Philol.* LXXVIII, pp. 46 ff., and from Sou. (*l.c.* pp. xlviii–lviii).

86. 340 c, d. In this remarkable passage Plato was probably thinking of Dion. For the kinship between the philosophic soul and the object which it apprehends cf. *Phaedo*, 79 d: "But when returning into herself she reflects, then she passes into the other world, the abode of purity, and eternity, and immortality, and unchangeableness, which are her kindred, and with them she ever lives, when she is by herself and is not let or hindered; then she ceases from her erring ways, and being in communion with the unchanging is unchanging. And this state of the soul is called wisdom" (Jowett's translation).

87. 340 d 3. A well-regulated life is necessary as a preliminary condition of philosophic study; when he is dealing with the critical and religious side of philosophy, a man's whole attitude must depend on what he is. Andr. compares *Rep.* 444 c ff., where it is shown that virtue and vice correspond to health and disease, and 518 b, c, where the need for following philosophy with the whole soul is compared to the similar need for turning, not only the eye, but the whole body to the light. The insistence on abstinence indicates that careful rules about diet formed a part of the life of the Academy. This tradition was not lost; it reappears in Shakespeare's *Love's Labour's Lost*, when, in Act I Sc. I, the king of Navarre turns his court into "a little Academe". For δόξαις ἐπικεχρωσμένοι cf. Sir T. Browne, *Christian Morals*, Pt I, Sect. 9,

"Persons lightly dipt, not grained in generous honesty, are but pale in goodness and faint hued in integrity". μαθήματα suggests especially mathematical studies; cf. *Laws*, 817 e 5, *Rep.* 503 e 4, *Epin.* 990 c 5.
88. 341 a 7. See Intr. Rem. to Ep. II, where I have given reasons for believing that the interview here described is the same as that which is said in Ep. II to have taken place in the garden under the laurels.
89. 341 b 5. The optative ἀκούοι shows that the word is in virtual or. obl.—"differing completely, I am sure, from what he then heard". Hack. (p. 91) interprets the virtual or. obl. as meaning that Dionysios claimed to treat the subjects of Plato's teaching in a wholly original way. But the point is, not that Dionysios claimed to be original, as of course he did, but that the mere fact of his having written such a handbook showed that he had failed to understand Plato's teaching. For τέχνη (= handbook) cf. Isokr. κατὰ τῶν σοφ. 19: οἱ τὰς καλουμένας τέχνας γράψαι τολμήσαντες.
90. 341 b 6. οἵτινες δέ. After "who they are", the reader expects "I do not know": for this Plato substitutes "they do not themselves really know". For the meaning cf. Milton, *Par. Reg.* IV, 309,

Alas! What can they teach and not mislead,
Ignorant of themselves, of God much more?

The rather curious turn, that the men do not themselves know *who* they are (οἵτινες), is reproduced by M. Antoninus, VIII, 52, who perhaps had this passage in his head. The writers to whom Plato alludes may have put forward materialistic views. Plato's reticence with regard to their names is characteristic. See Intr. pp. 26, 27.
91. 341 c 4. οὔκουν κ.τ.λ. With this emphatic disclaimer compare the similar statement in Ep. II, 314 c 1 with note 25 on that Epistle. In the next line ῥητόν has mathematical associations. "For the repeated play on the word ῥητόν cf. *Rep.* 546 b: here the word has primarily its literal sense, but there is a pretty clear allusion to the specially mathematical sense in which magnitudes commensurable with a 'proposed' standard are said to be ῥητά (Euclid, *Elementa*, x, def. 3)" (Tayl. *l.c.* p. 349).
92. 341 c 7. ἐξαίφνης κ.τ.λ. "The context, I think, shows that the ψυχή is that of the disciple which catches fire from the soul of the Master. One might indeed suppose that only one soul is referred to, and that the meaning is that in either soul a smouldering fire suddenly bursts into flame, but I feel that this would be Neoplatonic rather than Platonic" (Tayl. *l.c.* p. 354). The fuller description of the process of kindling the light at 344 b 3–8 makes it clear that the fire comes from the soul of the Master, and that συνουσία and συʒῆν refer, not to the prolonged solitary pondering over problems, but to intercourse with a teacher. The mention of ἔλεγχοι which proceed by question and answer places this beyond doubt; cf. *Laws*, 968 c 6, where διδαχὴ μετὰ συνουσίας πολλῆς is used to describe the education of the members of the Nocturnal Council. The point is important. Plato, like the sages of India, was

convinced that the higher truths of philosophy could only be apprehended by personal intercourse with a teacher, in whose mind the light
had been kindled. Those who omit the part played by the teacher,
as is done by Wtz. (*Pl.* I, 650, 651, II, 292) misapprehend Plato's
meaning.

93. 341 d 2-4. "This sounds arrogant, but the arrogance is only in
the sound. It is Plato's apology for giving to the public of his time only
'discourses of Sokrates', and not an exposition of his own philosophy.
If the Platonic philosophy could have been imparted to the world at
large in a book, Plato was obviously neglecting his duty in not writing
that book" (Tayl. *l.c.* p. 355). The points in his highest teaching which
admitted of formal statement, were few in number and not likely to be
forgotten by those who had mastered them; cf. 341 e 3, διὰ σμικρᾶς
ἐνδείξεως; 344 e 2, ἐν βραχυτάτοις; but dogmatic exposition of them would
be of no use except to minds which had already mastered them. The
following remarks of Mark Pattison illustrate Plato's attitude in his own
written works.

"The highest phase of the philosophic imagination is tentative, not
dogmatic. Philosophy cannot be presented as a system of truths for
defence or proof. It offers considerations for meditation, and not
fixed verities. It is an attempt to elevate the whole mind towards the
contemplation of the phenomena of the world from their ideal side.
Hence there is a close affinity between the mental state of the philosopher
and the poet. Plato's Dialogues, though not in verse, address the same
faculty of imagination to which poetry appeals. Poetry, philosophy,
and art, in their highest condition, meet on the same footing—that of
suggestion, not of affirmation" (Intr. to Pope's *Essay on Man*, p. 6).

94. 341 d 7. φύσιν. "It would probably be wrong to take the
reiterated allusions to φύσις, as the topic of the conversation with
Dionysios and of the alleged τέχνη, as concerned specially with φύσις in
the Aristotelian sense. φύσις throughout the passage apparently
represents the subject-matter of φιλοσοφία or ἐπιστήμη in general; that
is, it means τὸ ὄν or τὰ ὄντα. So when we read in *Theaetetus*, 173 e,
of the mind as πᾶσαν πάντη φύσιν ἐρευνωμένη τῶν ὄντων ἑκάστου ὅλου,
the context shows that this includes ethical reflexion as well as the
astronomy and geometry which have just been mentioned" (Tayl. *l.c.*
p. 350).

95. 342 a 3. The "Philosophical Digression", rejected as an interpolation by Rit. (*Ges. Komm.* pp. 371 ff.) and condemned as "skimble-
skamble stuff" and "nonsense" by Richards (*Plat.* pp. 278, 291),
begins at this point. For the reasons which render it impossible that the
Digression can be an interpolation see Tayl. *l.c.* pp. 350 ff. The singular
imperatives λαβέ and νόησον in 342 b show that at ἔστιν τῶν ὄντων Plato
starts by quoting material from some discourse addressed to a single
learner, apparently a beginner in philosophy, who has already had a
grounding in mathematics. But though it is clear where the quoted
matter begins, no one can say where it ends. We seem to come to a

214 NOTES

climax at 344 d 2, φρένας ὤλεσαν αὐτοί: but before that, e.g. at 344 b 3, ὅπερ ἐν ἀρχαῖς εἶπον, we begin to get references to things in the letter which precede the beginning of the discourse, and it is clear that before this point Plato has insensibly blended the quoted matter with his letter. It is characteristic of an old man to help himself out in this way with old materials (v. sup. note 37); but Plato, when doing so, soon begins to reconstruct the old material and adapt it to his present train of thought. It should be remembered throughout that he is not expounding his philosophy, but explaining why the exposition of it in a written treatise is not possible. This is done with something of the casualness of ordinary talk, which avoids exact terminology and presents ideas in the order in which they happen to occur to the speaker. It is, as How. calls it, an impressionist picture, and is intended to give to non-philosophical readers some notion of a process which they have not themselves been through.

96. 342 b 1. δεῖ ὅ. The translation follows Bt.'s text. Andr. returns to the original readings of A and O, διό, ἀληθές, and ὤν (for ὄν), with a colon after ἐστιν. He thinks that διό expresses "das dynamische der Idee", that with δεῖ ὅ the Idea appears "nur als statisches Erkenntnissgegenstand", and that ὤν is preferable, because unconnected sentences are less like Plato's later style. But the omission of connecting particles at the beginning of sentences is one of the points characteristic of the style of the *Laws* (see Jowett, *Intr. to Laws*, p. 15, 1875 edn.); and without δεῖ it is not easy to account for the infinitive τιθέναι; for it is not satisfactory either to supply ἀνάγκη or to regard it as infinitive for imperative. Bt.'s restoration is highly probable, and it is easy to see how corruption would arise.

97. 342 b 2. The parallelism between the five things mentioned here and the three things, ὄνομα, λόγος, and οὐσία in *Laws*, 895 d, is obvious; but Raed. (*P.P.E.* p. 397) is going too far when he argues that the passage in the *Laws* must have been written earlier. In the *Laws* Plato is working up to a definition of "Soul", and only wants to make it clear that a definition is λόγος τῆς οὐσίας. Here the point is that definition is only one instrument among others by which knowledge is gained, and that knowledge is a state of the mind attained by prolonged effort with the aid of instruments and a teacher.

98. 342 b 6. ῥημάτων. For the rendering "verbal forms" Tayl. refers to *Soph.* 262 b, and adds, "it is of course possible that the sense is more general, and that we should translate 'predicative phrases', so as to include adjectives used predicatively."

99. 342 c 1. τρίτον δέ. Under the third head, that of εἴδωλον, only concrete objects are mentioned here; but it is clear from 342 d 4–8 that the word covers all individual and perceptible instances of such things as the good, the beautiful, the pleasant and their opposites, all acts, feelings and mental characteristics leading to acts. It is not easy for the ordinary mind to follow abstract thought without the aid of concrete instances. This applies to the discussions of moral questions not less than to mathematics. A purely abstract exposition of Ethics is extremely difficult for beginners.

100. 342 c 4. τέταρτον δέ. Under the fourth head Plato groups everything that goes on in the mind in its attainment of knowledge: ἐπιστήμη is the final state in which the mind possesses scientific knowledge, and νοῦς is the active principle by means of which this state is reached. Both these are more akin to the object of knowledge, i.e. the ultimate truth of things, than the earlier stages of the process which come under the head of right opinion, ἀληθὴς δόξα. For the distinction between νοῦς and ἀληθὴς δόξα see Tayl. on *Tim.* 51 d 6 and 51 e 1.

101. 342 e 2–343 c 5. πρὸς γὰρ...ἄνδρα. γάρ introduces new thoughts, which are developed in a puzzling order. Plato has stated in a preliminary way that there are preparatory stages of imperfect knowledge, leading up to full scientific knowledge. He is thinking mainly of mathematical knowledge, and is going on to show that the difficulties which the earlier stages present arise from three causes, (1) the misleading features of all diagrams, (2) the defects of language as a medium of thought, (3) the difficulty of distinguishing between what is essential (τὸ ὄν) in that which is being studied, and what is merely a superficial characteristic of it (τὸ ποῖόν τι). Instead of taking these three points in order, he gives in the lines 342 e 2–343 a 4 a preliminary parenthetical mention of the second and third; then in 343 a 4–8 he deals with the first, the misleading features of diagrams, after which, at 343 a 9, he passes to the second, the defects of language. Finally at 343 b 7 he returns to the third, the distinction between τὸ ὄν and τὸ ποῖόν τι, which is most important. See note 105.

102. 343 a 2. εἰς αὐτό: sc. τὸ τῶν λόγων ἀσθενές. For the unalterable character of language when committed to writing cf. *Phaedrus*, 275 d, e.

103. 343 a 7. τοῦ γὰρ εὐθέος. "No actually described physical disc is ever absolutely circular. At any point you please you can make it coincide throughout a finite distance with a physical 'straight' line. So, one might almost say, in the diagrams of our Euclids, the so-called circle and tangent can always be seen by any one to coincide throughout a perceptible distance. But 'the circle itself', the 'mathematical' circle of which Euclid is speaking, only coincides with the tangent at a 'mathematical' point" (Tayl. *l.c.* p. 361).

104. 343 a 9. For the inadequacy of language Raed. compares Faust's words, "Name ist Schall und Rauch". In our day the transitory nature of philosophical terminology hardly requires illustration.

105. 343 b 8. The distinction between τὸ ὄν and τὸ ποῖόν τι was fundamental with Plato. Most of his earlier Dialogues are attempts in the sphere of Ethics to discover the τὸ ὄν or the τί of the moral virtues, and proceed by showing the inadequacy of explanations which give only the ποῖόν τι. The same distinction was all-important in the mathematical work of the Academy. See Tayl. *l.c.* pp. 358 ff. The pupil who studies geometry under a good teacher is largely occupied in learning to discriminate between what is essential and non-essential in the characteristics of lines and figures. In the highest regions of philosophic thought the same distinction was not less important (see note on Ep. II, 312 e 5). In c 4 παρεχόμενον ἕκαστον is not a repetition of ἕκαστον προτεῖνον, but is in apposition to τὸ μὴ ζητούμενον, and παρεχόμενον is passive. The accumulation of participles is awkward but not unparalleled.

106. 343 d 2. ἐν οἷς δ' ἄν. For mathematical illustrations see Tayl. *l.c.* pp. 363–4. In all controversy the attack is easier than the defence. The man who approaches fundamental problems of philosophy or religion from the point of view of τὸ ὄν or τὸ τί, and tries to make his interlocutors do the same, is easily exposed to ridicule by hostile critics. Sou. compares the parable of "The Cave" (*Rep.* 507 d 4) and the description of the man who, after seeing things in the light of day (i.e. τὰ ὄντα), descends again to those who have only seen what is discernible in the light of the Cave (τὸ ποῖόν τι), and is easily made to appear ridiculous when he takes part in their controversies.

107. 343 d 7, 8. There is a slight verbal confusion here: the "four things" include the group ἐπιστήμη, νοῦς and ἀληθὴς δόξα which do belong to the soul of the speaker. But this does not vitiate Plato's point. Nor would it be enough to confine the defects to the three instruments of knowledge. There are also defects of mind; and the man who has overcome these by efforts such as Plato describes, is not thereby enabled to impart his knowledge to others.

108. 343 e 1–344 a 2. For διαγωγή L. and S. give "instruction". I can find no parallel for this; but what is said below at 344 b 6 about "questions and answers" makes it clear that the process described is performed with the aid of a teacher. εὖ πεφυκότος is the ordered system of things, which, when fully apprehended, is the object of ἐπιστήμη. In what follows διέφθαρται has the same construction as πέφυκεν, and the clause, though after ἂν κακῶς φυῇ it is not strictly logical, is added as a sort of parenthetical afterthought to establish the point that a mind, which is well endowed on the intellectual and moral sides, may be corrupted by bad education or other causes. There is nothing misanthropic in the dictum ἡ τῶν πόλλων ἕξις κ.τ.λ. Plato never shut his eyes to the fact that most men have not the gifts which would fit them for the study of philosophy. See *Tim.* 51 e 5. Lynkeus is the keen-sighted hero of Greek fairy tales. Pindar (*Nem.* x) tells the story of the brothers Idas and Lynkeus, how Lynkeus looking from Mt Taygetos saw Kastor, when he was concealed in a hollow oak tree, and how the brothers, after killing Kastor, were themselves killed by Polydeukes and Zeus.

109. 344 a 2. At ἑνὶ δὲ λόγῳ Plato begins to sum up the results of his digression. The mention of justice and τὰ καλά and the truth about virtue and vice shows that he is dealing with philosophy in its widest sense—our ultimate views as to the order of things, physical and moral, and the way in which a man may hope to gain enlightenment in this region. For συγγενῆ *v. sup.* note 86, and Tayl. *l.c.* p. 365. "For the thought that Philosophy demands kinship between the Reality known and the mind that knows it see *Rep*. 490 b, οὐδ' ἀπολήγοι τοῦ ἔρωτος, πρὶν αὐτοῦ ὃ ἔστιν ἑκάστου τῆς φύσεως ἅψασθαι ᾧ προσήκει ψυχῆς ἐφάπτεσθαι τοῦ τοιούτου—προσήκει δὲ συγγενεῖ. The meaning is that mere quickness in learning and good memory will never make a philosopher. A special elevation of soul and a peculiar gift of insight is indispensable. Historically we can trace back the thought that the highest intelligence is akin in a special way to the worthiest objects of knowledge to the Orphic belief that while the body to which a soul is temporarily assigned consists of materials drawn from its physical surroundings, the soul itself, being a divinity, comes from heaven."

110. 344 b 2. τὸ ψεῦδος ἅμα καὶ ἀληθές. "In dialectic it is precisely by seeing where the unsatisfactory hypotheses are false that we are led on to a truer one" (Tayl. *l.c.* p. 366 n. 2). The word τριβή, which suggests friction as well as practice, prepares the way, as Tayl. points out, for the metaphor of the sudden breaking out of the flame in the next sentence.

111. 344 b 3–7. Note the striking change of construction, μόγις δὲ τριβόμενα πρὸς ἄλληλα....ὀνόματα καὶ λόγοι....ἐξέλαμψε φρόνησις. We should expect φρόνησιν ἐνέτεκεν as in 343 e 2. χρωμένων does not, as Sou.'s translation implies, agree with φθόνων, but with the men who carry on the ἔλεγχοι; it is an adjectival genitive parallel to εὐμενέσιν. There is no need to amend συντείνων to συντείνοντι with Eva Sachs and Wtz., or to συντεινόντων with Egermann: the word describes the activity of the enlightened intelligence. Two further points may be added:

(1) The description of the course of study, carried on by questions and answers under the guidance of the teacher, makes it quite impossible that the enlightenment here described is attained in a state of trance. Philosophers, as well as poets and saints, have had trance experiences. Among the Greeks Plotinus is a clear instance, and we can hardly give any other explanation to the experience of Sokrates described in *Symp*. 220 c, d. Tennyson's Ancient Sage is giving the poet's own experience of trances brought on by repetition of his name, when he tells of a state in which there is

no shade of doubt,
But utter clearness, and thro' loss of self
The gain of such large life as match'd with ours
Were Sun to spark—unshadowable in words,
Themselves but shadows of a shadow-world.

There is no evidence either in Plato's writings or in tradition that he ever had such experiences. How.'s suggestion (pp. 43, 44), that he carried on dialectical exercises as a sort of yogi-practice in order to throw himself into the trance state, deserves mention as one of the curiosities of criticism.

(2) Plato is trying to give to those who have not been through the course of study some notion of those moments of philosophic vision which come to those in whom the light has been fully kindled. We may perhaps suppose that in such passages as that about the Idea of the Good in *Rep*. 505–509, or the gradual ascent to the knowledge of αὐτὸ τὸ καλόν in the *Symposium*, we have indications of visions of the kind, belonging to the time when the light was kindled in him by Sokrates.

112. 344 c 4. The συγγράμματα, which consist either of laws or of works of any other kind, are, as Sou. points out, meant to suggest Plato's longer Dialogues. Such Dialogues as the *Philebus* and *Laws* do contain full treatment of important questions and certainly give us the teaching of Plato himself. But their object is to give light on certain isolated questions, and they must not be regarded as systematic expositions of his views on the greatest problems of philosophy. One crucial point illustrates this. A belief in God was evidently one of Plato's strongest convictions. In the 10th Book of the *Laws* he gives arguments by which unbelievers may be led to change their views. But he has nowhere given a statement to show how he brought this belief into relation with the rest of his philosophy, and it is not at all clear from his works how he did so. His modern interpreters have differed widely in their attempts to harmonise what he says about God with his teaching about the "Idea of the Good" (see Tayl. *Plato, the Man* etc. p. 232).

113. 344 c 7. κεῖται δέ που ἐν χώρᾳ τῇ καλλίστῃ. "That is, ἐν τῇ ψυχῇ, or more precisely ἐν τῷ νῷ; the truths which are of most moment in the opinion of a good and wise man are written on the 'fleshy tables of the heart', not on tablets of wax or sheets of parchment. He bears them about with him and does not need to store them in a library" (Tayl. *l.c.* p. 367). Andr. interprets χώρᾳ of the souls of the philosopher's pupils, comparing *Phaedrus*, 276 b 7; this is less likely. The absence of a subject to κεῖται is another mark of intentional informality of style. The right word can be supplied from σπουδαιότατα.

114. 344 d 1. ἐξ ἄρα κ.τ.λ. Plato slightly remodels the words of Paris to Antenor in *Il*. VII, 359–60,

εἰ δ' ἐτεὸν δὴ τοῦτον ἀπὸ σπουδῆς ἀγορεύεις
ἐξ ἄρα δή τοι ἔπειτα θεοὶ φρένας ὤλεσαν αὐτοί.

115. 344 d 3. μύθῳ τε καὶ πλάνῳ. For this use of μῦθος in the sense of "discourse", which is one of the Ionicisms found in Plato's later writings, see my note on *Epin*. 980 a 5. πλάνος is poetical, but occurs in *Phaedo*, 79 d. πλάνη is commoner in prose; cf. *Laws*, 683 a 3, τῇ πλάνῃ τοῦ λόγου. For Plato's digressional style cf. note on 324 b 8.

116. 344 d 8. εἰς ἀναρμοστίαν κ.τ.λ. I follow Tayl. in taking this as a description of the court circle of Dionysios. ἀναρμοστία is Plato's regular term for the opposite of ἁρμονία. The world of Syracuse is out of tune with philosophy.

117. 344 e 2. ἐν βραχυτάτοις. Cf. 341 e 3, διὰ σμικρᾶς ἐνδείξεως.

118. 345 a, b. "The general meaning is 'I only spoke with him once; hence the question arises why we did not go over the ground again and again'. The three possible explanations of Dionysios's conduct in not asking for a second interview, viz. that he thought himself after his first conversation competent to carry on his studies by himself, that he thought what he heard disappointing, that he felt unequal to the demands of philosophy on his intellect and character, correspond to the three results of the πεῖρα suitable to a prince enumerated at 340 b, c, d" (Tayl. *l.c.* p. 368). I have followed Tayl. in removing the comma after τρίτον in a 6, and in taking τοῦτο in a 2 as equivalent to "the compassing of the truth".

119. 345 a 3. For ἴττω Ζεύς see *Phaedo*, 62 a 8, with Bt.'s note.

120. 345 c 1. τὸν ἡγ. τ. κ. κυρ. A strong phrase for Plato to use of himself. But it cannot possibly, as one critic suggests, refer to Dion; and there is nothing to support the ingenious idea of Andr. that it may be a quotation of language used by Dionysios.

121. 345 c 4. From this point to 350 e we have a clear and picturesque narrative in chronological order which calls for few comments. Note Plato's fondness for direct speech in reporting his own thoughts and the words of others. This and the colloquial phrases are what we should expect from a writer of dialogues; cf. Ep. III, 319 c. The negotiations about Dion's property belong to the summer and autumn of 361 B.C., when Plato still had his quarters in the palace garden, from which he was moved for the festival of Demeter (see note 135). In 345 c 7 ἐπιστολῆς is the long letter mentioned in 339 b 5. Dionysios now abandoned the assumption that Dion was merely on his travels (v. 338 b 1), and treated him as an exile, so that the guardianship of Dion's son passed into his own hands.

122. 345 e 2. ὄφρ' ἔτι κ.τ.λ. *Od.* XII, 428; cf. Plut. *Dion*, 18.

123. 345 e 5. Dionysios probably felt that the presence of Plato at Syracuse guaranteed him from any aggression on the part of Dion.

124. 346 a 1. The ἀπόστολα πλοῖα are trading vessels, which, as may be gathered from this passage, usually made the journey in convoys. The sailing season was the early part of the summer; cf. 345 d 5.

125. 346 b 3. ἐν Πελοπ. It is not quite clear where Dion made his headquarters during his exile. He stayed for some time at Athens, first with Kallippos, and then on the property which he bought there and afterwards gave to Speusippos (Plut. *Dion*, 17). He must also have resided for a time at Sparta, where he was made a citizen. But his closest connections were with Corinth, and it was probably there that Dionysios assumed him to be residing. Corinth was the natural headquarters of a Syracusan in Greece proper (see Intr. p. 2), and is the only place mentioned by Diodoros in his brief account of Dion's exile (XVI, 6).

126. 346 c 7. εἰς ὥρας. 'When the season comes round.' Cf. Hom. *Od.* IX, 135, Theocr. XV, 74.

127. 347 a 2. ναύτην, the reading of the MSS, is justified by Soph.

Phil. 901 (quoted by Bt.); there is no need for the emendation αὐτῆς adopted by How. and Andr.

128. 347 a 7. τ᾽ αὖτ᾽. The corruption of the MSS may be due to the fact that αὖτε is not elsewhere used in prose. This would not have prevented Plato from using it; αὖ, which Hercher reads, causes an awkward hiatus.

129. 347 d 8. νεανικῶς; cf. Ep. III, 318 b 5. For discrepancies real and apparent between the narrative here and that of Ep. III see Intr. Rem. to that letter and note on 318 a 5.

130. 348 a 4. τῶν μισθοφόρων. The quarters of the main body of the 10,000 mercenaries were outside the walls of the akropolis (cf. 350 a and Intr. p. 8 note †. A large number of them were Campanians; some were Gauls and Spaniards. Plato was used to scenes of war; but the mutiny of these barbarians and their savage warcry evidently made a strong impression on him.

131. 348 b 5. λόγος δή τις. It seems probable, from this passage, that Herakleides at this time was actually in command of the bodyguard. For him and the other persons see the narrative in Intr. pp. 28, 29.

132. 348 c 3. τὰ μὲν οὖν ἄλλα κ.τ.λ. An anacoluthon of the nominativus pendens type: after the subject "Dionysios" we expect "enquired the whereabouts of Herakleides". But the narrative is continued in a fresh sentence.

133. 349 b 5. The denial of Dionysios and Plato's contradiction of him are quoted from memory by Demetrios, περὶ ἑρμ. § 290, in the following form: τοῦ αὐτοῦ εἴδους ἐστὶ καὶ τὸ Πλάτωνος, πρὸς Διονύσιον ψευσάμενον καὶ ἀρνησάμενον ὅτι 'ἐγώ σοι, Πλάτων, οὐδὲν ὡμολόγησα', 'σὺ μέντοι, νὴ τοὺς θεούς.' Demetrios pronounces the form of Plato's answer to be both "dignified and safe": it is not clear why he regarded such a flat contradiction as "safe".

134. 349 c 5. τὸ δὴ μετὰ τοῦτο. The Greek is rather ambiguous. But the words πρόφασιν ἄλλην ἀδελφὴν τῆς πρόσθεν, 349 d 6, show that Dionysios is represented as looking for an excuse, not for selling Dion's property, but for hostility to Plato. His real motive for this was irritation at the way in which Plato had contradicted him. But Plato's attitude with regard to Dion's property gave him a decent excuse: ἔχειν therefore means "provide". Plato's visit to Herakleides was another interference resembling his interference on behalf of Dion. I owe this explanation to Prof. Taylor.

135. 349 d 2. θυσίαν δεχήμερον. See Diod. v. ch. 5, § 4. The duration of the festival shows that it was not the Korea but the tendays' festival in honour of Demeter, which was held at the beginning of the sowing season, perhaps October. Plato was sent to the house of Archedemos for the ten days of the festival; but his visit may have been prolonged. His call on Theodotes occurred in the course of it. Quarters were subsequently assigned to him in the cantonments of the mercenaries outside the akropolis. For the chronology see Intr. pp. 28, 29.

136. 349 e 6. οὐκέτι μετεπέμψατο. Plato does not say that he had no further interview with Dionysios, only that he was not invited to return to his former lodging. Dionysios, no doubt, continued to treat him with an outward show of cordiality.

137. 350 a 1 ff. The ships' crews here mentioned belonged to the navy of Dionysios. The ships which he kept permanently in commission would be manned by paid crews, and it is interesting to observe that some of the men were enlisted at Athens.

138. 350 b 1. αὐτῶν ἕνα. Lamiskos was one of the Pythagorean School at Taras. The thirty-oared galley took Plato only as far as Taras (see Intr. p. 29). What professes to be the letter written on this occasion by Archytas to Dionysios is given by Diog. Laert. III, 21.

139. 350 d 6. διαλλάξεσιν. At this stage Plato's object was not the overthrow of Dionysios, but to effect a reconciliation between him and Dion (see Intr. Rem. to Epp. II, III).

140. 351 a 1. καίτοι. From this point to the climax in 351 e 2 Plato is defending the character and aims of Dion, who during the latter part of his career was generally charged with aiming at the tyranny for himself.

141. 351 a 4. Some departure from Bt.'s punctuation is necessary. Richards proposes a colon after αὐτοῦ. I have followed a suggestion of Tayl. and assumed a colon to stand after μέτριος. τὰ μέγιστα is constructed with εὐεργετῶν and ἐν ταῖς μεγίσταις with ἐν δυνάμει καὶ τιμαῖσιν: for the hyperbaton see Intr. p. 90. The repetition of ἐν is irregular, but belongs to the informal style of the letter.

142. 351 a 7. πένης. He is impoverished in soul like the man mentioned in 335 b 1; see note 60.

143. 351 b 1–3. Instances of the seizure of private property, such as those here described, had occurred in Sicilian States within recent memory. At Gela the elder Dionysios had induced the populace to confiscate the property of the rich, killing the owners. He used most of the spoil for the remuneration of his mercenaries; some of it, however, must have gone to his Geloan confederates.

144. 351 b 4 ff. Plato here shows political ideals in advance of those of most of his contemporaries. In the latter part of the sentence he is evidently glancing at the policy of Perikles with regard to the Athenian empire. Similar views had been expressed by Isokrates in his speech on the Peace, which was published about two years before this Epistle. Plato drew no line between Ethics and Politics, and would not have been in sympathy with the views about "Macht" which have found favour with some thinkers in our day.

145. 351 c 5. οὔ τι δι' ὀλιγίστων θανάτων. There is no need for Richards' emendation ὅτι δι' ὀλιγίστων. Plato has already twice (327 d 5 and 331 d 3) spoken of complete absence of bloodshed as a thing to be aimed at in connection with reforms such as Dion was planning. Here we have to face the fact that the ideal was abandoned by Dion when he consented to the murder of Herakleides. Plato probably disapproved of this, but he may have excused it as necessary under the circumstances. He may be alluding to it in the next sentence, when he speaks of the precautions taken by Dion.

146. 351 c 6. The view that it is better to suffer injustice than to do it is upheld by Sokrates, *Crit.* 49 b ff. and *Gorg.* 469 b, c. This doctrine, with its corollary that we must not render evil for evil, was a cardinal point in the ethical teaching of the Academy, as it was in the systems of Buddhism and Christianity. Such doctrines, however admirable as general principles, have disastrous results, if followed in dealing with turbulent men or groups of men in a State. Plutarch's narrative (*Dion*, 47), which probably rests on the credible evidence of an eye-witness, Timonides, shows that Herakleides and his gang were ready to take full advantage of Dion's desire to put such ideals into practice in his public policy. The fact that Timoleon succeeded where Dion failed was, in some measure at least, due to his prompt action in dealing with individuals of this type. The false step of Dion, mentioned in the next sentence, was not the murder of Herakleides, but the failure to take adequate precautions against his own murderers.

147. 351 d, e. This striking passage forms a worthy climax to Plato's Apologia. It is difficult to do justice to it in a translation. The ἀνόσιοι are Kallippos and his confederates whom Plato regarded as offenders against God and man; cf. ἀνοσιουργός, 352 c 3. The λαιμαργία is the greed which made Kallippos aim at the position of tyrant.

148. 352 a 1. τὰ νῦν ῥηθέντα. The murder of Dion.

149. 352 a 4. For the superfluous δεῖν see Intr. p. 96.

EPISTLE VIII.

1. 352 b 3. The formula of greeting, as in Ep. III, provides the material for the exordium.

2. 352 c 3. The ἀνοσιουργός is Kallippos. For the bearing of this sentence on the date of the letter see Intr. Rem. p. 192 note †.

3. 352 d 3, 4. A very Platonic expression of opinion; see note 146 on Ep. VII. Compare what is said about war and sedition in *Laws* 627 e ff. In Plato's opinion it was desirable that internal struggles should be ended not by a decisive victory in which one side crushes the other, but by mutual concession and a reconciliation of the parties leading to φιλοφροσύνη. For the superfluous δεῖν cf. 352 a 4.

4. 352 e 5. εὐχῇ προσέοικεν. Cf. *Rep.* 450 d, ὄκνος τις αὐτῶν ἅπτεσθαι, μὴ εὐχὴ δοκῇ εἶναι ὁ λόγος, and 499 c, οὕτω γὰρ ἂν ἡμεῖς δικαίως καταγελώμεθα, ὡς ἄλλως εὐχαῖς ὅμοια λέγοντες, where εὐχή means "something Utopian", and *Laws*, 736 d 2, εὐχὴ δὲ μόνον ὡς ἔπος εἰπεῖν λείπεται, where England translates "impossible aspiration". Here the word is first used in this way, and then in its ordinary sense of "prayer". In *Tim.* 27 c, Plato insists that every enterprise should be begun with prayer, and this was probably carried out in practice at the Academy. For similar teaching see *Phil.* 25 b, *Laws* 887 c, *Epin.* 980 c. For ἐπιχείρησις see Ep. VII, 341 e 1.

5. 353 a 3. σχεδόν must be taken with διὰ τέλους. For the hyperbaton cf. 318 e 6, and see Intr. p. 90.

6. 353 b 3. αὐτοκράτορας τυράννους. The reference is to the crisis in 406 B.C., when Akragas had fallen, and Gela was being besieged by Himilco; see Intr. p. 6. Plato's statement is in conflict with the story given by Diodoros, XII, 94, according to which Dionysios alone was appointed to the supreme command with the title στρατηγὸς αὐτοκράτωρ. Diodoros is probably right on both points. Plato's history of past events is often erratic; see note on 354 d 8. For the title see note 2 on Ep. I. The elder Hipparinos, though not officially partner of Dionysios, must have been closely associated with him. Aristotle (*Pol.* V, 5, 6) mentions him as an instance of an oligarch, who, having expended his property, supports an aspirant for tyranny. The series of marriages arranged by Dionysios shows that he regarded the connection with Hipparinos and his family as essential to his position.

7. 353 d 2. ἐν ἐλπίδι τοῦ οἴεσθαι. Explanatory genitive. For the pleonasm see Intr. p. 96.

8. 353 d 5. συμβαίνει γιγνόμενον. A periphrastic tense, "turns out to be"; cf. 327 c 6.

9. 353 e 4. Ὀπικῶν. Plato, while he was at Syracuse, may have heard of the rising power of the Romans, who made a treaty with Carthage in 348 B.C., and would be spoken of as an Oscan or Opican tribe. The passage shows that, though careless about the details of the past, Plato could make a sound forecast of the future.

10. 353 e 6. τέμνειν φάρμακον: the shredding of the herbs from which a medicine is concocted is a common metaphor in poetry; cf. Aesch. *Ag.* 17, Eur. *Androm.* 120. Plato has the same phrase in *Laws*, 919 b 3, and uses φάρμακον again below, 354 b 6, of the reforms of Lykourgos, which are the pattern of the reforms required at Syracuse. The prolixity of the following sentences resembles that of the passage leading up to his advice in Ep. VII, 330 c 9 ff.

11. 354 a 5. παλαιάν. This refers back to Plato's first visit to the younger Dionysios. It is not a reference to anything in Ep. VII, which could not be described as παλαιά. Egermann argues that Plato's correspondents would not have known the advice as 'old', unless they had learnt about it from Ep. VII. This is absurd. Plato's advice with regard to the tyranny was known to everyone in Syracuse, including the barbarian bodyguard; cf. Plut. *Dion*, 19 *ad fin.*

12. 354 b 2. τὸ τῶν οἰκείων γένος. In both States, as in Sparta, the royal family were Herakleidae.

13. 354 b 6 ff. Plato is not writing as a historian. For rhetorical purposes all Spartan institutions were ascribed to Lykourgos, as those of Athens were to Solon. A difficulty has been felt, because here, as in Herod. I, 65, both the Gerousia and the Ephorate are ascribed to

224 NOTES

Lykourgos, whereas in *Laws*, 691 e ff., though no names are mentioned, Plato evidently regards the two institutions as due to different lawgivers. England justly remarks, "Plato takes very little pains about the statement of historical facts. It is the point they are to illustrate that is important". Both passages are rhetorical in character.

14. 354 c 4. φεύγειν φυγῇ. Cf. *Epin.* 974 b, and *Symp.* 195 b with Stallbaum's note. εὐδαιμόνισμα does not occur elsewhere in classical prose; the word expresses the attraction which the position of tyrant exercised over the Greek mind. For this see the speech of Eteokles in Eurip. *Phoen.* 504 ff. and Isokr. *Evagoras*, 40, νῦν δ' ἅπαντες ἂν ὁμολογήσειαν τυραννίδα καὶ τῶν θείων ἀγαθῶν καὶ τῶν ἀνθρωπίνων μέγιστον καὶ σεμνότατον καὶ περιμαχητότατον εἶναι.

15. 354 d 8. κατέλευσαν βάλλοντες. The story of Diodoros (XIII, 92) is that after the fall of Akragas, 406 B.C., the Syracusans deposed Daphnaios and his colleagues and appointed ten new generals, among them Dionysios, who had led the agitation in the Assembly. Grote is no doubt right in supposing that Plato has confused this incident with another in the siege of Akragas, when the Akragantine populace did actually stone to death four of their generals. See Intr. p. 5. It is not possible, with Apelt, to evade the difficulty by reading, with one MS, κατέλυσαν for κατέλευσαν; for even if we follow him in the very improbable change of λαβόντες for βάλλοντες we are still left with κατὰ νόμον οὐδένα κρίναντες, which clearly presupposes something more than the deposition of the generals.

16. 354 e 3. In *Rep.* VIII, 564 ff., there is a description of the rise of despotism out of excess of liberty, which has suggested some of the phraseology of this passage; cf. 564 a, ἡ γὰρ ἄγαν ἐλευθερία ἔοικεν οὐκ εἰς ἄλλο τι ἢ εἰς ἄγαν δουλείαν μεταβάλλειν καὶ ἰδιώτῃ καὶ πόλει, and 569 c, ὁ δῆμος φεύγων ἂν καπνὸν δουλείας ἐλευθέρων εἰς πῦρ δούλων δεσποτείας ἂν ἐμπεπτωκὼς εἴη, ἀντὶ τῆς πολλῆς ἐκείνης καὶ ἀκαίρου ἐλευθερίας τὴν χαλεπωτάτην τε καὶ πικροτάτην δούλων δουλείαν μεταμπισχόμενος. Cf. *Ep.* VII, note 37.

17. 354 e 6. Tennyson's "God is law, say the wise" is a verbal parallel, but the point is different; Plato's νόμος is the law of the State, not the uniformity of nature. His point here is the same as in *Laws*, 715 c, on which passage England remarks: "Laws are the modern representatives of the δαίμονες of the golden age; they derive their authority from the divine element in us; obedience to them is, therefore, obedience to the Gods". τοῖς θεοῖς δουλεία occurs in *Laws*, 762 e, where service to the laws is said to be the same as service to the Gods.

18. 355 b 2. In *Laws*, 743 e, the same threefold division is expressed in similar language. In both passages Plato may be repeating material used in oral addresses.

19. 355 c 1, 2. Cf. *Laws*, 631 b 5, ἔχουσιν γὰρ ὀρθῶς (sc. οἱ νόμοι), τοὺς αὐτοῖς χρωμένους εὐδαίμονας ἀποτελοῦντες.

20. 355 c 8. δεξάμενοι. An anacoluthon of the nominativus pendens type. See Intr. p. 93. Strict grammar would require δεξαμένοις.

21. 355 d 3. μέσον τεμεῖν. The metaphor is that of cutting a road; cf. *Laws*, 793 a 4, with England's note.

22. 355 e 5. τὸν ἐμὸν υόν. For the historical difficulty see Intr. Rem. pp. 193 ff. For the two occasions on which Dion liberated the city see Ep. VII, note 48.

23. 356 a 5. ἐλευθεροῖ. The tense shows that Plato regards the struggle with Kallippos as still going on. See Intr. Rem. p. 193.

24. 356 a 7. The proposal to include Dionysios among the kings is startling. But it is possible, as suggested in Intr. p. 51, that he was already co-operating behind the scenes with the Dionean party. A hint of this may have been sent to Plato.

25. 356 b 4. The change of τάφους to τάφων, proposed by Stephanus, and adopted by some of the later editors, is unnecessary. The slight irregularity belongs to the informal manner of the Epistle.

26. 356 b 5, 6. Cf. 356 d 2. Plato leaves it doubtful whether the kings are to have some of the powers of constitutional monarchs or are to be mere figureheads. One can hardly believe that Dion contemplated ret'rement to a position in which he would have been powerless. He must have been aiming at a constitutional monarchy, with himself as sovereign. Plato's views probably inclined to an oligarchy of the kind described in the *Laws*.

27. 356 c 1. εἴρηται. c 6. πρότερον ἐρρήθη. These are not references to Ep. VII, 337 b. The speaker here is Dion, and he is referring to his own proposal to get commissioners sent from Corinth to draw up a new constitution. See Plut. *Dion*, 53. Egermann (*l.c.* p. 21), who wishes to find a reference to Ep. VII, argues that in these two clauses Plato is speaking parenthetically in his own person. This is quite impossible.

28. 356 d 4. Plato evidently intended the thirty-five Nomophylakes to be the real power in the State. Cf. *Laws*, 752 e 1 (with England's note), where a body of thirty-seven Nomophylakes is provided for the imaginary colony of Knossos. Their administrative and judicial powers correspond closely to those described here, and there is the same provision that for their judicial functions they shall have ex-magistrates associated with them. They correspond, as England points out, to the φύλακες παντελεῖς or τέλεοι of *Rep.* 414 b and 428 d.

29. 356 d 8. νῦν is not wanted, but the verbiage is characteristic of the informal style of a letter.

30. 357 a 4. ξενικαὶ Ἐρινύες. Cf. 336 b 4, νῦν δὲ ἤ πού τις δαίμων ἤ τις ἀλιτήριος, with note.

31. 357 b 7, 8. The turn given to the sentence is not quite what one expects; but that is a common feature in Plato's later works. Post's attempt (*Am. Journ. Phil.* Dec. 1924) to show that Plato's language "is influenced by his consciousness that he is speaking of an infant", is surely a forlorn hope.

32. 357 c 2. All the recent translators, except perhaps Andr., make this sentence refer to the future. This misses the point of the passage and ignores the tenses of συνομολογησάντοιν and συνδοκεῖν. Plato believes that Dion's son and nephew have *already* arrived at an agreement, that their views are shared by the main body of loyal citizens, and that there is enough general harmony to justify proposals for reform. See Intr. Rem. p. 193 note. **33.** 357 d 1. ὀνείρατα θεῖα. Dreams sent by the Gods, and therefore true.

EPISTLE IX.

Archytas has sent a mission to Athens on the public affairs of Taras and at the same time a letter to Plato commending to his care Echekrates, who is evidently a pupil at the Academy. Echekrates must be distinguished from his namesake of Phlious, who appears as a speaker in the *Phaedo*, and who must have lived at least fifty years before the date of this letter. But as he was a Pythagorean who had learnt from Tarentine teachers, there may have been some connection between the two. Tayl. suggests to me that the young Echekrates may have been the grandson of Echekrates of Phlious, and that his father, Phrynion, may have been dead, when this letter was written.

Enough has been said about Archytas in Intr. Sects. I and II. He was not only one of the leading mathematicians of the day, but also the author of ethical and metaphysical treatises, which are supposed to have given Aristotle some of his materials. Aristotle wrote a treatise on his philosophy which has been lost.

The sentence in 358 a, "each of us is born not for himself alone" etc., was a favourite with Cicero, who twice quotes it (*de Fin.* II, 14, 45, and *de Off.* I, 7, 22), and evidently had no doubt of the genuineness of the letter. It was probably from Cicero that George Gascoigne transferred it to his poem *The Steel Glass*, where it reappears in the lines:

> *O knights, O squires, O gentle bloods y-born,*
> *You were not born only for yourselves:*
> *Your country claims some part of all your pain;*
> *There should you live and therein should you toil,*
> *To hold up right and banish cruel wrong.*

The sentiment of 358 b 1, χώραν καταλιμπάνειν κ.τ.λ., is the same as that of *Rep.* 347 c, τῆς δὲ ζημίας μεγίστη τὸ ὑπὸ πονηροτέρου ἄρχεσθαι, ἐὰν μὴ αὐτὸς ἐθέλῃ ἄρχειν. A writer must be allowed occasionally to repeat his good things.

How. condemns the letter as containing only "factisch philosophische Gemeinplätze"; Post, because it contains nothing "that a mediocre forger could not have written". After reading it perhaps fifty times, I still find it delightful. The reader must judge, remembering that he is dealing with a letter of no great importance, written for a purely temporary purpose.

The fact that the name of Archytas appears in its Doric form in the superscription, whereas the Ionic form is used by Plato when he mentions Archytas in the course of Epp. VII and VIII, is no ground for suspicion. An Athenian, when mentioning Archytas in his correspondence, would naturally use the name in its Ionic form; but he would not necessarily do the same in the superscription of a letter addressed to Archytas himself.

1. 357 e 5. ἀσχολίας. Archytas was, no doubt, administering the government when he sent the envoys who conveyed his letter to Plato.

2. 358 a 1. οἷα καὶ σύ, i.e. the mathematical and philosophical work of Archytas.

3. 358 b 1. The form καταλιμπάνω is not used elsewhere by Plato; Wtz. calls it a Hellenistic word; but it is found in Thucydides and Antiphon, and is suitable to the rather formal style of this letter.

EPISTLE X.

This is a mere scrap. We have no knowledge of Aristodoros, whose name is given as Aristodemos by Diog. Laert. (III, 61); but he was probably a former pupil of the Academy, who had accompanied Dion in his expedition. It is not unlikely that Plato, when writing to Dion, sent short letters of encouragement to some of those who were supporting him. He may perhaps be thinking of these, when, in Ep. IV, he speaks of his zeal in supporting Dion.

The remark about other forms of wisdom and cleverness, which are more appropriately called accomplishments, may be an allusion to the School of Isokrates, who was fond of describing the subjects which he taught as φιλοσοφία. For Plato the term connoted moral qualities not less than intellectual gifts.

There are no grounds for suspecting the genuineness of the letter, if the reader will remember what it is that he has before him. How. classes the letter with Ep. IX, and condemns it on the same grounds. Post, on the other hand, sees in it the "characteristic touches of Platonic style and thought" which were absent from Ep. IX.

1. 358 c 3. πιστὸν καὶ ὑγιές. Cf. *Laws*, 630 b 2, πιστὸς μὲν γὰρ καὶ ὑγιὴς ἐν στάσεσιν οὐκ ἄν ποτε γένοιτο ἄνευ συμπάσης ἀρετῆς.

2. 358 c 6. κομψότητας. Cf. the κομψὸς ἀνὴρ ἴσως Σικελός τις ἢ 'Ιταλικός of *Gorg.* 493 a.

EPISTLE XI.

"Laodamas of Thasos was a great geometrician and scholar of Plato, who first taught him the analytic method" (Gray). See Diog. Laert. III, 24. The letter was most probably addressed to this Academician. We may assume that he was assisting in the foundation of a colony, and had applied to Plato for help in drawing up laws. Datos on the coast of Thrace, founded 360 B.C., has been suggested as probably the place referred to (Meyer, *Gesch.* vol. V, Sects. 977, 988). But there is no positive evidence. The text of the letter shows what has passed in the previous correspondence. Plato now informs Laodamas that laws will be of little use, unless there is some magistracy which exercises control over the conduct of the citizens. It will be remembered that both in the *Republic* and in the *Laws* an authority of this kind forms the central point in the constitution. Plato's unwillingness to risk failure by a personal visit is intelligible after his experiences in Sicily.

There is nothing in the contents of the Epistle which makes its genuineness doubtful. Zeller, however, speaks of it as an absurd letter (*Plato and the Older Academy*, p. 32 n. 65), and How. condemns it on the same ground as Epp. IX and X. Post in this case finds the style and thought Platonic. Wtz. (*Pl.* II, p. 280) condemns the style as un-Platonic, but without giving reasons. If the style is not that of Plato, it is a good imitation of it. The last ten lines are very characteristic of his later manner. It is not safe to speak with confidence about so short a letter. But I doubt if a forger would have confined himself to such sound advice.

1. 358 d 5. The reference is of course to Sokrates the Younger, who is introduced as a youth in the *Theaetetus*, *Sophistes* and *Politicus*. This letter shows that he continued till late in life to be associated with Plato in the Academy; and this is further supported by the references to him in Aristotle, for which see Tayl., *Plato the Man*, etc. pp. 393–4, and E. Kapp, *Philol.* LXXIX, pp. 325 ff.

2. 358 e 1. The periphrasis with περί, which makes Bury condemn the letter, is not more odd than others used by Plato; see Intr. p. 96.

3. 358 e 2. ἄσχημον. Here, as elsewhere in the Epistles, Plato is honest. He never shows that pose of freedom from weaknesses which lesser men assume. Failure to appreciate this point has led to the condemnation of this and other passages as unworthy of him.

4. 358 e 7. πάντα κινδύνων κ.τ.λ. In 362 B.C. Alexander of Pherai had equipped a fleet, and for the next three years his raids made the western side of the Aegean unsafe. He even made a descent on the Peiraeus. At the same time the disturbed state of northern Greece rendered travelling by land almost impossible. But similar dangers were of frequent occurrence, and it is quite as likely that the letter was written several years later.

5. 359 a 1. Hesiod, Fr. 229 (Rzach). The words, which were supposed to refer to *W. and D.* 483, have been recognised as a fragment, and restored as follows by Wtz. (*Pl.* II, p. 407): εἰπόντος μὲν ἐμοῦ φαῦλον, χαλεπὸν δὲ νοῆσαι.

6. 359 a 3. Bt.'s text, εἰ γὰρ οἷόν τε, does not give a satisfactory sense. Some word like οἴονται is wanted. Bekker reads οἴονθ' for οἷόν τε presumably from a conjecture. Perhaps our text has arisen from εἰ γὰρ οἴονθ' οἷόν τε. I have translated on this supposition.

7. 359 b 3. εὔχεσθε. Cf. 331 d 4, ἡσυχίαν δὲ ἄγοντα εὔχεσθαι, with the note there.

8. 359 b 4. σχεδόν κ.τ.λ. The Greek is not very clear here. "The point is that a good constitution is no guarantee of excellence without a vigilant executive authority; and the same thing applies to the cities of the past, which were well administered, if a man of character took advantage of some crisis to add to the constitution a proper supervising executive" (Tayl.). σύμβασις does not occur elsewhere in Plato: it became a Stoic term in the sense of "occurrences". The plural is like those mentioned in the note on 336 b 8.

EPISTLE XII.

This letter, if genuine, is Plato's answer to a letter from Archytas. He speaks in high terms of an unnamed Italian philosopher, notes of whose works have been sent to him by Archytas. He also forwards notes of an unnamed and unfinished work of his own. There is nothing in the letter itself which need give grounds for suspicion: but most of the MSS (six of the ten mentioned by Bekker) contain a note to the effect that the genuineness of the letter is doubted. Modern opinion has generally been adverse to the letter, and even Apelt, who accepts the other letters, surrenders this "without a sigh". But it is by no means clear that this verdict is right. The case against the letter rests on the fact that Diog. Laert. (VIII, 4) gives it along with what purports to be the letter from Archytas, to which it is an answer. That letter, which mentions by name Okellos, the Lucanian, and some of his supposed works, is certainly a forgery. One of the works mentioned is extant and belongs to a period considerably later than Plato and Archytas. "Ocellus Lucanus" has the distinction of being quoted, along with Manetho and Berosus, in the *Vicar of Wakefield* (ch. XIV). The following remarks, kindly communicated to me by Tayl., deserve consideration:

"As to XII, it is of course possible, as Zeller held, that it was forged along with the letter from Archytas, given with it in Diog. Laert., to accredit the pretended works of Ocellus Lucanus. But I am rather inclined to think that it is genuine. If it had been forged for the supposed purpose, I expect the forger would have made it clear that the unnamed person it refers to was Okellos, just as this is expressly said in the Archytas letter. I should rather conjecture that it was the existence of a genuine note of Plato, referring to an unnamed person recommended to him by Archytas, which suggested to the fabricator of works of Okellos to compose a letter in the name of Archytas identifying the unnamed person with Okellos. But this again is only a conjecture about the plausibilities of the case".

1. 359 d 2. ὡς ἕνι μάλιστα. Rit.'s suspicion of this phrase is uncalled for. If Xenophon (*Mem.* IV, 5. 9) could say ὡς ἕνι ἥδιστα, surely Plato may be allowed ὡς ἕνι μάλιστα.

2. 359 d 4. Μύριοι, Bt.'s text, is supported by almost all the MSS; but no satisfactory explanation of the allusion has been offered. The reading Μυραῖοι, which appears in the letter as quoted by Diog. Laert., means colonists from Myra in Lycia. Nothing is known of these. The emigrants who were said to have fled from Laomedon were the Elymaeans in Sicily, and How. conjectures Ἐλυμαῖοι here; but this is too remote even from Μυραῖοι.

3. 359 e 1. φυλακῆς has been explained as a reference to Plato's guardians in the *Republic*. It is more likely that the word simply means the custody of the notes. We may suppose that Plato and Archytas were agreed that notes on important philosophical questions ought not to be allowed to fall into the hands of such a person as Dionysios.

EPISTLE XIII.

This, if genuine, is the earliest of the Sicilian letters, and must have been written very shortly after Plato's return from the first of his two visits to Dionysios II, 366/5 B.C.; for one of the grandnieces, who lost their mother in the course of his visit, was less than a year old when he was writing. Beginning as a letter of introduction for Helikon, the astronomer, the Epistle goes on to speak of commissions which Plato has carried out for Dionysios, presents which he is sending to the monarch's family, requests for assistance for himself in certain matters and for small presents for one or two of his friends. In connection with these matters Plato gives Dionysios advice about financial arrangements in cases where expenditure on his behalf is required at Athens. The letter concludes with seven unconnected paragraphs, added as afterthoughts, on various subjects.

A good deal of the letter is written in a rather playful style. In a friendly letter dealing with private affairs there is no reason why an eminent philosopher should not write in such a style, and it is not unsuitable to the state of relations between him and Dionysios at the end of his first visit, as described by Plato himself in the 7th Epistle (see 330 a, b). The sentences in which Helikon is introduced give a strong impression of genuineness (see notes 3 and 4). Hack. is certainly right, when he sees "a genuine Platonic touch" in this passage. The request for assistance in portioning the eldest of his four grandnieces and for meeting public expenses, is quite in accordance with Athenian usage. The presents to the wife and children of Dionysios are not inappropriate, if it is remembered that Plato had been treated as a member of the family. The advice about money matters is very sensible, if the character and circumstances of Dionysios are considered. In the opening sentences of the letter there is, perhaps, a touch of egoism, but not more than we have in Ep. VII; cf. 333 d 1.

The letter with the presents is to be conveyed to Syracuse by Leptines, who had perhaps been the bearer of a letter from Dionysios to Plato (see ἐπέστελλες, 361 a 1). Leptines may have been the son or grandson of the Leptines who was brother of the elder Dionysios, and he was probably the same person who, jointly with Kallippos, seized Rhegion in 351 B.C., made himself tyrant of Apollonia and Engyon in Sicily a few years later, and was finally deposed and deported to Corinth by Timoleon (Diod. Sic. XVI, 45; Plut. Timol. 24). Helikon stayed for some time at Syracuse, and during Plato's last visit gained some credit by foretelling an eclipse of the sun, for which he was rewarded with a talent of silver by Dionysios. Plutarch who records this (Dion, 19) speaks of him as εἶς τῶν Πλάτωνος συνήθων. Rit., who uses this passage to prove that Helikon accompanied Plato on his journey, and therefore could not have been introduced by this Epistle, has forgotten that Plutarch was familiar with the Epistle, and quotes it as genuine (Dion, 21).

The question of the genuineness of this letter is still hotly discussed, and there has not been the decisive swing of the pendulum in its favour which has taken place with regard to the 7th and 8th letters. The attacks of Kar., the worthlessness of which, in the case of those two letters, is recognised, are still repeated as if they held good against the 13th. It was the first of the collection to be attacked. Ficinus disliked its contents and omitted it from his translation. The words ἀντιλέγεται κ.τ.λ. which follow Ep. XII were misapplied by Ralph Cudworth to Ep. XIII, and his suspicion was further aroused by the language used about the σύμβολον in 363 b. The letter was warmly defended by Bentley (see Dyer's edn. of Bentley's Works, III, pp. 410 ff.), whose opinion with regard to a letter ought still to carry weight. It was condemned by Karsten and E. Zeller, and more recently has been the object of savage attacks from R. Adam (Über die Echt. der Pl. Br. pp. 27–28), C. Ritter (N.U. pp. 328 ff.), U. von Wilamowitz–Möllendorff (Pl. I, pp. 645–6), and Howald (l.c. pp. 13–16). It is regarded as genuine by others, whose opinion is entitled to respect, as Grote, E. Meyer, J. Burnet, A. E. Taylor, and R. Hackforth. One of its defenders, R. F. Unger (Philologus, N.F. IV, pp. 191 ff.), thinks it the only one of the thirteen letters which is genuine.

The style gives no decisive evidence either for or against the letter. It is free from those marked peculiarities of language which the 7th and 8th Epistles share with the Laws, and is written throughout in the simple and unconventional manner which might be expected in a letter to a friend, who is addressed in terms which imply intimacy. It is natural that there should be signs of negligence such as the repetition of particles of transition, e.g. τὸ δὴ μετὰ ταῦτα. But it is hypercriticism of Rit. to object to the repetition of οἰκεῖος after an interval of twelve lines and of εὔνους after an interval of twenty-eight lines, to ἔφης (for ἔφησθα), when he allows that the form is found twice in the *Gorgias*, and to the use of χαρίεις without any suggestion of irony, which occurs in *Rep.* 605 b (see below, note on 363 c 5). Any stone seems to be good enough to throw at the 13th Epistle.

A good defence of the letter is given by Hack., who, as he agrees with Rit. in condemning Epp. II and VI, may be regarded as an impartial critic. He deals both with the style and with the contents of the letter, taking *seriatim* the points attacked by Rit. and showing that they give no real ground for suspicion.

The question really hinges, not on indications of style nor on matters of fact, but on the view we take with regard to the tone in which Plato is likely to have addressed Dionysios. Zeller complains of "der kamerädschaftliche Ton" of the letter, Rit. that it ascribes to Plato "ärmliche und kleinliche Züge", that it shows him as a "niedrigen Höfling und feilen Tyrannenknecht", and a "widerwärtiger Gesell". In Ad.'s opinion the letter is the "Bettelbrief eines Parasiten". Wtz. sees Plato in it as a "verächtlicher Bettler um Geld", and as "politischer Agent des Tyrannen".

Language of this sort shows a complete misapprehension of the actual circumstances of Plato and Dionysios. The critics have forgotten the unique position which Dionysios occupied during the early part of his reign,—that he was, for the moment, the one really great power in the Greek world, and that this fact could not be ignored by Plato, if he wished to have any influence over him. They lose sight also of what is not less important, the neglect of the young man's education (Plut. *Dion*, 9), which must have made it by no means easy to decide on the tone which it would be wise to adopt in dealing with him. It is clear also that he had been completely alienated by the stiff and unbending deportment of Dion. Plato's care to avoid this may have led him into what Zeller feels to be a "kamerädschaftlicher Ton", hardly to be expected from a person whose σεμνότης became proverbial. But there is nothing in the tone of the letter which is unworthy of Plato or inappropriate to the very exceptional position in which he was placed. The violent language of Rit. and others condemns itself and need not be further referred to. The wisest criticism on the whole is that of Grote, who says: "When we consider both the character and station of Dionysios, it is difficult to lay down beforehand any assured canon as to the epistolary tone in which Plato would think it most suitable to address him" (*Gk. Hist.* ch. 81).

Those who condemn the letter have different theories to account for its existence. All are agreed that it belongs to a time very shortly after Plato's death, if not before it. In view of the author's accurate knowledge of matters of fact no other supposition is possible.

Ad. thinks that it is the work of a sophist whose object was to produce a caricature which would discredit the character of Plato. Wtz. regards it as a piece of propaganda written with a similar purpose, by someone belonging to the court of Dionysios. How. accounts for it as an attempt to give a depreciatory and gossiping view of history and of the characters of the great. Rit. thinks that Letters II, VI and XIII are all the work of the same forger, a man working in the Schools of Rhetoric, shortly after the death of Plato; but he assigns no special motive for the forgery. This last view has no evidence in its favour; for the features of style, which Rit. quotes as shared by the three letters, all appear in other letters as well as these three. It is also condemned by the fact that one of the three letters (Ep. VI) avoids illegitimate hiatus, while the other two do not. This feature presents no improbability, if we suppose the three letters to have been written by Plato himself at different periods of his life, the 6th belonging to the close of it. But it is incredible that all three can be the work of the same forger.

Those who read the letter without seeing anything discreditable to Plato in its contents, will not need to discuss the theories of Ad. and How. The view of Wtz. has in its favour the fact that Dionysios had been most anxious to secure Plato's friendship, and might have put abroad a document which certainly shows that there had been between them relations of a cordial nature. But it is most unlikely that a creature of Dionysios would have put into Plato's mouth the excellent advice on financial matters which is given in the letter; and it is scarcely probable that such a person would have used the language in which the character of Helikon is described. But if Dionysios wished to prove intimacy between Plato and himself, may he not have done so by publishing a genuine letter? The picture which we have in the letter of the relations between the two harmonises well with Plato's own description of the position at Syracuse just before the close of his first visit to the younger Dionysios. It is not impossible that the letter may have been written by Plato, and put into circulation by Dionysios. If this was what happened, and if the letter, thus made public, was added subsequently to a collection of letters formed from papers left by Plato and preserved at the Academy, we have a possible explanation of the otherwise puzzling fact that it is tacked on at the end of the collection, though in date it precedes all the other letters of the Sicilian group. But this is all pure conjecture, and the transposition of the letter from its proper place before Ep. II may have been due to other accidental circumstances either at Athens or at Alexandria.

Post, who accepts the letter as genuine and gives an able defence of the main part of it, inclines to the view that it was published by Dionysios. But he adds that Dionysios may have "found it amusing to add details that would alienate Plato's friends and scandalise the whole philosophic circle". A somewhat similar impression is recorded by the poet Gray, who remarks: "I know not what to determine; unless we suppose some parts of it to be inserted by some idle sophist who was an enemy to Plato's character". Both these criticisms arise from dislike for certain things which occur in the seven short paragraphs which are tacked on at the end of the letter. I have dealt with the more important of these in the notes, and will here only ask the reader to remember how natural it is that a letter should terminate with a series of such afterthoughts. In Ep. II we have a similar series, which is actually in the form of a postscript, following the final greeting. Is it likely that the forger, to whom adverse critics attribute the letter, had the dramatic power to give it such a conclusion? Let those who think so go through a course of reading in the Epistolographi Graeci.

1. 360 b 1. The frequent recurrence of τότε in this letter is regarded as suspicious by Rit. Hack. (pp. 182, 193) has shown that it is a feature of Plato's later style.

2. 360 b 7. τῶν τε Πυθαγ. καὶ τῶν διαιρ. There is nothing to be gleaned from the letter as to what the specimens of Pythagorean work were. They may have been merely mathematical exercises. The διαιρέσεις were probably exercises in "dichotomy", like those introduced into the *Sophistes* and *Politicus*. Such exercises, doubtless, formed a regular part of the work of the Academy. Diog. Laert. (IV, 5) mentions διαιρέσεις in his list of the works of Speusippos. Or the reference may be to such διαιρέσεις as those attributed to Plato in Diog. Laert. III, 80, for which see Ritter, *N.U.* p. 367 note.

3. 360 c 1. Ἀρχύτης. For the Ionic form see Ep. VII, 338 c 6 note.

4. 360 c 3. Plato had pupils in the Academy from Kyzikos and the neighbourhood, e.g. Athenaios of Kyzikos, and Menaichmos (the inventor of conic sections), and his brother Deinostratos, who came from an island close by. Unger in his paper on Eudoxos (*Philologus, l.c.*) asks why Plato does not mention Eudoxos himself as his authority for the character of Helikon, and considers that Eudoxos was dead when the letter was written. This is unlikely; but the letter may have been written after his return to Knidos. By τὰ ἐκείνου is meant the teaching of Eudoxos in mathematics and astronomy. For a summary of his contributions to these see Sir T. Heath's *History of Greek Mathematics*, I, pp. 320–34.

5. 360 c 5, 6. For Polyxenos see Ep. II note 2. He is spoken of here as still unknown to Dionysios. From what is said about him in Ep. II it is clear that at some date between the two letters he too went to Syracuse with a letter of introduction from Plato. The name of Bryson had, no doubt, often been mentioned during Plato's visit. For his connection with Plato see Bt. *Phil.* pp. 254, 263. Theopompos charged Plato with extensive plagiarism from his works (Theop. Fr. 247, Clar. Press). By τούτοις we must understand the associates of Isokrates, and what follows is explained by the rivalry between the two Schools. It should not be taken too seriously, but in the spirit in which similar remarks are made among themselves by members of rival Universities.

6. 360 c 7. ἐλαφρός implies cheerfulness or gaiety, as in *Laws*, 657 d 4; Theocr. II, 124.

7. 360 d 2. οὐ φαύλου ζῴου κ.τ.λ. quoted by Plutarch, περὶ δυσωπ.

EPISTLE XIII 235

533 c and by Clem. Alex. *Strom.* VI, 625 A; cf. *Laws* 777 b 4, δύσκολόν ἐστι τὸ θρέμμα ἄνθρωπος.

8. 360 d 7. σχολάζῃς. Dionysios was occupied with the war, mentioned 338 a 4.

9. 360 e 3. εὐδοξῆς. For Plato's views about the pursuit of honour see Intr. Rem. to Ep. II, p. 165.

10. 361 a 3. Leochares, whose "floruit" Pliny places in Ol. 102 (*N.H.* XXXIV, 8), became a sculptor of scarcely less celebrity than his contemporaries, Scopas and Praxiteles. Plutarch (*Alex.* 40) couples him with Lysippos. Copies are still extant of his famous group of Ganymede and the eagle of Zeus; the best of these is in the Vatican. Recent authorities regard the Apollo Belvedere as an imitation of an Apollo by him; see Farnell, *Cults*, IV, p. 394.

11. 361 b 1. Athenian figs were celebrated; cf. the story quoted in Athen. XIV, 652 B. For the practice of storing them cf. Sokr. Ep. IX, 2, τῶν τε ἰσχάδων ἀποτίθεσο, where the writer was probably thinking of this passage.

12. 361 b 6, 7. There is something like intentional negligence in the Greek here. ἡμέτερον must refer to Plato personally and it is natural to assume the same with regard to ἡμῖν in the line before; but this word follows μοι so closely that it may be meant to apply to Plato and Dionysios jointly. Two lines farther on ὑμῖν is meant to cover the wife and family of Dionysios. The ship is probably that which was chartered for Plato's journey from Syracuse to Athens. The price would not be excessive for a ship specially chartered. The low rates for travelling by sea which Rit. quotes from Böckh are for the fares of individuals. Rit. suggests that Leukadia may have been the name of a trireme, for which Dionysios is supposed to have contributed as Trierarch. But Plato seems to be referring to expenditure incurred for himself.

13. 361 d 1, 2. Rit. sees in this one of the intentional mystifications of a forger. It is much more likely that we have a description of something that actually happened after Plato had received at Syracuse the news of the death of his nieces. Cicero (*Leg.* II, 63), describing the Athenian funeral customs, and contrasting them with those of Rome, says "sequebantur epulae quas inirent propinqui coronati". May we not suppose that Dionysios provided Plato with a funeral banquet and pressed him, perhaps unceremoniously, to adhere to all the details of Athenian custom? In a more recent paper (*Philologus*, N.F. XXII, pp. 332 ff.) Rit. allows that Ep. XIII contains trustworthy information about Plato's family and the ages of his grandnieces, and conjectures that the wedding banquet during which Plato died may have been that of the youngest of the grandnieces mentioned here, who must have been about twenty years old at that time. He suggests that the same feast is referred to in the fragmentary passage in the *Index Herculanensis*, ed. S. Mekler, p. 20.

14. 361 e 3. Plato has been criticised for not conforming with the rules laid down in his *Laws* (742 c, 774 c, 959 d), where dowries are forbidden altogether and expenses over trousseaux limited by sumptuary laws. But he was an Athenian, not a Knossian. At Athens the relatives of girls who were left orphans were compelled by law to provide dowries, and a magistrate who failed to enforce the law was liable to a fine of 1000 drachmae. For the amount which Plato thought suitable to his circumstances we may compare the case of Mantitheos, who, in the speech written for him by Lysias (ch. 10), takes credit for the fact that, though he had only very moderate means, he gave 30 minae as dowry to each of his two sisters.

15. 361 e 5. Ten minae would probably cover the cost of a handsome piece of sculpture, such as some of those in the Street of Tombs at Athens. Such a monument would be suitable for a lady who had been a prominent member of one of the best families at Athens. Plato speaks as if her death were not likely to be long delayed. As he was about sixty years old, and was considerably younger than his brothers, Glaukon and Adeimantos, she may have been about ninety. It seems clear that Plato was the only one of her sons still surviving. Plato makes no suggestion as to the amount which Dionysios might contribute towards the tombstone or the dowry. He evidently expects the monarch to help him with a part of the cost, in the same way as Dion had helped with the other dowries.

16. 362 a 4. The words "on your behalf" are not expressed in the Greek; but there is no doubt that this is the meaning. As an Athenian citizen, Dionysios was liable to such services. The citizenship was conferred on him when it was conferred on his father, B.C. 369/8 (Dittenberger, 1, Insc. 89).

17. 362 b 1. Dionysios I had had connections with Aegina, and Andromedes may have been his agent there. There is no reason to suppose, as Ad. does, that he was at Athens; in that case it would not have been necessary to send Erastos to him. Plato writes as if Erastos were known to Dionysios, and he may have accompanied Plato in his visit to the sovereign. He was probably the same person who afterwards went to Skepsis with Koriskos (see Ep. VI).

18. 362 b 4. ἐπέστελλες evidently refers to a letter from Dionysios, which may have been brought by Leptines. We can only conjecture what were the μείζονα which the monarch wished Plato to send. Professor Taylor suggests to me that he probably wrote about something more important than statues, and may have asked Plato to try to raise a loan for him.

19. 362 c 2 ff. Plato's conduct in volunteering to send reports of this kind has been adversely criticised. But it was not unsuitable that, as a personal friend of the monarch, he should give any information that he could about agents of this sort, over whom it was difficult for Dionysios to exercise any control. The advice which follows is certainly not that of a flatterer, and is calculated to be most useful to a young man, who was still inexperienced in the management of affairs.

20. 362 e 2–8. Plutarch (*Dion*, 21) has given his explanation of this,

THE FAMILY OF PLATO

(Adapted from J. Burnet, *Thales to Plato*.)

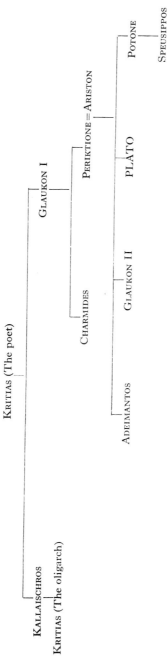

Note. Plato also had nieces; there is no evidence as to their parentage. See the mention of them in Ep. XIII 361 c, d, from which passage it may be inferred that there were two of them, who died at or about the same time during Plato's first visit to Dionysios the younger, *c*. 366 B.C., leaving four daughters, the eldest of whom was married to Speusippos.

and, though what he says is not entirely accurate, he is probably right in supposing that Dionysios had asked Plato to sound Dion with regard to a scheme for the rearrangement of marriages in the royal family, which the monarch had in view, and by which Dion would be asked to divorce his wife Aretê. There is no reason why we should be shocked at this proposal. The marriages in the royal family had all been arranged by Dionysios I with a view to strengthening his political position at Syracuse. The present proposal was, no doubt, made with similar objects. Timokrates, to whom Aretê was transferred, was a person employed in positions of trust. During the absence of Dionysios he took command of the troops at Syracuse (Plut. *Dion*, 26). Plato expresses no approval of the scheme, and merely informs Dionysios in plain terms that there was no chance of Dion's consenting to such a proposal. See Tayl. *Plat.* pp. 272–3.

21. 363 a 1. Κρατίνῳ. This friend of Plato is not otherwise known. His brother, Timotheos, is the celebrated general, who also was on intimate terms with Plato. See Aelian, *V.H.* 11, 10 and 18.

22. 363 a 7. The discussion about the soul is Plato's *Phaedo*, in which the Pythagoreans, Simmias and Kebes, are, along with Sokrates, the principal speakers. The sympathy of Dionysios with this School is tacitly assumed, and there is nothing inappropriate in the present which he is asked to send.

23. 363 b 1. συμβόλου. Bentley (*l.c.*) explains: "The 'symbol' he here speaks of made no part of the letters, nor began the first paragraph of any of them.—'Twas extrinsic (if I mistake not) to the letter, and was a mark at the top in these words, σὺν θεῷ if it was a serious letter; otherwise, σὺν θεοῖς. These two were the common forms in the beginning of writings or any discourse of importance, and in their usage were equivalent and indifferent".

This is the only probable explanation of the σύμβολον which has been suggested. The passage is interesting, because the doubts which it raised in the mind of Cudworth (*Intell. Syst.* 11, p. 66) led him to pronounce the letter a forgery, and so started the controversy about the genuineness of the Epistles. Deissmann (*Licht vom Osten*, p. 133) compares the use of σύμβολον here with that of σημεῖον in Paul, II *Ep.* *Thess.* iii, 17.

24. 363 b 7. Nothing is known from other sources about the missions mentioned in this paragraph. The ambassadors first spoken of must be an embassy sent by Dionysios to Athens. But it is not clear who Philaides was. The name can hardly be that of a Syracusan; and if he had been sent by Dionysios to the king of Persia, he would surely have gone straight back to Syracuse, instead of waiting at Athens. He may have been an Athenian.

25. 363 c 4, 5. ἂν μὲν αὐτὸς κ.τ.λ. For the brachylogy see Hack. p. 282. It is condemned by Rit. (*N.U.* p. 357) because none of the other numerous instances of brachylogy in Plato is an exact facsimile of it. He also condemns the use of χαρίεις without any suggestion of irony as

un-Platonic. In the fourth century the word was a common colloquialism in the sense of "a man of sound views"; cf. Isokr. *Ep.*
4, § 9, ἅπαντες οἱ χαρίεντες τοὺς τοῖς σπουδαίοις τῶν ἀνδρῶν ὁμιλοῦντας
ἐπαινοῦσι; *Panathen.* § 8, περὶ ὧν οἱ χαριέστατοι τῶν Ἑλλήνων καὶ
μνησθεῖεν ἂν καὶ διαλεχθεῖεν ὡς σπουδαίων ὄντων. Nothing is known of
Terillos or Teison, unless the latter is the same as Teisias, mentioned
349 c 3. The word ἐπολιάνομει shows local knowledge; magistrates of
this title are mentioned in an inscription of the fourth century B.C. at
Heraklea Siris in Sicily.
26. 363 d 1. συσφαιριστάς. These are evidently the young men who
play with Dionysios. Aristokritos is mentioned in Ep. III, 319 a 3.

ADDENDUM TO NOTES

1. Epistles I and XII. Novotný prefixes to his notes on these Epistles
a full and valuable discussion of the question of genuineness. In Ep. I
there is much in common between his treatment of the question and
that given in the Introductory Remarks to my Notes. In the case of Ep.
XII he arrives at the same conclusion in favour of the letter, and supports
it by arguments which, though stated with more detail, closely resemble
those used by Prof. Taylor in the letter quoted in my remarks. In
both cases it seems better to let my remarks stand in the same form in
which they left my hands some months ago.
2. 312 e and 323 d. Novotný comments at length on these two
cryptic passages, giving a full collection of parallel passages illustrating
them, including the statements of Christian writers. His own explanations are as follows:
In Ep. II the King is the Idea of the Good; the δεύτερα are the νοητά
and the δεύτερον to which they belong is the act of thought (including
ἐπιστήμη, νοῦς and δόξα); the τρίτα are the αἰσθητά, and the τρίτον to
which they belong is the act of αἴσθησις.
In Ep. VI the view of Plotinus is adopted, that the ἡγεμὼν καὶ αἴτιος
is νοῦς and the Father of νοῦς is the Idea of the Good.
3. 314 c 1–4. With Taylor, Burnet, and most others, I have assumed
that τὰ νῦν λεγόμενα means "the writings now called mine", i.e. the
Platonic Dialogues which were in circulation at the time. Novotný in his
notes on this passage and on 341 b 6 explains τὰ νῦν λεγόμενα in Ep. II as
συγγράμματα written by some other person and purporting to describe
Plato's views. He thinks that Heraclides Ponticus may be the person
referred to in Ep. II, and that he is spoken of sarcastically as "alter
Socrates". It seems unlikely that, if he wrote such treatises, they would
have disappeared without leaving a trace. Aristotle would surely have
alluded to them.
Novotný adopts a similar line of interpretation with regard to ἄλλους
γεγραφότας in 341 b 5. He thinks that Plato is referring to those who are
said by Simplicius (Arist. Fr. 28, Rose) to have published accounts of

Plato's lecture on the Idea of the Good, Aristotle, Speusippos, Xenokrates, and the rest. But it seems hardly possible that men who remained in close association with Plato to the time of his death published accounts of his lecture during his lifetime.

4. 336 a 2. ἐπεὶ τὴν δουλείαν. Novotný has a long and important note on Greek ceremonies connected with manumission. He illustrates fully the change of dress denoted by σχήματι. For φαιδρύνας he quotes passages of poetry in which the word is associated with λουτρά and he suggests that λουτρά also formed a part of the ceremony, the details of which in the case of Greek manumission are not fully known.

5. 353 a 3, 4. Νῦν ὑμῖν—διὰ τέλους. I have tacitly assumed that Plato is here thinking of the whole period from the accession of the elder Dionysios, and this is the view taken by the other editors who have touched on the point, Howald, Souilhé and Bury. But Novotný is more likely to be right in regarding πόλεμος as the war which began with Dion's expedition, and συγγένεια as meaning the younger Dionysios on the one side, and on the other Dion, and later Dion's nephew, Hipparinos.

6. 354 d 8. τοὺς δέκα στρατηγούς. Novotný declines to accept Grote's explanation of the difficulty, considering, with some reason, that there is too great a divergence between Plato's statement and the action taken by the Akragantines against their generals. He suggests that Plato is mentioning an incident not known from other sources, and that the generals to whose stoning he refers were the colleagues of Dionysios, whose deposition preceded his appointment as στρατηγὸς αὐτοκράτωρ. There would only be nine of them; but Plato might have spoken of them loosely as ten. Nothing is said by Diodoros about their ultimate fate, and Novotný can only refer to his general statement (XIII, 96) that Dionysios killed the leading men among his opponents. On the whole it seems unlikely that such an incident as their stoning by the populace would have been left unmentioned by other authors; and in the absence of any better explanation it is safer to accept that of Grote.

7. 360 d 2. οὐ φαύλου ζῴου. Novotný interprets φαῦλος as "simplex", "stabilis", "immutabilis", and regards it as antithetical to εὐμεταβόλου, comparing Diog. Laert. III, 63, where φαῦλος in the sense of ἁπλοῦς is mentioned as one of Plato's special uses of words, and *Theaet.* 147 c, where the word clearly has this meaning.

8. 363 e 5. ὁ αὐτὸς ἴσθι. Novotný reads αὐτὸς ἴσθι with A and two other MSS used by him, and states a strong case in favour of that reading. He takes ἴσθι as from εἰδέναι, with object supplied from τὴν ἐπιστολήν and translates the words "ipse nosce hanc epistulam", i.e. "hanc epistulam tibi soli scriptam puta".

INDEX I

ENGLISH.

References are to pages.

INDEX II

GREEK

References are to the divisions in the Clarendon Press Text, and in most cases to passages on which something is said in the Notes.

CAMBRIDGE: PRINTED BY W. LEWIS, M.A., AT THE UNIVERSITY PRESS

HISTORY OF IDEAS
IN
ANCIENT GREECE

An Arno Press Collection

Albertelli, Pilo. **Gli Eleati: Testimonianze E Frammenti.** 1939

Allman, George Johnston. **Greek Geometry From Thales To Euclid.** 1889

Apelt, Otto. **Platonische Aufsätze.** 1912

Aristotle. **Aristotle De Anima.** With Translation, Introduction and Notes by R[obert] D[rew] Hicks. 1907

Aristotle. **Aristotle's Psychology.** With Introduction and Notes by Edwin Wallace. 1882

Aristotle. **The Politics of Aristotle.** A Revised Text With Introduction, Analysis and Commentary by Franz Susemihl and R[obert] D[rew] Hicks. 1894. Books I-V

Arnim, Hans [Friedrich August von]. **Platos Jugenddialoge Und Die Entstehungszeit Des Phaidros.** 1914

Arpe, Curt. **Das** τί ἦν εἶναι **Bei Aristoteles** and Hambruch, Ernst, **Logische Regeln Der Platonischen Schule In Der Aristotelischen Topik.** 1938/1904. Two vols. in one

Beauchet, Ludovic. **Histoire Du Droit Privé De La République Athénienne.** 1897. Four vols.

Boeckh, Augustus. **The Public Economy of Athens.** 1842

Daremberg, Ch[arles]. **La Médecine: Histoire Et Doctrines.** 1865

Dareste, Rodolphe [de la Chavanne]. **La Science Du Droit En Grèce: Platon, Aristote, Théophraste.** 1893

Derenne, Eudore. **Les Procès D'Impiété Intentés Aux Philosophes A Athènes Au Vme Et Au IVme Siècles Avant J. C.** 1930

Diès, A[uguste]. **Autour De Platon: Essais De Critique Et D'Histoire.** 1927

Dittmar, Heinrich. **Aischines Von Sphettos:** Studien Zur Literaturgeschichte Der Sokratiker. 1912

Dugas, L[udovic]. **L'Amitié Antique D'Après Les Moeurs Populaires Et Les Théories Des Philosophes.** 1894

Fredrich, Carl. **Hippokratische Untersuchungen.** 1899

Freeman, Kathleen. **The Work And Life Of Solon,** With A Translation Of His Poems. 1926

Frisch, Hartvig. **The Constitution Of The Athenians.** 1942

Frisch, Hartvig. **Might And Right In Antiquity.** "Dike" I: From Homer To The Persian Wars. 1949

Frutiger, Perceval. **Les Mythes De Platon: Étude Philosophique Et Littéraire.** 1930

Heidel, William Arthur. **The Frame Of The Ancient Greek Maps.** 1937

Heidel, W[illiam] A[rthur]. **Plato's Euthyphro, With Introduction and Notes and Pseudo-Platonica.** [1902]/1896. Two vols. in one

Hermann, Karl Fr[iedrich]. **Geschichte Und System Der Platonischen Philosophie.** 1839. Part One all published

Hirzel, Rudolf. **Die Person:** Begriff Und Name Derselben Im Altertum and Uxkull-Gyllenband, Woldemar Graf, **Griechische Kultur-Entstehungslehren.** 1914/1924. Two vols. in one

Kleingünther, Adolf. ΠΡΩΤΟΣ ΕΥΡΕΤΗΣ : Untersuchungen Zur Geschichte Einer Fragestellung. 1933

Krohn, A[ugust A.] **Der Platonische Staat.** 1876

Mahaffy, J. P. **Greek Life And Thought From The Age Of Alexander To The Roman Conquest.** 1887

Martin, Th[omas] Henri. **Études Sur Le Timée De Platon.** 1841. Two vols. in one

Martin, Th[omas] H[enri]. **Mémoire Sur Les Hypothèses Astronomiques.** 1879/1881. Three parts in one

Milhaud, Gaston. **Les Philosophes-Géomètres De La Grèce.** 1900

Morrow, Glenn R. **Plato's Law Of Slavery In Its Relation To Greek Law.** 1939

Plato. **The Hippias Major Attributed To Plato.** With Introductory Essay and Commentary by Dorothy Tarrant. 1928

Plato. **The Laws Of Plato.** The Text Edited With Introduction and Notes by E. B. England. 1921. Two vols.

Saunders, Trevor J. **Bibliography On Plato's Laws, 1920-1970:** With Additional Citations Through May, 1975. 1975

Plato. **The Platonic Epistles.** Translated With Introduction and Notes by J. Harward. 1932

Raeder, Hans. **Platons Philosophische Entwickelung.** 1905

Ritter, Constantin. **Neue Untersuchungen Über Platon.** 1910

Ritter, Constantin. **Platon:** Sein Leben, Seine Schriften, Seine Lehre. 1910/1923. Two vols.

Sachs, Eva. **Die Fünf Platonischen Körper.** 1917

Schwartz, Eduard. **Ethik Der Griechen.** 1951

Shute, Richard. **On The History Of The Process By Which The Aristotelian Writings Arrived At Their Present Form.** 1888

Snell, Bruno. **Die Ausdrücke Für Den Begriff Des Wissens In Der Vorplatonischen Philosophie.** 1924

Tannery, Paul. **La Géométrie Grecque.** 1887

Tannery, Paul. **Recherches Sur L'Histoire De L'Astronomie Ancienne.** 1893

Taylor, A. E. **Philosophical Studies.** 1934

Wallace, Edwin, compiler. **Outlines Of The Philosophy Of Aristotle.** 1894

Zeller, Eduard. **Platonische Studien.** 1839

Zeno And The Discovery Of Incommensurables In Greek Mathematics. 1975